D1565024

# THE ROOT AND THE BRANCH

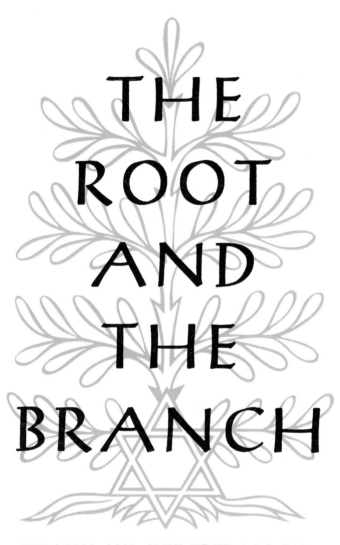

# THE ROOT AND THE BRANCH

JUDAISM AND THE FREE SOCIETY

BY

ROBERT GORDIS

THE UNIVERSITY OF CHICAGO PRESS

LIBRARY OF CONGRESS CATALOG CARD NUMBER: 62-17133

THE UNIVERSITY OF CHICAGO PRESS, CHICAGO & LONDON
THE UNIVERSITY OF TORONTO PRESS, TORONTO 5, CANADA

ⓒ 1962 BY THE UNIVERSITY OF CHICAGO
COMPOSED AND PRINTED BY THE UNIVERSITY OF CHICAGO PRESS
CHICAGO, ILLINOIS, U.S.A.

*For Fannie*

# PREFACE

Perhaps because the ancients lived closer to nature than do their modern descendants, they were more likely to picture life in general and human existence in particular through metaphors borrowed from the world of plants, flowers, and trees. This tendency has entered the warp and woof of all language and is reflected in virtually all the scriptures of mankind.

Thus the Book of Genesis tells us how the first human pair in the Garden of Eden was granted the boon of immortality by being given access to the fruit of the tree of life, while being denied the bittersweet fruit of the tree of knowledge. Isaiah, the greatest poet among the Hebrew prophets, depicted the preservation of the Saving Remnant of his people and the destruction of the useless and corrupt majority by comparing Israel to an oak tree in the autumn season, whose leaves fall away, while the stock, or holy seed, remains. He proceeded to foretell the advent of the Messiah, the redeemer of Israel and of mankind, who will be descended from the House of David, in the words, "There shall come forth a rod out of the stem of Jesse, and a branch shall grow out of his roots." The direst of curses in the ancient Semitic world was that a man might have his roots cut off from below and his branches from above. The Hebrew term for "offspring" was "seed" or "sprout," and even the ordinary term for "son" was used of a vine.

One of the most moving passages in the Book of Job contrasts the destiny of a tree, which may be transplanted and thus revived, with that of a man, who, once he dies, cannot be restored to life. The poignancy of the passage derives in no slight measure from the fact that man's life is generally pictured as a tree.

Now, the power of a figure of speech resides not only in the vividness of the image which it evokes, but, more profoundly, in its capacity to suggest more than it explicates, its nuances being at least as meaningful as its overt content. This is pre-eminently true of the metaphor of the tree. Thus, in a moving parable, the Upanishads emphasize that the branches, the leaves, and the fruits of a tree may seem to be disparate and unrelated to each other, but actually they are all nourished by the sap coming from the same root. For the Hindu thinker, the divergences are illusory; only the underlying unity is real.

This conviction of the unity of all creation is, of course, basic to the Hebraic world view. It goes far to explain the uncompromising monotheism that has always characterized Judaism from the biblical era onward. But the prophets and sages of Israel went beyond the Hindu poets, for they would not dismiss the differences among men as a mere illusion from which men should liberate themselves. Nor would they regard these distinctions within the human family as an error or a corruption of the social order that men should strive to eliminate. On the contrary, they united their deep conviction of the unity of mankind with a lively appreciation of its diversity. For them, both attributes are inherent and potentially valuable characteristics of the human condition. To put it in the language of faith, both aspects of human nature are expressions of the will of God.

Less poetic but more illuminating than the Hindu parable is the comment of the Talmud, which compares God the Creator to a human mintmaster, with one difference: whereas all coins struck from the same mold by the hand of man are identical, each human being, though fashioned in the form of Adam, remains uniquely different. To revert to the metaphor of the tree, the stock is one, but the branches, the leaves, and the fruits are many, and equally real. Moreover, without them, the root itself would have no function or value. So, too, the family of mankind is one in essence, yet multifarious in form.

Abraham Lincoln has been credited with the saying that God must love the poor because he made so many of them. With greater justice, we may declare that God must abhor monotony because he made a universe constantly reaching out for variety. The evidence is written large in the evolutionary history of the plant and animal kingdoms, as disclosed by biology and underscored for man by psychology and anthropology as well.

These differences among men, to be sure, have all too often proved a curse instead of a blessing. History teaches, however, that every effort to suppress them in favor of a pattern of uniformity has produced far greater ills than those which it was designed to cure. This was true of the attempt of the Hellenizing Seleucid kings of Syria after the death of Alexander the Great to impose the Greek way of life upon all the peoples under their rule. It was this effort which precipitated the first war for freedom of conscience in human history, the revolt of the Maccabees in 168 B.C.E. Their victory is to be credited with the preservation of the Hebrew Bible and of its teachings in the realm of religion and ethics, as well as with the survival of Judaism and the emergence of Christianity. The most recent effort in this direction is the most tragic— the bloodstained campaign of the Nazis on a global scale to achieve the *Gleichschaltung* of all those whom they did not succeed in exterminating.

How are the divergences of men—religious, racial, and national—to be utilized for the enhancement of life instead of for its destruction? Upon the answer to this, the crucial issue of our day, the survival of men as human beings depends.

The present volume seeks to bring one source of wisdom and experience, the oldest living component of Western culture, the Jewish tradition, to bear upon these issues. It is my hope that our generation may thus be helped to discover how to cherish the ideals of liberty and diversity within the context of the unity of the human race.

A preface is intended to perform a twofold function. On the one hand, it should afford the reader an insight into the basic concern which led to the writing of the work and the need which it is designed to serve. On the other, it should set forth the basic assumptions, or, if you will, the prejudices, of the author, with regard to the issues under discussion.

The first of these purposes is met by the first chapter in this book, which seeks to present the motives which led to these studies on the teaching of Judaism in the tension-laden areas of group relations. As for the second purpose, it is a truism, or should be, that the need for building a world community is of critical urgency today. This conviction is no novelty for one who, like the author, began his studies in biblical and post-biblical thought many years ago. I have always counted myself fortunate to have been introduced in earliest boyhood to the Bible as a whole and to the Hebrew prophets in particular by teachers who, whatever their personal commitment to religion, stressed the social and ethical content of the tradition.

This overriding concern with the content of the Bible rather than with the means by which its message was communicated to man is somewhat out of fashion, at least for the present. No doubt, this approach affords only a partial view of that mountain range of the spirit which is the Bible. Yet it is no more limited, and perhaps is more fruitful, than the contrary emphasis now in vogue, which is preoccupied almost exclusively with discussing man's confrontation with

the divine and is scarcely at all interested in the substance of
the divine conversation. For the religious spirit, revelation is
both process and product. In being concerned with the process, modern theology is entirely within its rights. It is, however, in error when it excludes the product of revelation
from its attention, neglecting the results of the encounter.
For, after all is said and done, the insights, attitudes, and actions which the divine imperative commands constitute the
goal and purpose of revelation. For Moses and all the prophets, the experience of the divine was not an end in itself, as
it is for the mystic. What mattered supremely is not how
they met God but what they learned from the meeting.

The sense of the one human community which was nurtured by the pages of Scripture and the teaching of the sages
early became central in my thinking. The reader interested
in intellectual excavation will find this concern expressed
in a work entitled *The Jew Faces a New World*, published
in 1941, in which the effort is made to set forth the insights
of Judaism that have a bearing on religious differences and
on the problems posed by modern nationalism.

The intervening years have, I hope, deepened my knowledge and understanding of the tradition as surely as they
have increased my awareness of the tragic dimensions of the
problems that are involved in translating its ideals into reality. In the interim, the demands of my congregational activity and the commitments of my academic career have been
heavy. But they have not led me to lose sight of the central
character of these issues for the survival of the free society
and of the human race itself.

On the contrary, I have been increasingly drawn into this
area. This is largely due to my activity as a consultant on
religion for the Center for the Study of Democratic Institutions, which now has its national headquarters in Santa Barbara, California. I owe a debt beyond the power of words
to express to its president, Dr. Robert M. Hutchins, who

invited me to spend the academic year 1960–1961 in residence at the Center in Santa Barbara, and to the extraordinary
warmth of his friendship and encouragement in all phases
of my work. The writing of this volume is a direct consequence of his inspiration. It was rendered possible by the
superb facilities for thinking, discussion, and research af-
forded by the unique Center which he has called into being.
My colleagues and friends in Santa Barbara have taught me
far more than they may themselves be aware of, though of
course they bear no responsibility for the opinions or errors
that may be found in the present work.

I am also very grateful to my good friend, Dr. A. William
Loos, executive director of the Council for Religion and International Affairs, formerly the Church Peace Union, on
the board of trustees of which I have the honor to serve.
His invitations to me to participate in the educational semi-
nars which the Council conducts on ethics and international
relations throughout the United States stimulated my thinking in this all-too-neglected area so crucial to the future of
the world.

My thanks are expressed to the Center for the Study of
Democratic Institutions, the Council for Religion and International Affairs, and the Union of American Hebrew Congregations, as well as to the *Christian Century*, the *Hibbert
Journal*, the *Jewish Frontier*, and the *Jewish Spectator* for
permission to utilize, in modified form, material which originally appeared under their several auspices.

Even a modest work by an individual author represents
the fruit of co-operation. My son David, who read the first
draft of the book with the loving and critical eyes which
only a son has for his father, has placed me greatly in his
debt. I am similarly indebted to my dear friend, Dr. Abraham I. Shinedling, whose wide erudition and painstaking attention to detail have enhanced the accuracy of every page.
He was also kind enough to prepare the Indexes. I am deeply

grateful to my devoted and gifted secretaries, Miss Patricia
Douglas and Mrs. M. B. Cohen, whose labors on the book
went far beyond the line of duty.

My heartfelt thanks are extended to my beloved congregation, Temple Beth-El of Rockaway Park, New York, to
which I have ministered for three decades, and to Dr. Louis
Finkelstein, chancellor of the Jewish Theological Seminary
of America, where I have served nearly as long as professor
of biblical exegesis. It was due to their combined kindness
that I was able to enjoy this sabbatical year, which proved
fruitful in so many respects.

Beyond all words is my sense of thanksgiving to my dear
wife, whose boundless love, understanding, and care,
through the mercy of God, preserved me during a period
of trial and illness. Gently but firmly, she has led me from
the ivory tower of technical research into the open field of
human concern, where men live and hope and struggle, often
failing but never quite bereft of their vision of the ideal. To
her, I say, "For from thee is all, and out of thy hand do I
return it to thee."

ROBERT GORDIS

BELLE HARBOR, NEW YORK
March 1962

# CONTENTS

# 1

# JEWISH TRADITION IN THE MODERN ERA

As the free world girds itself for a life-and-death struggle, it is seeking everywhere to find resources for its survival. It is no wonder, therefore, that the great religious traditions, which at one time dominated Western civilization, and which even today help shape its character, are being laid under contribution in this war for the world. With increasing seriousness, men are exploring the insights which Christianity affords, or can be made to yield, for dealing with the problems and tensions of a pluralist society. The papal encyclicals on social, economic, and political issues are being studied as never before. The implications of the Protestant Reformation and the ideas of its leading thinkers, both past and present, from Luther and Calvin to Tillich and Niebuhr, are proving of interest to men otherwise far removed from theological concerns.

In all this significant intellectual activity, the potential contribution of Judaism is almost totally missing. This state of affairs is particularly to be deplored, because it is clear that in its highest and most creative hours Judaism was firmly rooted in its own country but its vision embraced the world. This is true not only in the biblical period to which we owe the Law of Moses, the Prophets, and the Wisdom literature, but also in the talmudic era and in the medieval epoch.

1

Even when external conditions conspired to limit the perspective of Jewish thought, they never succeeded in destroying completely the unique capacity in Judaism for keeping both the more limited attachments to folk and nation and the broader perspective of world allegiance. Thus the prophets and sages of Israel never denied the reality of national loyalties or their right to exist. On the contrary, they accepted them as legitimate elements in the human situation and proceeded to ethicize them, thus transforming them into instruments for men's personal self-fulfilment and the spiritual enrichment of society. They then turned to the resources within their tradition in order to evolve a world view that would find room for creeds, races, and nations other than their own. They thus pointed the way realistically to the concept of a world community.

In the days of Amos, when most men never moved more than a few miles from their birthplace during their entire lifetimes, only a prophet or a son of a prophet could conceive of so recondite a doctrine as the unity of mankind, including all its divisions and transcending them. But in our age of virtually instantaneous world-wide communication and jet transportation, only the wilfully blind, whose ranks are, unfortunately, still too numerous, can fail to recognize that the interdependence of mankind is not a pious platitude, but the basic reality of human life. Our tragedy is that we are citizens of the world but do not know it. What Benjamin Franklin sought to teach his fellow Americans is the message of the age to the world: "We must all hang together, or assuredly we shall all hang separately." In fact, death by hanging will prove too good for us—it will almost surely be extinction by nuclear bomb.

The free world literally cannot afford to leave untapped any resources that are available for motivating men to grapple with their problems. Among them the oldest living religio-ethical tradition in the West, that of Judaism, has been largely ignored. The reasons for this state of affairs, unfortunate as it is, are not far to seek.

In the first instance, Judaism is the tradition of a people whose role in the social order has been passive for two thousand years of exile, during which it lived on sufferance as an alien element in the general population in Europe, Asia, and North Africa. Even while domiciled in Palestine, the Jewish people was rarely master of its own destiny. It enjoyed—if that is the word—political independence for less than four hundred years during the biblical era, from the reign of King David to the destruction of the state and the burning of the Temple in Jerusalem by the Babylonians in the year 586 B.C.E. During the Second Commonwealth, its fitful independence lasted for less than eighty years, from 142 B.C.E., when Simon the Maccabee wrested freedom for his people, until 66 B.C.E. In that year the Maccabees' descendants invited the Romans to take over the hegemony of Palestine. Truth to tell, the world conquerors would probably have done so even without an explicit invitation. Thus the Jewish group lacked independence, or even full autonomy, for the greater portion of its history. It would therefore seem a foregone conclusion that it would feel no responsibility and hence have little initiative for thinking deeply on the problems of intergroup relations, whether they were religious, racial, or national. Its major concern would be the desperate battle for its own survival.

Moreover, the classic literature of Judaism is remote in time, spirit, and idiom, having been written centuries ago, under radically different conditions, and in a language not easily accessible to the Western world. This inaccessibility is more than a matter of translation from the Hebrew. The Jewish genius, as embodied primarily in the Bible and the Talmud, was originally not speculative in temper, with the result that theoretical or doctrinal discussions are rare in both these great classics. Hence the mere translation of ancient

Hebrew sources often proves unilluminating. What is required is a transposition of the content of the tradition into the modern key, through a creative reinterpretation. While avoiding a distortion of its essential spirit, the modern expositor of the tradition must be endowed with both scholarship and sympathy. He must be able to discover the general principles behind the concrete illustrations so characteristic of talmudic law and know how to penetrate into the involved rabbinic interpretations of biblical passages. Modern readers unfamiliar with the ancient modes of thought may see in them farfetched casuistry and no more. The task of the modern interpreter is to reveal the valuable insights in the religio-ethical outlook of Judaism embedded in these apparently unpromising sources.

That is not all. Judaism is the religion of a tiny fraction of mankind, only twelve million out of the two and a half billion inhabitants of this planet, or less than one-half of one per cent. Judaism is a minority faith everywhere in the world, except in the State of Israel, itself a tiny country. Hence it is natural that the majority should, often without any malice whatsoever, overlook its very existence.

Moreover, the ubiquity of the phrase "the Judeo-Christian tradition" has lent color to the assumption that whatever insights Judaism might possess have been absorbed by Christianity and indeed carried further in the tradition of the daughter faith.

This last assumption, let it be clearly stated, is mistaken. Judaism continues to bear a twofold significance, one historical, the other contemporary. First, Judaism has been the major source of the two other great religions of the Western world, Christianity and Islam. Recent scholarship has made it clear that the extent of this indebtedness is far greater than was previously suspected. It was once generally believed that the faith and the ethics of Christianity were largely Jewish in origin, while the theology and the ritual of the church reflected the influence of Hellenistic thought and oriental religion. Scholarly research in the Dead Sea Scrolls has now led to the striking and totally unexpected conclusion that much of the content of early Christian thought and practice, previously attributed to extra-Jewish circles, emanated from the life and outlook of the Jewish Dead Sea sectarians. Less striking, but impressive, nevertheless, are the results of recent research into the rabbinic sources of the Koran. Hence, neither "daughter religion"—neither Christianity nor Islam—can be fully understood without constant recourse to its background in Judaism.

In referring to Christianity and, in lesser degree, to Islam as "daughter religions" of Judaism, we are underscoring an important historic truth. Christianity did not derive directly from the Old Testament, but from rabbinic Judaism, which was already flourishing in the days of Jesus, the Apostles, and Paul. Thus, the faith represented in the primitive church rested upon the thought and practice of post-biblical Judaism. Such elements in Christianity as the concept of God as Father, the faith in the advent of the Redeemer, the method of interpretation of biblical texts in the Gospels and in the Epistles of Paul, the belief in the resurrection of the dead, as well as the system of ritual observances in the Gospels, which include the Sabbath, the festivals, diet, and family relations—all these are not simply Old Testament religion but the way of life of rabbinic Judaism. The Hebrew Bible had been completed several centuries before the rise of Christianity.

The concept of a mother-daughter relationship is fruitful in other respects as well. It recognizes that each possesses a distinct individuality. A child is never the facsimile of its parent, if only because another progenitor is involved in the process. In addition to normative Judaism or Pharisaism, there were other important influences which helped fashion the character of Christianity. These included elements from oriental religion, Greek philosophy, the mystery cults, as well as non-Pharisaic minority sects in Judaism, as the Qumran Scrolls dramatically reveal. Moreover, the mother continues to live and grow older—one hopes wiser, too—even after the birth of her daughter! Thus, both Christianity and Judaism have followed their own separate paths subsequent to their separation, though it must always be kept in mind that a close genetic relationship continues to exist between them.

The historical impact of Judaism upon Christianity and Islam has been tremendous. It is, however, not in its historical influence but in its intrinsic content that the major significance of the Jewish tradition resides. Yet as modern men seek to meet the multiple challenges of the age, one basic question arises: Is it necessary to turn to the specifics of Judaism for the values that Western man cherishes and strives to conserve and develop? Are not all these attitudes to be found in the religious and ethical content of Christianity or, to use a broader term which has gained great currency in our time, in "the Judeo-Christian tradition"?

This question is of far more than theoretical importance. For the threat to democracy, which reached one climax in the bloody struggle of World War II, is being fought with equal vigor in the slightly less sanguinary, but equally perilous, battles of the "cold war." In seeking to defend ourselves against the threat of totalitarianism in all its colors—brown, black, or red—statesmen and educators, perhaps even more than religious spokesmen, have invoked the resources of "the Hebraic-Christian heritage" or the Judeo-Christian tradition. For more and more men are becoming convinced that the only enduring foundations of democracy are spiritual in character.

As the struggle between the Communist world and the free nations rises in intensity, it is becoming increasingly clear that the future of democracy depends upon a delicate balance between the sanctity of the individual on the one hand and the need for social justice and group action on the other. In preserving this vital tension and in rooting the ideals of freedom and justice in the one God, Judaism and Christianity share a deep community of outlook.

The conception of a Judeo-Christian tradition is therefore no imaginary notion, newly concocted to serve apologetic ends or political purposes. It is surely obvious that both religions are far closer to each other with regard to many elements of their world view than either is to Buddhism, to Zoroastrianism, or even to Mohammedanism. This is true, not only because Christianity began as a sect within Judaism, but also because Christians and Jews have lived together in Europe and America for nineteen centuries. Basic to both religions is the same sacred history, which extends for two millennia from Abraham to the closing days of the Second Temple, a record of revelation enshrined in the same sacred Scriptures, from Genesis to Chronicles. The Bible and the history which it records serve as the source of many basic attitudes on God, man, and the universe. Moreover, both religions in their classic forms derive many additional elements of their outlook, which are not to be found in the text of the Bible, from the various currents of post-biblical Judaism, both Palestinian and Alexandrian, expressed in rabbinic as well as in apocryphal literature.

The substantial elements shared in common cannot be disregarded, as some zealous partisans of one or the other tradition have attempted to do. At the same time, it is equally misleading to overlook the vital differences in the two components of the Judeo-Christian tradition.

It is undeniable that both possess a common background, but even the same sources have developed far-reaching variations. Truth, Renan reminds us, lies in the nuance. Given subtle differences in emphasis and in timbre, a new individuality emerges. The Hebrew Scriptures, to be sure, are sacred

to Christianity as well as to Judaism. But while Judaism ac-
cords primacy to the Torah over the Prophets, Christianity
stresses the Prophets, while practically discarding the Law.
For Judaism, they are a vital commentary on the Torah,
which is the fountainhead of the life of faith, and hence they
are secondary to the Torah in importance. For Christianity,
the Prophets replace the Law as the most significant element
of the Old Testament.

This difference points to an even more important divergence. For classical Judaism obedience to the Law is the
unique instrument for the fulfilment of the will of God. On
the other hand, classical Christianity, in the formulation of
Paul, is strongly antinomian, denying the validity and authority of the Torah. Indeed, Paul went much further, argu-
ing that the Law was an instrument increasing the consciousness of sin and thus contributing to the sinfulness of man.

Thus Paul explains:

> Sin indeed was in the world before the law was given,
> but sin is not counted where there is no law. . . . While we
> are living in the flesh, our sinful passions, aroused by the
> law, were at work in our members to bear fruit for death.
> But now we are discharged from the law, dead to that
> which held us captive, so that we serve not under the old
> written code but in the new life of the spirit . . . [Romans
> 5:13; 7:5-7, R.S.V.].

The rabbis, on the other hand, declare, "The Holy One,
blessed be He, wished to add merits to Israel. Therefore, He
increased for them the Law and the Commandments, as it
is said, 'God was pleased for the sake of His righteousness
to magnify the Torah and make it glorious' " (*Mishnah,
Makkoth* 3:16). While Judaism regards the Law as the path-
way to God, Christianity substitutes the person of Christ,
belief in whom constitutes the road to salvation. No matter
how much one may reduce the importance of loyalty to the

Law in Judaism and stress the value of Law in Christianity, a substantial margin of difference will remain.

Even where both traditions accept the validity of a given passage, the varying stress accorded it often becomes significant. In Judaism, the call "Hear O Israel, the Lord our God, the Lord is One," known as the *Shema*, which precedes the commandment to love Him (Deuteronomy 6:4–9), holds a central place. This is the classic affirmation of the fundamental Jewish doctrine of the unity of God. It is accordingly recited at the close of the Day of Atonement and by each Jew on his deathbed as the Confession of Faith. Jesus as a professing Jew assigned to it the same importance. According to Mark (12:28–34), he quoted the verse when answering the question as to which is the greatest commandment. The *Shema* holds no such central position in Christianity, and, in the version in Matthew (22:35–40), Jesus' reply to the same question does not include it.

On the other hand, the Adam and Eve narrative in Genesis has served as the source for the central Christian concept of the Fall of Man, which has been elaborated with incredible depth in twenty centuries of Christian thought. In traditional Judaism, the paradise tale is of course familiar and famous, but, aside from a few minor references, it has developed no theological significance whatever.

Similarly, traditional Christianity has always made much of the seventh chapter of Isaiah, in which it found a prophecy of the Virgin Birth of the Savior more than seven centuries later. That a palpable error in translation underlies this view of the passage has long been recognized by virtually all Christian scholars. But this fact has little affected the use of the verse in contemporary Christian life. The new *Standard Revised Version* now correctly renders the Hebrew word *almah* as "young woman." On this score, it was vigorously attacked by several fundamentalist groups and by individual fundamentalist Christian preachers throughout the country. Similarly, the fifty-third chapter of Isaiah, which depicts the Suffering Servant of the Lord, has been regarded in traditional Christian circles as a prophecy of the career of Jesus. It has therefore played an incalculable role in Christian thought. On the other hand, Jewish commentators, like many Christian exegetes, have interpreted it as a portrayal of the tragi-heroic function of the people of Israel as God's witness in a pagan world. Yet the moving figure of the Suffering Servant, which has had such an impact on the Christian conception of the Savior, never became equally basic to the traditional Jewish world view. Thus, practically none of the beautiful "Servant Songs" were chosen for the *Haftarot*, the prophetic readings in the synagogue liturgy.

Nor are the differences between Judaism and Christianity limited to proof-texts. The early Christian church, to be sure, took over the body of Jewish ideas and a mass of Jewish practices which were current in first-century Jewish Palestine. This legacy, however, was subjected to a very complex process. The ritual practices were largely surrendered, especially when Gentile Christians began to predominate over the Judeo-Christians in the ranks of the new church.

With regard to the ideas taken over from Judaism, there were elements which Christianity accepted, but many which it modified, others which it discarded or overlooked, and still others which it reinterpreted or replaced entirely. Such Christian doctrines as the Fall of Man, Original Sin, the superiority of asceticism, and vicarious atonement are, it is true, slightly adumbrated in Judaism, and some few passages may be adduced to support them from Jewish sources. But the student who is truly at home in Judaism recognizes that they are not in the mainstream of the tradition, being secondary in character. There were, of course, many basic dogmas which became uniquely characteristic of the Christian faith, such as the Virgin Birth, the Incarnation, and the

Passion, which have no counterpart in Judaism, and which added immeasurably to the individuality of Christianity.

On the other hand, Judaism retained and developed various insights of its own. These are to be found less often in abstract formulations of creed than in the context of legal practice and institutional forms. Throughout its history, the Law has been the life of Judaism, interpreted and developed in the pages of Scripture, the discussions of the Talmud, the formulation of the Codes, and the decisions of the *responsa*, a process of growth and development still going on today.

It has been one of the great merits of Christianity to focus attention upon the fate of the individual and the means available to him for his salvation. This is not to deny the existence of a deep and ongoing interest in the needs and problems of society. Conversely in Judaism, while the individual soul has certainly not been lost sight of, the genius of the tradition has placed the destiny of the group, be it the family, the nation, or the human race, at the center of its concern. Through the centuries of its experience, Judaism has garnered some insights in these areas. Their significance, we believe, is by no means limited to Jews but can be of great value in the struggle to save what is most vital in the civilization of the West.

That some of these ideas have become part of the Christian outlook as well does not reduce their role as normative in Judaism. The Decalogue remains a supreme contribution of the Hebraic spirit, even though, or, to be more accurate, precisely because, it has become part of the warp and woof of Western civilization. But there remain many other elements of great value in the Jewish tradition which have been overlooked or set aside or have remained not fully understood during the past two millennia. Many of them are to be found in the tension-laden areas of group relations, religious, racial, and national. When interpreted in depth, against the background of the history and the secular culture of Western man, these aspects of the Jewish tradition can help point the way to the building of the world community.

To recapitulate, several factors are responsible for the fact that the humanistic and universal values embodied in Judaism have not been adequately recognized. That they are expressed in a foreign idiom and recondite literature is one reason. That they were the heritage of a small, disfranchised pariah group is another. Moreover, paradoxical as it seems, the existence of the Judeo-Christian tradition was a third cause. For while the tradition preserved many of these Hebraic insights, it also ignored others of equal value.

There remains one additional factor that helps to explain why these insights have been overlooked. It derives from the historical experience of the modern Jew. For the Jews, the Middle Ages did not end with the Crusades or the conquest of Constantinople by the Turks, with the Renaissance or the discovery of America, with the Protestant Reformation or even with the Industrial Revolution. For them, the modern era began fitfully and partially in the eighteenth century with the French Revolution, and then only for the relatively small Jewish communities living in western and central Europe, in France, Germany, Italy, and the Low Countries, which were overrun by the armies of France. Throughout the thousand years between Charlemagne and Napoleon which constituted the medieval era for the Jews, they were largely isolated from the main stream of Western civilization.

For the vast majority of Jews who were living in the East, within the confines of the sprawling Russian and Austro-Hungarian Empires, the Middle Ages persisted even longer, until the end of the nineteenth century and the beginning of the twentieth. Most of them continued to live under medieval conditions, political, economic, and cultural. They or their children re-entered Western society only when millions of them emigrated from eastern Europe to North and

South America, South Africa, and Israel—and thus escaped the total annihilation decreed for them by the Nazis.

When, at the end of the eighteenth century, the Jews of western Europe were first offered the blessings of the Emancipation and the Enlightenment, it was made clear to them that the rights granted them were not being offered freely as their due, but proffered as an exchange, a *quid pro quo*. The price demanded was the surrender, or at least the attenuation, of the distinctive Jewish tradition and the dissolution of the organic Jewish community which constituted the way of life by which their ancestors had lived in the Ghetto. Most Western Jews in Europe and America were enthusiastic about the exchange. With a few exceptions, like some communities in Holland, they were more than willing to pay this price for the sake of the blessings of civic equality, political enfranchisement, economic opportunity, and the broadening of cultural horizons which came with integration into citizenship in the modern state.

That this gift was warmly appreciated by modern Jews is abundantly clear from the far-flung contribution which they have made to every aspect of modern life, its commerce and industry, its science, literature, music, and art, its political institutions and its social progress. Such seminal minds as Marx, Einstein, and Freud and countless other figures of only slightly lesser magnitude testify to the flowering of talent within the Jewish community which enriched every phase of contemporary culture. When the Nazis charged that the Jews had poisoned the wells of the German spirit, they were paying a perverted tribute to the extensive debt that modern Germany owes the grandchildren of the Ghetto.

One of the most significant contributions of modern Jews, which has often proved an embarrassment and a potent source of anti-Semitic prejudice as well, has been their high level of social consciousness, their responsiveness to human needs, their hatred of oppression and exploitation, their passion for justice.

This is not to suggest that these qualities are universal among Jews or lacking in others. Yet it is undeniable that the Jewish group contains a disproportionately high percentage of men and women in whom the old messianic fervor of Judaism still burns with a gemlike intensity, though often in thoroughly secularized form. Indeed, these advanced spirits have frequently been far removed and even totally estranged from the God-centered view of life basic to the Bible and the Jewish tradition.

Nonetheless, their sensitivity to oppression and their passion for justice were part of their unconscious inheritance as Jews. This legacy was compounded of two major elements: the Hebrew prophets, who set forth their fundamental ideals in winged words, and the Talmud, which sought to concretize biblical ethics in an elaborate system of jurisprudence. The prophetic legacy these modern Jews often left unacknowledged; the rabbinic contribution, of which they knew less than nothing, they scorned. Yet willy-nilly, these idealists remained, in the words of the Talmud, "if not prophets, at least sons of the prophets."

A unique exception to the rule is the career of Moses Hess, who was dubbed "the Communist Rabbi" and was credited with converting Karl Marx to socialism. Hess was conscious of his debt to his Jewish past and sought to synthesize nationalism, religion, and socialism in his *Holy History of Mankind* and *Rome and Jerusalem*, books totally neglected in his own age and little read since. Yet it was not purely an accident that Karl Marx, who after his baptism at the age of eight probably never set foot in a church again, and surely never crossed the threshold of a synagogue, and whose hostility to religion became a basic article of faith to his disciples, was a descendant of a long line of rabbis.

This preoccupation, if not obsession, with justice and equality, the English writer and scientist C. P. Snow originally felt to be a specifically Jewish trait. He has described it as "the sharp-edged passion for justice, argumentative, repetitive, but quite incorruptible." Years ago, Thorstein Veblen explained the role of the Jew in the vanguard of progress as stemming from the fact that he was *in* Western society but not quite *of* it, so that he was able to preserve a degree of detachment which is basic to the critical stance. In our day, Reinhold Niebuhr has repeatedly paid tribute to the involvement of Jews in movements dedicated to social progress.

Probably this social idealism has been exaggerated by sympathetic observers, but it is real. It has undoubtedly been nourished by the position of Jews as members of a highly conspicuous and frequently discriminated-against minority group. As a result, the rabbinic injunction, "Be of the persecuted, and not of the persecutors," was for them not merely an abstract ethical injunction but an unavoidable and universal fact of life. Experience showed that anti-Jewish attitudes usually went hand in hand with other varieties of reaction and prejudice, be they racial or religious, and that economic injustice proved a fertile breeding ground for rabble-rousers, who found in the Jew the ideal scapegoat for all the ills of society.

In sum, both tradition and destiny have conspired to endow many modern Jews with a high degree of sensitivity to oppression and with a passionate sense of dedication to the goals of justice, freedom, and peace.

At the same time, most modern Jews of enlightened views, recognizing that their entrance into Western society derived from the eighteenth-century Age of Reason, have retained its strong bias in favor of individualism. Many of them have continued to assume that the group relations of men are divisions that are at best artificial and at worst irrational, and that they will wither away under the sun of reason and intelligence. Often their position has not gone beyond that of the great apostle of Jewish emancipation in France, Clermont-Tonnère, who felt no sense of restriction in his ringing offer of emancipation to the Jews: "To the Jews as Jews, nothing; to the Jews as men, everything."

This emphasis upon the individual, upon man as man, is the measure both of the greatness and of the limitations of the eighteenth century. It found its classic expression in the American Declaration of Independence, which declared that "all men are created equal," and in the very name of its French counterpart, "the Declaration of the Rights of Man." It was, of course, an expression of the burgeoning Industrial Revolution, the economic expression of which was to be found in the laissez faire theory, according to which each individual, be he employer or worker, was a free and equal participant in the economic process and in the political theory that that government is best which governs least. Hence, the democratic political order, which had its origin in this period, ignored as well as it was able the various group associations of men, whether they were religious, social, economic, or racial.

The task of the twentieth century is not to negate the ideals of the eighteenth but to fulfil them; not to accept the limitations of the eighteenth century but to transcend them. The stress upon the essential equality and unity of mankind needs to be underscored in our day. But we must also reckon with the collective loyalties of men, including the most powerful of all, that of nationalism, and must recognize them as inherent elements of the human situation. We are beginning to understand that the freedom of the individual is an illusion unless he also possesses freedom of spiritual self-determination, the right to maintain the voluntary group associations which are the hallmarks of human functioning. As a result, one of the basic issues confronting a democratic society is how to relate the aspirations and rights of these groups to the life and unity of the total society. It is in the relations among religious groups, races, and nations that the areas of maximum tension in the Western world are to be found today.

Increasingly, modern men, whatever their religious or ethnic backgrounds, are sensitive to the impact of these issues. Yet, unlike his Christian fellow citizen, the modern Jew all too often is estranged from any religio-ethical tradition of his own to which he can turn, either for guidance or for governance. Those Jews who are at home in their tradition are often unaware of the complex problems of intergroup relationships, having established for themselves an enclave within Judaism. On the other hand, those Jews who are aware of these tensions in the modern world are not at home with their tradition. In a word, Jews who are committed to Judaism are often unconcerned with the world; those who are concerned with the world are not committed to Judaism.

As a result, when Jews have sought to deal with questions of racial, national, and religious relationships, they have tended to solve them on an *ad hoc* basis. Both as individuals and through organizations, Jews have often been in the forefront of the battle for interfaith understanding, social progress, civil rights, and international peace. The conscious motivations, however, have often been sociological, economic, or political. The feeling is general that in adopting the particular positions Jews have been moved in largest degree by the effects which such positions were likely to have upon their status and that of their fellow Jews in various communities. Rarely has the Jewish world view, its teaching concerning man and the universe, been invoked on its own merits and utilized as the basis for a concept of the world community.

The tragedy for modern Jews in the present situation is

self-evident. Frequently, the most idealistic among them are the most uprooted, totally alienated from the sources of their being. The disease of "Jewish self-hatred," in varying degrees of virulence, has often attacked the most gifted and creative sons and daughters of the Jewish people. It is by no means limited to the least worthy members of the community. The situation is equally disastrous for the Jewish tradition, which is thus allowed to languish and disappear where it could illumine and direct.

Finally, the world is impoverished by this failure to utilize the content of the Jewish tradition on these issues, and this on two grounds. First, within Judaism there are attitudes and insights on group relations which are lacking in the younger member of the Judeo-Christian tradition, if only because of the greater individualistic emphasis in Christianity and the greater stress upon the group in Judaism. Moreover, as Jacques Maritain has suggested, there is need for a "charter of agreement" for Western man on the fundamental principles by which he seeks to live. A charter of agreement, Maritain points out, will necessarily be based upon a diversity of defenses stemming from the variety of philosophic, cultural, or religious backgrounds of modern man. In helping to achieve such a charter, Judaism has its own distinctive contribution to make. The present volume is a modest effort to advance this undertaking.

# 2

# JUDAISM—ITS CHARACTER AND CONTENT

An understanding of the insights of the Jewish tradition in any area of life necessarily presupposes an appreciation of the nature of Judaism. This is not so easy to come by as is sometimes imagined. As is entirely natural, most descriptions of Judaism seek to place it in a comparative context with Christianity, Islam, or the oriental religions. Unfortunately, this leads to a very considerable degree of error. It is the same with efforts to categorize Jews as analogous to other groups of human beings. The fact is that neither Judaism nor the Jewish group fits into any of the established norms with which theologians or sociologists operate.

Because of the obvious bond between the Jewish group and its religion, Judaism is often defined as an "ethnic religion." While this description has elements of truth, it is not adequate for comprehension in depth. To be sure, it emphasizes the central role of the historic experience and the collective consciousness of the Jewish group within the structure of Judaism. The communal character of Jewry has had a profound impact upon the religious and ethical content of Judaism, as well as upon its ritual practice. Virtually all Jews today, except for tiny splinter groups, would reaffirm this organic link between faith and folk. Most non-

Jews, too, would recognize this relationship as a reality in the lives of their Jewish neighbors.

Yet the designation "ethnic religion" fails to do justice to what is most significant in Judaism. Virtually all nations in ancient times had group religions expressive of their ethnic character, whether they were Babylonians, Egyptians, Syrians, Greeks, or Romans. Even then, however, Judaism was an ethnic religion "with a difference," set apart fundamentally from that of its contemporaries. From its inception, biblical religion possessed a strong universalistic outlook which transcended national boundaries. This trait is reflected in the early traditions of the origin of the human race depicted in Genesis, in the emphasis upon one God and his moral law embodied in the Decalogue, and in the persistent demand made even by the earliest prophets for righteousness from all men and nations, including their own people.

*The history of Judaism reveals the uniqueness of its character.* As Yehezkel Kaufmann has pointed out, biblical Judaism, the heritage of a tiny, weak nation clinging precariously to the shores of the eastern Mediterranean, proved the only ethnic religion of the ancient world that succeeded in winning the allegiance of millions of men who were not ethnically Jews. This was true also of the *sebomenoi tou theou*, "the fearers of God," in the Hellenistic and Roman periods, who were semiconverts, and ultimately were absorbed either into Judaism or into nascent Christianity. It remains true today of hundreds of millions of Christians who are not merely "spiritually Semites" but regard themselves as the New Israel. It is also true of hundreds of millions of Moslems for whom Judaism is the rock upon which their religion has been reared.

Nor does the term "ethnic religion" do justice to the capacity of Judaism, unique in human history, to survive and grow creatively during two millennia of exile, without land, government, or central sanctuary, and, as we shall see, without a centralized religious authority. In the modern world, where ethnic religions have all but disappeared, the uniqueness of Judaism, or, if you prefer, its "sore-thumb quality," is all the more evident.

*Equally impervious to accepted norms is the character of the Jewish group.* It may be pointed out that this stress upon the unique category into which Israel falls has ample scriptural warrant. King David proclaimed: "Who is like unto thy people Israel, one people upon the earth!" (II Samuel 7:23), and the Gentile prophet, Balaam, the son of Beor, declared, "Behold, here is a people dwelling apart, not to be reckoned among the nations" (Numbers 23:9). What was praise for the psalmist and the prophet may be a pitfall for the philosopher, who quite naturally prefers neat pigeonholes for his categories. Hence scholars are frequently driven to exasperation by this intractable conglomeration of human beings. No wonder Arnold Toynbee called Jews "a fossilized remnant of Syriac society." But they are surely the liveliest fossil on record!

The fact remains, however, that any one of the accepted sociological categories represents a dangerous distortion of reality. We may recall the storm which arose when David Ben-Gurion asked the question, "What is a Jew?" and the vast torrent of words which poured forth in response, marked by a tremendous variety of outlook. None of the usual terms like "race," "nationality," or "religious denomination" is really appropriate.

The bloodstained term "race," as most competent anthropologists agree, would best be expunged from men's vocabularies, not merely on humanitarian grounds but because of its total lack of scientific validity. Nonetheless, it continues to be invoked in connection with Jews, because it suggests the idea of common descent and ethnic homogeneity. This sense of kinship is undoubtedly present and is indeed basic.

Yet historical research has demonstrated that the Jewish group, like all others, represents a vast mixture of ethnic and racial stocks, from the earliest biblical times to the present. The term "nationality," with its connotation of political allegiance, and often of geographic contiguity, manifestly cannot apply to the Jewish group, which shares no common political loyalty and is scattered over the face of the globe. The term "religious sect" or "denomination" is also inadequate, both because Judaism includes elements not to be paralleled in other religions and because the Jewish group includes many for whom religion is of little or no consequence, who yet are stamped as Jews by their own consciousness and in that of the world.

As we have therefore urged elsewhere, the least objectionable term to apply to the Jewish group would be the least specific, namely, "people," and it, too, would need to be defined afresh as referring to a religio-cultural-ethnic group.

> The only term which is sufficiently inclusive to be used to describe the Jews is the old biblical word " 'am," meaning "a people," from a Semitic root probably connoting "togetherness." Jews the world over differ in social outlook, political citizenship, economic status, and religious attitude. Yet the overwhelming majority are conscious of the fact that they are members of one people, sharing a common history and a sense of kinship inherited from the past, a common tradition and way of life in the present, and a common destiny and hope for themselves and for the world in the future.[1]

In sum, both Judaism and the Jewish people are not to be subsumed under any of the usual categories in vogue in our day.

The term "ethnic religion," as we have seen, is inadequate as a description of the complex reality which is the Jewish

---

[1] Robert Gordis, *Judaism for the Modern Age* (New York, 1955), p. 47.

tradition. *More directly germane to our theme, it fails to do justice to the innate balance between particularism and universalism which characterizes Judaism.* Judaism is the religion of the Jewish people, but its God is not a national God and its group interests do not constitute the boundaries of its ethical concern. In a truly national religion, the god is the defender and the protector of the collective interests. To be sure, an early outlaw and freebooter like Jephthah in the Book of Judges could conceive of the relationship of the God of Israel to His people as paralleling that of other national deities. Hence, in his negotiations with the Ammonites he could say: "Indeed, that which Chemosh thy god has expropriated, you will possess. And what the Lord our God has expropriated for us, that we will possess" (Judges 11:24).

The authentic teachers of Judaism, however, never saw their God as less than the father of all men, the arbiter of history, and the source and sanction of righteousness in human affairs. Thus the Torah describes the patriarch Abraham as bargaining for the lives of the sinful people of Sodom because "the God of all the earth must surely do justice" (Genesis 18:25). Amos saw the God of Israel, whose seat is in Zion, exacting retribution from all nations guilty of barbarism and treachery against one another (Amos, chaps. 1, 2). Biblical Judaism conceived of God as universal, but as choosing Israel as the instrument for his transcendent truth and therefore consigning his chosen people to contumely and pain until all the nations would recognize its role in history as the teacher of mankind (Isaiah 42:1-4, 19-22; 52:13—53:12). For this prophet, as for all Jews to the present, there was no contradiction between a passionate concern for the spiritual welfare of mankind, on the one hand, and, on the other, a constant preoccupation with the Jewish people's return from exile and the reconstitution of its national life in the land of Israel (Isaiah 40:1 ff.). In the same utterance, the prophet could welcome proselytes who had accepted the faith in the one God and observed the Sabbath and could see them dwelling in Jerusalem, offering the ritual sacrifices enjoined by the Law: "Their burnt-offerings and sacrifices will be acceptable upon My altar, for My house shall be called a house of prayer for all peoples" (Isaiah 51:6–7).

It is true that many biblical critics have found it impossible to understand this tension. Hence they have proceeded to apply the scalpel of deletion to the various prophetic texts, eliminating either the particularist passages in order to refashion the prophet into a pure universalist image or excising the universalist passages in order to create a narrowly nationalistic figure. As great a contemporary scholar as Otto Eissfeldt, speaking of Amos, declares: "Bei ihm ist Gott alles, Israel nichts" ("For him God is everything, Israel nothing"). This is a conceivable position for a German theologian; it is meaningless for a Hebrew prophet, for whom God and Israel are linked in an indissoluble covenant.

In the post-biblical centuries when Jews underwent exile and persecution, the experience inevitably tended to narrow the perspective of the Jewish world view. Yet particularism and universalism both remained in evidence. We may cite the *Alenu* prayer which Solomon Schechter called the "Marseillaise of the Jewish spirit." It was composed in Babylonia in the third century C.E. by the great talmudist Rab and is the concluding prayer of every Jewish service of worship. Its first paragraph stresses particularism in uncompromising fashion, while the second underscores the universalistic hope of Judaism:

> It is our duty to praise the Master of all, to exalt the Creator of the universe, who has not made us like the nations of the world and has not placed us like the families of the earth; who has not designed our destiny to be like theirs, nor our lot like that of their multitude. . . .
> We therefore hope, O Lord our God, speedily to behold

Thy majestic glory, when the abominations shall be removed from the earth, and the false gods destroyed; when the world will be perfected under the reign of the Almighty, and all mankind will call upon Thy name, and all the wicked of the earth will turn to Thee. May all the inhabitants of the world perceive and know that to thee every knee must bend, every tongue must swear loyalty. For the kingdom is Thine and to all eternity Thou wilt reign in glory, as it is written, "The Lord shall reign forever and ever," and it has been foretold, "The Lord shall be king over all the earth, on that day the Lord shall be one and His name one."

Throughout its long history, Judaism kept in tension its particularistic origin and function and its universal vision and thrust. All the various modern interpretations of Judaism that possess any degree of authenticity recognize and share this preservation of a specific group loyalty linked to an attachment to universal values.

This balance has always been natural to Jews but has often appeared as a stumbling block or a scandal to some and as a pretense or a contradiction to others. The sober, historical fact is, however, that both elements in this balance have survived in Jewish consciousness and thought for millennia. It is also the key to the understanding of the unique Jewish attitude toward national and religious loyalties outside of its own, with which we shall be concerned later.

Another basic fact about Judaism is that *the nexus binding the Jewish group together is a common historical experience rather than a confession of creed*. From its inception, Judaism has been the distillation of a group experience, including within its confines a vast variety of attitudes, insights, and temperaments. The Jewish biblical scholar, A. B. Ehrlich, at the beginning of the present century, expressed the hope that the recognition would soon come to scholars that the Hebrew Bible, in contradistinction to the New Testament, is not a collection of tracts by like-minded believers, but "a national literature upon a religious foundation." He may have been less than fair to the variety of outlook in the New Testament and the early church, but his view of the Hebrew Bible was basically sound.

The three elements of the Hebrew Scriptures, the Torah, the Prophetic books, and the Wisdom literature, represent the three differing emphases among the spiritual and intellectual leadership of ancient Israel. The priest, the prophet, and the sage have all left their spiritual legacy in the Bible, which accordingly encompasses the widest possible gamut of outlook and insight, embracing the polarities of the man and the Jew, the individual and society. The Torah is basically concerned with law and observance, but that includes ethics as well as ritual and an overriding concern with the national destiny of Israel. The prophets are pre-eminently caught up in their vision of the one God and his categorical imperative of ethical living, but the future of Israel within the family of mankind evokes their highest hopes as well. The sages of the Wisdom literature are interested in a workable, personal morality for the individual, but their speculations explore the deepest areas of man's relation to God in a world where evil is omnipresent. Similarly, the rationalist and the mystic are both to be found within the pages of Scripture, often in the same book. The greatness of the Hebrew Bible lies precisely here—the various insights and attitudes toward life are not blurred, but each is expressed with passionate intensity.

Normative Judaism is the result of this interaction of lawgiver, priest, prophet, singer, and sage, each of whom has contributed to the variety of Jewish religious experience. As a result, adherence to Judaism could never be construed in terms of belief or credal conformity. Instead, it was the way of life, the pattern of ethical and ritual practice in which the fundamental outlook of Judaism was expressed

that united the various elements of the Jewish people and became the touchstone of Jewish allegiance.

Moreover, *Judaism is not congenitally speculative in character*. The representative personality of Judaism at its best
is not the philosopher, but the prophet. Plato in *The Republic* might discourse on the relationship of power and justice. Aristotle might analyze the concept of justice, and
Greek ethics could be concerned with elucidating the proper path for man's conduct. For the prophets the answer lay
in the realm of conduct, and theoretical presuppositions
were not investigated: "He hath told thee, O man, what is
good, and what the Lord doth require of thee: to do justice,
to love mercy, and to walk humbly with thy God" (Micah
6:8).

The contrast between the Greek and the Hebrew ethos
can be, and frequently is, overdrawn. Aeschylus, the most
Hebraic of the Greeks, is a brother in spirit to the prophets,
while the biblical sage, Ecclesiastes, though not a formal
student of Greek thought, undoubtedly was influenced by
Greek ideas, which pervaded the atmosphere in his day.[2]
Moreover, biblical religion did concern itself with theological issues, though its method of argument differed from the
canons of Greek and Western logic. The nature of God,
his relation to man, the problem of evil, the role of Israel,
the meaning of history, the purpose of life—all these were
subjects of passionate discussion, not only in Job and in
Ecclesiastes, but also in the Prophets, in the Psalms, and
even in the Torah.

Hence, when Judaism came into direct contact with
Greek thought, it did not retreat into a totally rejecting,
extreme antirationalism. At its first meeting with Hellenism,
Judaism produced Philo. In the second period, that of the
earlier Middle Ages, the confluence was more lasting and

---

[2] See Robert Gordis, *Koheleth—The Man and His World* (New York,
1951; 2d ed., 1955), chap. vi.

produced a long galaxy of thinkers from Saadia through Moses Maimonides to Hasdai Crescas. These philosophers attempted to give a rational, structured character to the faith of Judaism, and in large measure they were successful. Nonetheless, they were unable—nor was it their intention—to transform the innate character of Judaism, which remained wedded to concrete modes of thought and expression.

It is probably no accident that medieval Hebrew borrowed and naturalized the Greek term *philosophia* but never used the Greek term *theologia* in all its vast literature. For Judaism, the love of wisdom rather than a precise formulation of the doctrine of God lies at the heart of its conception of life and faith.

*The historical record discloses that Judaism never developed an ecclesiastical structure or a centralized religious authority.* In this connection, it should be pointed out that the figure of Ezra, who in the fifth century B.C.E. returned from the Babylonian exile, has often been downgraded in the history of Judaism. Actually, the Talmud made no such error and assigned to him a position second only to that of Moses. Ezra was a *priest* by descent and a *sopher*, a "scribe," better rendered "master of the Book," by vocation. Standing at a transition point in history, Ezra could have thrown the weight of his influence behind the hereditary priesthood as the dominant religious influence in Second Temple Judaism, as it had been in the past. Instead, he used the weight of his office and the prestige of his example to buttress his function as an expounder and an interpreter of the Book. While the priests continued to officiate in the Temple, as explicitly commanded in the Torah, the leadership and the dynamic influence in Second Temple Judaism were transferred to the new, democratic body of scholars whose authority depended only upon their learning, character, and personal influence, and whose seat was in the synagogues and schools. Hence not only Judaism, but Christianity, too, owes Ezra a debt insufficiently acknowledged. By giving primacy to the scribes and the rabbis in Judaism, rather than to the hereditary priestly clan of the Aaronides, Ezra indirectly helped to fashion the democratic character of the Catholic priesthood and of the Protestant ministry.

At all events, Judaism never created or recognized a centralized religious authority which could issue a binding formulation of creed, demand a pattern of ritual uniformity, or lay claim to infallibility.

Finally, *religious authority in Judaism depends primarily upon the personality and prestige of the individual scholar.* On every issue, the normative decision was established only by the assent of the majority, who had to be persuaded of the truth of the given position. Nonetheless, the minority remained active, articulate, and accredited members of the group. Basing themselves upon a passage in the Bible, Exodus 23:2, the rabbis established the principle, "one is to follow the majority." Claims to divine intervention or personal illumination were treated more or less respectfully but were rigorously excluded from deciding questions of law. Thus, in a famous controversy between the aged and pious Rabbi Eliezer and the remainder of his colleagues, in which the majority of the court was ranged against him, the Talmud declares that a heavenly voice was heard pronouncing in his favor. The presiding member of the court proceeded, however, to declare, "We pay no attention to heavenly voices. The Torah was not given to angels, but to human beings. We follow our God-invested authority, and decide the law on the basis of the views of the majority" (*Baba Metzia 59b*).

These attributes of Judaism, organically blended into an

all-encompassing tradition, are the key to its frequently unique approach to the problem of reconciling liberty and unity in a world marked by religious pluralism, racial differences, and national diversities. These realities of the human situation can prove either stumbling blocks or stepping-stones to the building of the free society.

# 3

# RELIGIOUS LIBERTY—IDEAL
# AND PRACTICE

In one sense, it can be maintained that every religious sect is passionately committed to the ideal of religious liberty—for itself. Actually, the term may be properly used in three distinct though not unrelated senses.

In the first instance, religious liberty may be equated with the right, which a religious group claims for itself, to practice its faith without interference from others. There have been communions which have conceived of religious liberty almost exclusively in terms of their right to observe their own beliefs and practices. For such a group the degree of religious liberty in a given society is measured by the extent to which it, and it alone, has been free to propagate its faith. Religious liberty is defined as "freedom for religion," and "religion" is equated with the convictions of the particular group.

This conception of religious liberty has a long and respectable history behind it. When the Puritans left England and later emigrated from Holland to Massachusetts, they were actuated by a passionate desire for religious freedom, but in this sense only. Protestant dissenters, Catholics, Jews, and non-believers could expect scant hospitality in the Bay Colony, and when any members of these groups appeared within its borders, they were given short shrift. Various

31

disabilities for non-Protestants survived in some New England states as late as the nineteenth century.

In our day, those who would restrict religious liberty to their own group frequently fall back on the doctrine that "error has no rights." It should be added that in the modern age, the Roman Catholic church, particularly in democratic countries, has generally recognized that Protestants and Jews, and even heretics and non-believers, have a right to religious freedom. This the church has conceded as a matter of practice, though it has not officially revised its theory.

Undoubtedly, this aspect of religious liberty as the right which every religious community demands to practice its tenets without interference or discrimination is a legitimate, indeed, an essential, component of the concept, and Judaism is no exception in so regarding it. By and large, however, the Jewish group has regarded the right to perpetuate its religion as self-evident, and little ink has therefore been spilled on an elaboration of this theoretical principle. Where that right has been interfered with, either overtly or covertly, whether by ecclesiastical authorities or by the secular state, through the law or group pressure, be it under fascism, communism, or democracy, Judaism has regarded the action as a sign of injustice, an act of discrimination and persecution to be opposed, rather than as a philosophy to be analyzed.

It is generally this practical phase of the subject which appears in the arena of public controversy and concern today. It attracts the attention of the sociologist, the legal expert, the community leader, and the politician, because Judaism is a minority religion and so is perpetually exposed to the disabilities of that status.

It is, however, the two other aspects of religious liberty, more theoretical in character, which are much more significant for the preservation of the ideals of a free society. The first of these is the theory and practice of *religious liberty within Judaism*—the attitude of the Jewish tradition toward dissidents within its own community. The second is the theory and the practice of *religious liberty toward non-Jews* —the attitude of the Jewish tradition toward the rights of non-Jews seeking to maintain their own creeds, and the legitimacy of such faiths from the purview of Judaism.

In order to comprehend the Jewish attitude toward religious differences within the community, one must keep in mind that Judaism has always been marked by a vast variety of religious experience and articulate expression. We have already noted that the Hebrew Bible contains within its broad and hospitable limits the products of the varied and often contradictory activities of the priest and the lawgiver, the prophet and the sage, the psalmist and the poet. It reflects the temperaments of the mystic and the rationalist, the simple believer and the profound seeker after ultimate truth.

This characteristic of the Bible set its stamp upon all succeeding epochs in the history of Judaism. It is not accidental that the most creative era in its history after the biblical era, the period of the Second Temple, was the most "sect-ridden." Even our fragmentary sources disclose the existence of the Pharisees, the Sadducees, the Essenes, and the Zealots, to use Josephus' classic tabulation of the "Four Philosophies." We know from the Talmud, which is a massive monument to controversy, that the Pharisees themselves, who were the dominant group in number and influence, were divided into various groups which held strongly to opposing positions, with hundreds of individual scholars differing from the majority on scores of issues. Unfortunately, very little is known about the Sadducees, but the same variety of outlook may be assumed among them. With regard to the Essenes, the discovery of the Dead Sea Scrolls has indicated that the term is best used of an entire conspectus of sects who differed among themselves as well. The Samaritans were also a significant group of dissidents, highly articulate in their divergence from a Jerusalem-centered Judaism. It was in this atmosphere that the early Jewish sect of Christians first appeared, adding to the charged atmosphere of vitality and variety in Palestinian Judaism. There were also countless additional viewpoints in the various Diaspora communities.

All these groups in Judaism obviously shared many fundamentals in their outlook. They were united by the faith in one God as the creator of the universe and the ruler of man, the concept of Israel as the elect people, and devotion to the Torah as his revealed Will. In addition they looked forward eagerly to the advent of the Messiah and to the triumph of his cause through the establishment of righteousness and peace for Israel and the world. Yet on other major aspects of the tradition, including the meaning of some of these very doctrines, controversy raged. Thus the crucial debate between the Pharisees and the Sadducees revolved about the divine origin and authority of the oral law and the belief in the resurrection of the dead, two central doctrines which the former affirmed and the latter, with equal vigor, denied.

In the realm of practice, always basic to Judaism, there were equally fundamental differences. Thus the Pharisees and Sadducees disagreed as to the date of the Shavuot festival and on the mode of observing Sukkot. So, too, one of the few relatively assured results of Dead Sea Scrolls research is that the Qumran sectarians differed from normative Judaism on the calendar, evidently sharing the viewpoint of the *Book of Jubilees*. Hence the great festivals, including the Day of Atonement, were observed on different dates by the various groups. The Talmud records that among the Pharisees the differences between the schools of Hillel and Shammai were deep-seated and broke out into physical violence at one point (*Sanhedrin* 88*b*; *Shabbat* 17*a*). Nonetheless, the Talmud declares, the Shammaites and the Hillelites did not hesitate to intermarry and "He who observes according to the decision of Beth Hillel, like him who follows the school of Shammai, is regarded as fulfilling the Law," because "both these and the others are the words of the Living God" (*Mishnah, Eduyot* 4:8). No such encomiums were pronounced on the Sadducees, who contradicted the fundamentals of normative Judaism. Those holding Sadducean views were stigmatized as "having no share in the world to come" (*Mishnah, Sanhedrin* 10:1). In this world, however, it is noteworthy, neither they nor any others of these sects were ever officially excommunicated.

In the Middle Ages a variety of factors combined to contract this latitude of religious outlook. On the one hand, the constantly worsening conditions of exile and alien status required, it was felt, a greater degree of group homogeneity. Second, most of the earlier dissident viewpoints disappeared. Thus the standpoint of the supernationalist Zealot revolutionaries was now totally meaningless, while that of the Sadducees, who centered their religious life in the Temple at Jerusalem, was completely irrelevant to the life of an exiled people.

Third, the widespread emphasis on religious conformity imposed by the medieval world on its aberrant sects also proved a model and example. Father Joseph Lecler points out in his massive two-volume work, *Toleration and the Reformation*, that Thomas Aquinas was "relatively tolerant toward pagans and completely intolerant toward heretics." Thomas explicitly stated that "to accept the faith is a matter of free-will, but to hold it, once it has been accepted, is a matter of necessity."

No such precise and logical theory was ever elaborated in Judaism. The Jewish community lacked the power to compel uniformity of thought, even in the relatively rare instances when the leadership was tempted to embark upon such an enterprise. Nonetheless, some efforts were made to restrict religious liberty in the Middle Ages. The history of these undertakings is significant for the intrinsic nature of the Jewish tradition.

Somewhat paradoxically, the attempt to impose a measure of uniformity in religious belief was due to the emergence of medieval Jewish philosophy, which was nurtured in Aristotelianism and to a lesser degree in Platonism. The sprawling and unprecise character of traditional Jewish belief proved distasteful to many a theologian. Maimonides, the most influential thinker in the group, was the least patient with unclarity and vagueness. Thus he confidently proposed his "Thirteen Principles," which he hoped would serve as a creed for Judaism. Their all-embracing character, the lucidity of their formulation, and the importance of their author gave them wide popularity, and they are printed in the traditional prayer book as an appendix. Lesser men, however, did not hesitate to quarrel with both the content and the number of articles of belief in the Maimonidean Creed, and it never became an official confession of faith.

An even more striking illustration of the enduring vitality of the right to religious diversity in Judaism may be cited. Uncompromisingly rationalistic as he was, Maimonides declared that to ascribe any physical form to God was tantamount to heresy and deprived one of a share in the world to come. Nowhere is the genius of Judaism better revealed than here. On the same printed page of Maimonides' *Code*, where this statement is encountered, it is challenged by the comment of his critic and commentator, Rabbi Abraham ben David of Posquières, who writes: "Better and greater men than Maimonides have ascribed a physical form to God, basing themselves on their understanding of Scriptural passages and even more so on some legends and utterances, which give wrong ideas." The critic's standpoint is clear. He agrees with Maimonides in denying a physical form to God, but he affirms the right of the individual Jew to maintain backward ideas in Judaism without being read out of the fold on that account! The right to be wrong is the essence of liberty.

Nonetheless, the spirit of medieval Judaism was far less hospitable to religious diversity than was rabbinic Judaism in the centuries immediately before and after the destruction of the Temple. Thus, while none of the earlier sects was ever excommunicated, the Karaites received less lenient treatment. This sect, which arose in the eighth century and denied the authority of the Talmud under the banner of strict adherence to the letter of Scripture, proved a major threat to normative Judaism. A very lively polemic literature developed for several centuries. Efforts were made to excommunicate the Karaites *in toto* by some individual scholars. Later a more liberal attitude toward them came into existence, when the sect no longer threatened the vitality of rabbinic Judaism. Karaism, which was originally a highly creative and stimulating force in Jewish scholarship and thought, ultimately shriveled up into a tiny group. It finally became segregated, and in this form has vestigial remains in our day. But this segregation was due at least as much to its own volition as to the antagonism of the majority. In recent years, the Karaites were impelled to deny their connection with the Jewish people by the desire to avoid the discriminations which various regimes, notably Czarist Russia, imposed upon traditional Jews.

In the Middle Ages, the *herem*, the "ban" or "excommunication" which is already referred to in the Talmud, became a frequently utilized instrument of community life, but it rarely served as a weapon for enforcing religious conformity. A detailed study of the ban in talmudic and medieval Judaism makes it clear that it was primarily invoked to enforce the authority of the community in the case of three principal threats: (*a*) the weakening of the authority of the Jewish courts; (*b*) the violation of religious or ethical standards; and (*c*) malfeasance in office by community officials.

Curiously enough, the best-known example of the use of excommunication in Judaism is an exception rather than the rule. The philosopher, Baruch Spinoza, was publicly excommunicated by the Jewish community of Amsterdam on July 27, 1656. This act is frequently, though erroneously, cited as an instance of the enforcement of religious conformity by ecclesiastical fiat. Undoubtedly, religious intolerance played its part in shaping the spirit of the community, many of whose members, including Spinoza's own family, had managed to escape from Spain and Portugal at great peril, after agonizing years spent as Marranos, under the surveillance of the Inquisition. The iron of persecution had surely entered their souls, and their passionate loyalty to the faith which they had won at so great a cost made them intolerant of deviants.

However, it should be noted that Spinoza had already taken up residence outside of the Jewish community before his excommunication. That the basic motivation for the ban was practical is revealed by the fact that the act was at once communicated to the Amsterdam magistracy. It was obvious that the Jewish community, living on sufferance even in free Holland, was fearful lest its status be jeopardized by its harboring and tolerating a heretic whose views were regarded as subversive of all religion. These fears were not groundless, as is clear from the fact that Spinoza's *Tractatus Theologico-Politicus* was published in 1670 anonymously and was promptly proscribed by the synod of Doort and the States-General of Holland, Zealand, and West Friesland.

Excommunication against religious diversity was invoked again in the eighteenth century, this time against Hasidism, a folk movement, pietistic in character, which arose in eastern Europe. As the tide of Hasidism threatened to inundate all of east European Jewry, the great rabbinic luminary,

Elijah, the Gaon of Vilna (1720–97), was prevailed upon twice to lend his august authority to a ban against the sect, in 1777 and again in 1781. As he himself anticipated, this *herem* did not avail. Ultimately, the sect abated in its hostility against rabbinical Judaism, and today the Hasidim and their "opponents," together with a mediating group, are all within the household of Orthodox Judaism.

In the nineteenth century, when the Reform movement first began to appear in central Europe, some Orthodox rabbis in central and eastern Europe sought to stem the tide by invoking the ban against the innovators. It had proved largely ineffective in the field of ideas even in the Middle Ages; now, however, it was completely useless. It served only to drive deeper the wedge between the traditionalists and the non-traditionalists and was tacitly abandoned.

The effort to enforce religious conformity reached the level of bathos in the United States over a decade ago. A modernist prayer book was issued by the Reconstructionist group headed by Professor Mordecai M. Kaplan. A public protest meeting at a New York hotel was convened by an Orthodox rabbinical association, and a copy of the book was burned. It is, however, characteristic of the anti-authoritarian temper of traditional Judaism that the book-burning reportedly took place in private and was later disavowed by the sponsoring organization as being the act of an over-zealous individual. Indeed, it is often denied that the book-burning took place at all!

In sum, religious liberty within the Jewish community exists *de facto*. It is recognized *de jure* by all groups in Reform and Conservative Judaism and by substantial elements in Orthodoxy as well. Some right-wing groups in contemporary Orthodoxy have sought to arrogate to themselves alone the stamp of legitimacy and to stake out a claim to sole possession of the truth, but these efforts have not proved successful and are not likely to be so. The long tradition of dissent in Judaism militates against any such claim to unique authority. It is significant that Orthodoxy itself exhibits literally dozens of variants and possesses a lesser degree of cohesion than do the non-Orthodox interpretations of Judaism.

An observation is in order with regard to the status of religion and state in Israel. The Israeli cabinet includes a minister of religions (in the plural), who is charged with the supervision and maintenance of the "holy places" of all the three great religions and with the support of their institutional and educational requirements. There is full freedom of religion in Israel for everyone—except Jews. Catholic and Protestant Christianity, Islam, Bahai—all enjoy the fullest freedom of expression, including the opportunity for zealous missionary activity among Jews, which has aroused not a little antagonism. In addition to the ministry of religions, Israel has a chief rabbi for each of its principal communities, a scholar of unimpeachable Orthodoxy, except for those Orthodox groups who deny his authority! In accordance with the legacy of Turkish and British law, the chief rabbi (like his Christian and Islamic counterparts) has authority in the field of personal status, notably marriage, divorce, and inheritance, and, to a lesser degree, in the maintenance of religious observance in the army and public institutions, and in the supervision of religious education.

At present, there exists a type of union of religion and state in the state of Israel. In spite of the attempt to invest the contemporary situation with the halo of tradition, the historical truth is that such a formal union was not normative in Judaism. To be sure, it existed officially during the period of Jewish independence in the Maccabean age, which lasted, all told, less than eighty years (142 B.C.E. to 63 B.C.E.). The descendants of the Maccabees were priest-kings, theoretically combining in their own persons the secular and the religious authority. It is noteworthy, however, that their priestly legitimacy was strenuously and often bloodily denied by the Pharisees, the most numerous and influential group, as well as by the Dead Sea sectarians and other elements. Moreover, as we have noted, the priestly role was not the most significant one even during this period, when the Temple worship with its panoply of ritual was maintained and honored by most of the people. The dynamic source and center of the Jewish religion in this era was not to be found in the Temple in Jerusalem but in the far less pretentious synagogues and schoolhouses, and here not the priests, but the lay scholars, were the dominant influence. The creation of the office of a chief rabbi in Israel today represents, therefore, not a return to tradition but an innovation, the value of which is highly debatable. It is much more an imitation of Christian prototypes than a link in the chain of authentic Jewish tradition.

With the chief rabbinate as its symbol, Orthodoxy is the only officially recognized religious group in Israel today. Yet here, too, the innate tradition of dissent finds uninhibited expression. Thus, when the new and magnificent headquarters of the chief rabbinate was erected in Jerusalem, many of the leading Orthodox scholars announced that it was religiously prohibited to cross the threshold of the building! Side by side with these tensions within Israeli Orthodoxy are various other groups, along a wide spectrum of modernism, that have already established a foothold in the country and ultimately will demand and receive recognition. It is obvious that the present privileged status of Orthodoxy represents a transition stage that cannot endure. It is the result of a temporary political alliance that has subsisted uneasily between the non-religious progressive and labor parties left of center, headed by Prime Minister David Ben-Gurion, and the group of small Orthodox political parties during the first decade of Israeli independence. The motivation is to provide the necessary majority for a working coalition in the government.

No long-term conclusions may therefore be drawn from the present union of religion and state in Israel. It is partial and subjected to increasing strain and stress. Whether the ultimate pattern of religion-state relationships will approximate the American structure is problematic, though the American experience is frequently invoked as an ideal. The disestablishment of religion in any sectarian form is, however, inevitable.

The conclusion is unassailable that the nature of Judaism, buttressed by its historic experience, makes the freedom of religious dissent a recognized reality for virtually all members of the community *de facto*, even by those who would not recognize it *de jure*.

The attitude of Judaism toward religious liberty for those professing other creeds derives, in large measure, from the deeply rooted tension between particularism and universalism, which, as we have pointed out, is characteristic of the Jewish tradition. It is the resultant of two forces: the retention of the specific Jewish content in the tradition, on the one hand, and, on the other, an equally genuine concern for the establishment among all men of the faith in one God and obedience to his religious and ethical imperatives.

It is frequently argued that, with the appearance of Judaism, intolerance became a coefficient of religion. It is undoubtedly true that in a polytheistic world view tolerance of other gods is implicit, since there is always room for one more figure in the pantheon, and the history of religious syncretism bears out this truth. On the other hand, the emergence of belief in one God necessarily demands the denial of the reality of all other deities. The "jealous God" of the Old Testament who forbids "any other god before Me" therefore frequently became the source of religious intolerance. So runs the theory.

It sometimes happens, however, that a beautiful pattern of invincible logic is contradicted by the refractory behavior of life itself. An apposite illustration may be cited. The famous Semitic scholar Ernest Renan declared that it was the monotony of the desert that produced a propensity for monotheism among the ancient Hebrews, whereas the variety in the physical landscape of Greece, for example, with its mountains and hills, its valleys, rivers, and streams, necessarily suggested a multitude of divinities indwelling in them. This plausible theory enjoyed a good deal of vogue until it was learned that the pre-Islamic nomadic Arabs, who inhabit the vast stretches of the Arabian Desert, possessed a very luxuriant polytheism and that all the Semitic peoples, whose original habitat was the same desert, also had very elaborate pantheons. Thus the list of gods in the library of King Ashurbanipal contains more than 2,500 gods, and modern scholars have added substantially to the number.

Now, Judaism was strongly exclusivist in its attitude toward paganism. It insisted upon the uncompromising unity of God and refused to admit even a semblance of reality to other gods. Nonetheless, biblical Judaism reckoned with the existence of paganism from two points of view. Though logicians might have recoiled in horror from the prospect, the fact is that Hebrew monotheism, the authentic and conscious faith in the existence of one God, did accord a kind of legitimacy to polytheism—for non-Jews. In part, this may have derived from a recognition of the actual existence of flourishing heathen cults. In far larger degree, we believe that it was a consequence of the particularist emphasis in Judaism, which, being dedicated to preserving the specific group character of the Hebrew faith, was led to grant a similar charter of justification to the specific ethos of other nations, which always included their religion. No book in the Bible is more explicitly monotheistic than Deuteronomy, not even Isaiah or Job: "Know therefore this day, and consider it in thine heart, that the Lord He is God in heaven above, and upon the earth beneath; there is none else" (4:39). Yet the same book, which warns Israel against idolatry, speaks of "the sun, the moon and the stars" . . . *which the Lord thy God has assigned to all the nations* under the sky" (4:19; cf. 29:25). Thus the paradox emerges that the particularist element in Judaism proved the embryo of a theory of religious tolerance.

The second factor that helped to accord a measure of value to non-Jewish religion is one more congenial to sophisticated religious thinkers. A broad-minded exponent of monotheism would be capable of recognizing, even in the pagan cults against which Judaism fought, an imperfect, unconscious aspiration toward the one living God. Perhaps the most striking expression of this insight is to be found in the post-exilic prophet Malachi: "For from the rising of the sun even unto his going down, My name is great among the nations; and in every place incense is burnt and there is offered unto my name, even a pure offering; for great is My name among the nations, saith the Lord of hosts" (1:11).

Nor is this the only instance in our biblical sources. The universalism of the author of Jonah, who exhibits the pagan sailors in a far more favorable light than he does the fugitive Hebrew prophet, the broad compassion of the Book of Ruth, and the Book of Job, which pictures the patriarch not as a Hebrew observer of the Torah but as a non-Jew whose noble creed and practice are described in his great "Confession of Innocence" (chap. 31), all testify to the fact that it was possible to maintain the unity and universality of God, while reckoning with the values inherent in the imperfect approximations to be found in pagan cults. Thus the two apparently contradictory elements of the biblical world view, the emphasis upon a particularist ethos and the faith in a universal God, both served as the seedbed for the flowering of a highly significant theory of religious tolerance in post-biblical Judaism. To this concept, known as the Noachide Laws, we shall return.

Nonetheless, it was self-evident that a universal God who was the father of all men deserved the allegiance and loyalty of all his children. A steady and unremitting effort was therefore made to counteract the blandishments of paganism and to win men for Jewish monotheism through the use of persuasion. The biblical Deutero-Isaiah, the apocryphal *Sibylline Oracles*, the lifelong activity of Philo of Alexandria, indeed, the entire apologetic literature of Hellenistic Judaism, were all designed to win the allegiance of men for the one living God of Israel.

Forcible conversion to Judaism was ruled out, not merely because of the innate weakness of the Jewish group, but because of ethical considerations. Two exceptions are known. The Maccabean prince John Hyrcanus (135–104 B.C.E.) forced the Idumeans, hereditary enemies of the Jews, to accept Judaism. His son, Aristobulus, Judaized part of Galilee in the northern district of Palestine (Josephus, *Antiquities*, XII, 9, 1; 11, 3). These steps were dictated less by religious zeal than by practical considerations, the universal characteristic of mass conversions which persists to our own day. The whole tenor of rabbinic thought, which hedged the path of would-be converts with many safeguards in order to be assured of their sincerity, constitutes evidence that Jewish tradition was opposed to proselytization achieved either through force or through the pressure of ulterior motives.

Holding fast to their conviction that Judaism alone represents the true faith in the one God, the prophets had looked forward to its ultimate acceptance by all men: "For then will I change unto the people a pure language, that they may all call on the name of the Lord, to serve Him with one accord" (Zephaniah 3:19). "And the Lord will be king over

all the earth; on that day shall the Lord be one, and His
name one" (Zechariah 14:9).

This faith for the future did not cause devotees of Judaism to overlook the realities of the present. They did not
deny the values to be found in the religious professions and
even more in the ethical practices of many of their pagan
fellow men. From these facts there emerged one of the
most distinctive concepts of monotheistic religion, a unique
contribution of Judaism to the theory of religious liberty:
the doctrine of the Noachide Laws, which actually antedates the Talmud. The apocryphal *Book of Jubilees*, written before the beginning of the Christian era, could not conceive of untold generations of men before Moses living
without a divine revelation. It therefore attributes to Noah,
who was not a Hebrew, a code of conduct binding upon all
men:

> In the twenty-eighth jubilee, Noah began to enjoin
> upon his sons' sons the ordinances and commandments
> and all the judgments that he knew and he exhorted his
> sons to observe righteousness and to cover the shame of
> their flesh and to bless their Creator and honor father and
> mother and love their neighbor and guard their souls from
> fornication and uncleanness and all iniquity [*Jubilees* 7:22].

This injunction is elaborated in the rabbinic tradition under
the rubric of the Laws of the Sons of Noah (*B. Sanhedrin
56a–60a; Tosefta, Abodah Zarah* 8:4–8). According to this
rabbinic view, all human beings, by virtue of their humanity, are commanded to observe at least seven fundamental
religious and moral principles. These commandments include the prohibition of idolatry, of murder, and of theft;
the avoidance of blasphemy and of cruelty to animals by
eating the limb of a living creature; and the establishment
of a government based on law and order. When these principles, upon which all civilized society depends, are observed, Judaism declares the non-Jew to be as worthy of sal-

vation as the Jew who observes the entire rubric of Jewish law. Hence, there is no imperative need for the non-Jew to accept the Jewish faith in order to be "saved."

These Laws of the Sons of Noah, it may be noted, seem to be referred to in the New Testament as well:

> But that we write unto them, that they abstain from pollutions of idols and from fornication, and from things strangled, and from blood. . . . That ye abstain from meats offered to idols, and from blood and from things strangled and from fornication: from which if ye keep yourselves, ye shall do well. Fare ye well [Acts 15:20, 29].

This doctrine of the Noachide Laws is extremely interesting from several points of view. It represents in essence a theory of universal religion which is binding upon all men. Characteristically Jewish is its emphasis upon good actions rather than upon right belief as the mark of the good life. Ethical living rather than credal adherence is the decisive criterion for salvation. Its spirit is epitomized in the great rabbinic utterance, "I call Heaven and earth to witness, that whether one be Gentile or Jew, man or woman, slave or free man, the divine spirit rests on each in accordance with his deeds" (*Yalkut Shimoni* on Judges, Sec. 42). Significantly, the equality of all men in the rabbinic formulation does not derive from common doctrinal belief nor does it depend upon it but requires only loyalty to a code of ethical conduct.

Many contemporary religious thinkers are now seeking a theory which will combine complete loyalty to a specific tradition while accepting wholeheartedly the postulates of a democratic society, which is committed to pluralism as a reality and to religious liberty as a good. The issue is one which profoundly agitates Americans in our day because of its practical importance in government and politics.

There is more than academic interest, therefore, in this rabbinic adumbration of a theory of religious tolerance rest-ing upon a concept of "natural law." This doctrine of the Noachide Laws, be it noted, was not the product of religious indifference. It arose among devotees of a traditional religion who loved their faith and believed that it alone was the product of authentic revelation. Yet they found room for faiths other than their own in the world, as of right and not merely on sufferance.

Unorganized missionary activity and the conversion of individual non-Jews to Judaism through personal conviction remained entirely possible and, indeed, was far from rare throughout the Middle Ages, which were marked by untold accessions to Jewish ranks. Perhaps the most notable instance was the Tartar kingdom of the Chazars, which flourished in central Russia from the eighth to the eleventh century, and in which the royal house, the court, and a substantial proportion of the people accepted Judaism. It is noteworthy that the Chazar kingdom was the first state in history to establish thoroughgoing religious tolerance for all religions within its borders, for Christianity and Islam as well as for Judaism.

The principle of the Noachide Laws had originated in a pagan world. It obviously proved even more valuable when two monotheistic religions, Christianity and Islam, replaced paganism. Both "daughter faiths" sought energetically to displace the mother and deny her authenticity. The mother faith sought to repulse these onslaughts as effectively as possible by calling attention to what she regarded as their errors. But she did not, on that account, ignore the elements of truth which her younger and more aggressive offspring possessed.

The attitude of Judaism toward these two religions necessarily differed with the personality of each particular authority, his environment, and his own personal experience. The teaching of the second-century sage Rabbi Joshua, "The righteous among the Gentiles have a share in the

world to come" (*Tosefta, Sanhedrin* 13:2), which underscored the principle that salvation was open even to those
outside the Jewish fold, remained normative and served as
the basic principle underlying the Noachide Laws. The
medieval poet and philosopher Judah Halevi wrote:
"These peoples [i.e., Christianity and Islam] represent a
preparation and preface to the Messiah for whom we wait,
who is the fruit of the tree which they will ultimately recognize as the roots which they now despise" (*Kuzari* 4:23).

Rabbi Menahem Meiri, who lived in thirteenth-century
France, a land from which expulsions of Jews were common, wrote:

> Those among the heathens of the ancient days who ob-
> serve the seven Noachide precepts, i.e., refrain from idol
> worship, desecration of God's name, robbery, incest,
> cruelty to animals, and have courts of justice, enjoy the
> same rights as Jews; how much the more so in our days,
> when the nations are distinguished by their religion and
> respect for law! We must, however, treat equally even
> those who have no systems of law, in order to sanctify
> the Name of God [cited in Bezalel Ashkenazi's *Shittah
> Mekubbetzet* (1761), p. 78*a*].

He distinctly declares that "in our days idolatry has ceased
in most places" and describes both Muslims and Christians
as "nations disciplined by the ways of their religions."

Moreover, even the trinitarian concept of Christianity,
which Judaism emphatically repudiated as impugning the
unity of God, was not generally regarded as sufficient to
deny to Christianity the character of a monotheistic faith.
The twelfth-century talmudic commentator Rabbi Isaac
the Tosafist set forth a legal basis for the view that belief in
the Trinity was legitimate for Christians in his statement:
"The children of Noah are not prohibited from *shittuf*, i.e.,
associating the belief in God with that in other beings"
(*Tosafot, B. Sanhedrin* 63*b*). This utterance achieved such

wide scope and authority that it was frequently attributed by later scholars to the Talmud itself.

Maimonides, with his penchant for systematic canons of thought, was strongly critical both of Christianity and of Islam. Living all his life in Islamic countries, with few direct contacts with Christians, he tended to react negatively to the trinitarianism of Christianity and to its messianic claims for Jesus as the Savior. On the other hand, the uncompromising emphasis upon the unity of God in Mohammedanism, with which he was in constant contact, gave him a greater degree of tolerance for Islam, though he castigated the sensuality of the prophet Mohammed. Even the adoration of the Ka'abah, the black stone of Mecca, Maimonides regarded as a vestige of polytheism which had been reinterpreted in Islam, a remarkable anticipation of modern research.

In a passage in his great code, *Mishneh Torah*, which appears mutilated in the printed texts because of the censor, Maimonides rejects the claim that Jesus was the Messiah on the ground that he failed to fulfil the messianic function as envisioned in Scripture and tradition. He then proceeds:

> The thought of the Creator of the world is beyond the power of man to grasp, for their ways are not His ways and their thoughts are not His thoughts. All the words of Jesus the Nazarene and of Mohammed, who arose after him, came into being, only in order to make straight the road for the King Messiah, who would perfect the world to serve God together, as it is said, "Then I shall turn all the peoples into a clear speech, that they may all call upon the Lord and serve Him shoulder to shoulder."
>
> How is that to be? The world has already been filled with the words of the Messiah, and the words of the Torah and the commandments. And these words have spread to the furthermost islands among many people uncircumcised of heart or of flesh, who now discuss the Commandments of the Torah. Some declare that these commandments were true, but are now no longer obligatory and have fallen into decline, while others declare that there are

secret meanings within them, not according to their obvious intent, and that the Messiah had come and disclosed their secret connotations.

But when the true King Messiah will arise, he will succeed and be raised to glory and then they will all return and recognize that they had inherited falsehood, and that their Prophets and ancestors had misled them [*Hilkhot Melakhim* 11:4].

Elsewhere Maimonides goes further than the warrant of his rabbinic sources and the attitude of most of his contemporaries when he declares that Christians are idolators because of their trinitarian beliefs (*Mishneh Torah, Abodah Zarah* 9:3; *Commentary on the Mishnah, Abodah Zarah* 1:3).

On the other hand, his great predecessor Saadia (882–942), the first great figure in medieval Jewish philosophy, who also lived under Islam, declared that the Christians' belief in the Trinity is not an expression of idolatry but the personification of their faith in life, power, and knowledge (*Emunot Vedeot* 2:5). In his negative view, Maimonides not only ignored the talmudic passage quoted above but was in sharpest variance with most Jewish scholars like Rashi and Meiri, who lived in Christian countries, knew Christians at first hand, and recognized their deeply rooted belief in the one God.

In the eighteenth century, Moses Mendelssohn wrote a famous reply to the Protestant minister Johann Caspar Lavater. In it, he expounded the traditional Jewish doctrine, speaking in the accents of the eighteenth-century Enlightenment:

> Moses has commanded us the Law; it is an inheritance of the congregation of Jacob. All other nations we believe to be enjoined to keep the law of nature. Those conducting their lives in accordance with this religion of nature and of reason are called "virtuous men from among other nations," and these are entitled to eternal bliss (*sind Kinder der ewigen Seligkeit*).

There was an obvious apologetic intent and a consequent exaggeration in his next statement:

> The religion of my fathers, therefore, does not desire to be spread. We are not to send missions to Greenland or to the Indies in order to preach our faith to these distant nations. The latter nation, in particular, observing as it does the law of nature better than we do here, according to reports received, is in the view of our religious doctrines an enviable nation.

It is true that an active missionary campaign has not been carried on in Judaism ever since the pre-Christian centuries, when Hellenistic Judaism won untold pagans for "reverence for God" and thus helped lay the foundation for the rapid spread of Christianity. In the Middle Ages the external facts of history united with the inner nature of Judaism to preclude large-scale efforts to win non-Jews to Judaism. Today, some voices are being raised in the Jewish community in favor of an active campaign to bring the message of Judaism to the non-Jewish world, though without employing conventional missionary techniques. A warm controversy on this question is now going on among Jewish religious leaders and laity. But both those who favor and those who oppose such an active effort are at one in recognizing the legitimacy of non-Jewish faiths, the availability of salvation to all who observe the basic spiritual and ethical principles embodied in the Noachide Laws, and the right of all men to the fullest liberty of religious practice and belief.

The attitude of Judaism toward religious liberty may now be summarized as follows:

1. It accepts the existence of differences within the Jewish group and the right of dissidents to their own outlook and practice, at least *de facto*.

2. It recognizes the existence of other religions among men and their inherent right to be observed *de jure*.

There inheres a measure of naïveté, as there is of over-simplification, in Albert Einstein's utterance, "I thank God that I belong to a people which has been too weak to do much harm in the world." But more than mere incapacity inheres in the Jewish attitude toward religious liberty. The balance between the universal aspirations of Judaism and its strong attachment to the preservation of its group character impelled it to create a theory that made room in God's plan —and in the world—for men of other convictions and practices.

Moreover, the deeply ingrained individualism of the Jewish character, its penchant for questioning, and its insistence upon rational conviction have made dissent a universal feature of the Jewish spiritual physiognomy. As a result, all groups have achieved freedom of expression and practice, though efforts to limit or suppress this liberty of conscience have not been totally lacking and undoubtedly will recur in the future. But they are generally accompanied by a bad conscience on the part of the apostles of intolerance. They thus reveal their weak roots in the tradition that they are ostensibly defending and betray their predestined failure to achieve their ends.

Finally, the millennial experience of Jewish disability and exile in the ancient and the medieval world has strengthened this attachment to freedom of conscience among Jews. In addition, the modern world has demonstrated that the material and intellectual position and progress of Jews, individually and collectively, is most effectively advanced in an atmosphere of religious liberty. Thus, all three elements, tradition, temperament, and history, have united to make religious freedom, both for the Jewish community and for the larger family of mankind, an enduring ideal and not merely a temporarily prudential arrangement. The standard of liberty has not always been maintained with consistency, but it has generally been espoused with fervor and cherished with tenacity.

# 4

# GROUND RULES FOR A CHRISTIAN-JEWISH DIALOGUE

We have seen that the ideal of religious liberty has deep roots within the Jewish tradition. It is an even more pronounced feature of the spiritual landscape of American life. It is noteworthy that the First Amendment to the Constitution is dedicated to safeguarding freedom of religion, even before all other rights are set forth.

This emphasis upon religious liberty, imbedded deeply in the law of the land, has developed the unique American doctrine of the separation of church and state. It informs and complicates every discussion of the status of religion in society and of the extent and limits of the rights of organized religion in such fields as education and public morals.

Upon this platform of religious freedom, the American people has sought to build a structure of religious understanding and mutual respect. No phenomenon on the social scene is more characteristic of the optimism and basic good will of the American people than the "interfaith movement." Thirty years have elapsed since the interfaith movement was launched with genuine idealism and high hopes, and in the interim it has grown in prestige, program, and personnel. Yet, today, one seems to detect a widespread recognition that much more needs to be done, that there has been too much concern with the shadow rather than with the substance of intergroup relations. It will not do to content ourselves with affirmations of good will and mutual admiration. It is not enough to stress "the things that unite us," genuine though they be, unless we also come to grips with the controversial issues—which is to say, the live issues—that divide Americans of various religious persuasions and of none. If our religious and ethical tradition is to prove a blessing and not a curse, we cannot evade the problems, both ideological and practical, that bedevil intergroup relations in twentieth-century America.

The conviction that a new approach is needed is now widespread. Some of the leading agencies in the area of interfaith work are therefore reaching for new goals and new techniques. From all sides, the American people is being called upon to cease repeating avowals of brotherhood and to begin practicing it in the field of ethnic relations, both at home and in our relations with other nations abroad. In the area of religious differences, a Christian theologian has expressed the growing recognition "that Christians need to reopen discussions with the ancient people of God as well as with the other great faiths of the world."

There undoubtedly exists a genuine need for a fruitful dialogue between Christianity and Judaism, the two religions of the Western world that are linked together in a unique embrace of kinship and difference. It has been repeated time without number—and yet it remains true—that there are substantial areas of agreement between these two faiths, which share a common historical background and revere the same Scriptures as the Word of God. No theological subtlety should obscure the similarity of outlook between Judaism and Christianity with regard to the nature of God, the duty of man, and many other aspects of their respective world views,

It is, however, necessary to recognize that similarity is not identity. As we have already noted, each tradition possesses a varying emphasis, a difference in timbre that gives even to the elements they have in common a well-marked individuality. Hence what is dominant in one religion is frequently recessive in the other, and biblical texts of unassailable sanctity in both traditions occupy widely different positions in the hierarchy of values in each.

There is no need to add further examples. The Christian-Jewish dialogue, if it is to be fruitful, must reckon with the elements of similarity and of difference—and with the subtler and more significant aspects that partake of both. The enterprise therefore requires high resources of mutual sympathy, insight, learning, and candor.

It is this last-named quality that suggests the importance of some ground rules, if we are to have a true dialogue between the participants and not merely a monologue moving in one direction. In order to advance this significant enterprise, it is essential to keep in mind five principles that should be self-evident but all too often are ignored.

1. The time is overdue for *abandoning the well-worn contrast constantly being drawn between "the Old Testament God of Justice" and the "God of Love of the New Testament."* Every competent scholar, Christian and Jewish alike, knows that the Old Testament conceived of God in terms of love as well as of justice, just as Jesus' God manifested himself in justice as well as in love, for justice without love is cruelty, and love without justice is caprice. Professor J. Philip Hyatt of Vanderbilt University has been particularly articulate in emphasizing the attribute of love in the Old Testament conception of God.

It is, of course, not enough to use a biblical concordance to find the word "love" and to use the statistics of its occurrence as a proof. Often it is necessary to penetrate beneath the vocabulary to the meaning. Thus, in pleading with God for the wicked Sodomites, Abraham calls out, "Shall not the judge of all the earth do justice?" (Genesis 18:25). The term that is used as "justice," not "love," but the God who is prepared to spare the sinful city of Sodom for the sake of ten righteous men is manifestly a God of love.

In the Decalogue itself, God is similarly described as punishing evildoers to the fourth generation but as showing mercy to his loved ones to the thousandth (Exodus 20:5–6; Deuteronomy 5:9–10). Central in the Hebrew tradition is the theophany which follows upon God's forgiving the Israelites for the grievous sin of the Golden Calf. In phrases echoed throughout the Hebrew Bible, God is praised as "merciful and gracious, long-suffering, and abundant in goodness and truth," and the same distinction is drawn: "He *keeps mercy unto the thousandth generation*, forgiving iniquity, transgression, and sin; and not destroying utterly, though He *visits the iniquity of the fathers* upon the children, and upon the children's children, *unto the third and unto the fourth generation*" (Exodus 34:6–7).

When we move from the Mosaic age to the period of the later prophets, the emphasis is even stronger. The prophet Hosea had suffered a deep personal tragedy; his affection for his wife and trust in her were cruelly betrayed by her unfaithfulness. But his love triumphed over his indignation, and he saw in his relationship to his erring wife a prototype of God's love for his people, which he expressed in the language of the marriage covenant:

And I will betroth thee unto Me forever,
Yea, I will betroth thee unto Me in righteousness and justice,
In loving-kindness and compassion.
And I will betroth thee unto Me in faithfulness;
And thou shalt know the Lord [Hosea 2:21–22].

God's love for his wayward children finds expression both in his affection as well as in his exasperation:

When Israel was a child, then I loved him,
And out of Egypt I called My son. . . .
I drew them with cords of a man,
With bands of love: . . .
And I fed them gently [Hosea 11:1–4].

O Ephraim, what shall I do unto thee?
O Judah, what shall I do unto thee?
For your goodness is as a morning cloud,
And as the early morning dew [Hosea 6:4].

Amos is conventionally described as the stern prophet of
the God of justice. That he stresses divine justice is true, but
that he ignores divine love is not. One has only to penetrate
beneath the surface of his prophetic soul to sense the love
that he knows God feels for his sinful children:

Hate evil and love good,
And establish justice in the gate.
Perhaps the Lord, the God of hosts,
Will have compassion on the remnant of Joseph [Amos
5:15]

O Lord God, forgive, I beseech Thee;
How shall Jacob stand, for he is small?
The Lord repented concerning this;
"It shall not be," saith the Lord [Amos 7:2, 5].

The same spirit lives in Amos' vision of national forgiveness
and restoration:

In that day will I raise up
The tabernacle of David that is fallen,
And close up the breaches thereof,
And I will raise up his ruins.
And I will build it as in the days of old [Amos 9:11].

And I will turn the captivity of My people Israel,
And they shall build the waste cities, and inhabit them;
And they shall plant vineyards, and drink their wine;
They shall also make gardens, and eat their fruit [Amos
9:14].

To cite one more instance, the Book of Jonah reaches its
poignant climax in God's own words to the Hebrew

prophet, spoken with reference to the capital city of the archenemy of Israel, the Assyrians:

> And the Lord said: "Thou hast had pity on the gourd, for which thou hast not laboured, neither madest it grow, which came up in a night, and perished in a night; and should not I have pity on Nineveh, that great city, wherein are more than sixscore thousand persons that cannot discern between their right hand and their left hand, and also much cattle?" [Jonah 4:10–11].

Finally, the Hebrew word for "righteousness," *zedakah*, is frequently joined in the Old Testament to that most tender of all divine and human virtues, *hesed*, the full depth of which eludes the most skilful translator. Even the renderings "loving-kindness" and "steadfast love" seek in vain to transmit its meaning. No wonder that *zedakah*, "righteousness," became the Hebrew term for "charity" as well.

In order that the dialogue be genuine, let it be remembered that the God of both components of the Judeo-Christian tradition is the God of justice and of love.

2. Closely related to this unwarranted distinction is the *widespread practice of contrasting the primitivism, tribalism, and formalism of the Old Testament with the spirituality, universalism, and freedom of the New*, to the manifest disadvantage of the former.

This contrast between the Testaments is achieved by placing the lower elements of the Old Testament by the side of the higher aspects of the New, but the process is as misleading as would be the results of the opposite procedure. Thus, one of the most sympathetic and appreciative students of the New Testament, Claude G. Montefiore, writes in an eloquent passage in his *Synoptic Gospels* (II, 326):

> Such passages as Matt. XXV:41 should make theologians excessively careful of drawing beloved contrasts between Old Testament and New. We find even the liberal theologian Dr. Fosdick saying: "From Sinai to Calvary—was

ever a record of progressive revelation more plain or more convincing? The development begins with Jehovah disclosed in a thunder storm on a desert mountain, and it ends with Christ saying: 'God is a Spirit: and they that worship Him must worship in spirit and in truth'; it begins with a war-god leading his partisans to victory, and it ends with men saying 'God is love; and he that abideth in love abideth in God, and God abideth in him'; it begins with a provincial Deity, loving his tribe and hating his enemies, and it ends with the God of the whole earth worshipped by a 'great multitude, which no man could number, out of every nation and of all tribes and peoples and tongues'; it begins with a God who commands the slaying of the Amalekites, 'both man and woman, infant and suckling,' and it ends with a Father whose will it is that 'not one of these little ones should perish'; it begins with God's people standing afar off from His lightnings and praying that He might not speak to them lest they die, and it ends with men going into their chambers, and, having shut the door, praying to their Father who is in secret." (*Christianity and Progress*, p. 209.)

Very good. No doubt such a series can be arranged. Let me now arrange a similar series. "From Old Testament to New Testament—was ever a record of retrogression more plain or more convincing? It begins with, 'Have I any pleasure at all in the death of him that dieth,' and it ends with, 'Begone from me, ye doers of wickedness.' It begins with 'The Lord is slow to anger and plenteous in mercy'; it ends with, 'Fear him who is able to destroy both body and soul in Gehenna.' It begins with, 'I dwell with him that is of a contrite spirit to revive it'; it ends with 'Narrow is the way which leads to life, and few there be who find it.' It begins with, 'I will not contend for ever; I will not be always wroth'; it ends with 'Depart, ye cursed, into the everlasting fire.' It begins with, 'Should not I have pity upon Nineveh, the great city?'; it ends with, 'It will be more endurable for Sodom on the day of judgment than for that city.' It begins with, 'The Lord is good to all, and near to all who call upon him'; it ends with, 'Whosoever speaks against the Holy Spirit, there is no forgiveness for him whether in this world or the next.'

It begins with, 'The Lord will wipe away tears from off all faces; he will destroy death for ever'; it ends with, 'They will throw them into the furnace of fire; there is the weeping and the gnashing of teeth.' " And the one series would be as misleading as the other.

3. Another practice which should be surrendered is that of *referring to Old Testament verses quoted in the New as original New Testament passages*. Many years ago, Bertrand Russell, whose religious orthodoxy is something less than total, described the Golden Rule—"Thou shalt love thy neighbor as thyself"—as New Testament teaching. When the Old Testament source (Leviticus 19:18) was called to his attention, he blandly refused to recognize his error. This, in spite of the fact that both the Gospels and the Epistles are explicit in citing the Golden Rule as the accepted Scripture. Jesus refers to it as "the first and great commandment written in the law" (Matthew 22:38; Luke 10:27), and Paul describes it as "a commandment comprehended in this saying" (Romans 13:9).

In an excellently written tract ("I Believe in the Bible," published by the Congregational Christian Churches, p. 7), the author contrasts the God who "orders Agag hewn to pieces before the altar" with the God "who taught through St. Paul, 'If your enemy is hungry, feed him' (Romans 12:20)." If Paul were citing chapter and verse in his labors, would he have failed to point out that he was quoting Proverbs 25:21 verbatim?

4. Moreover, the dialogue between Judaism and Christianity can be mutually fruitful only if it is always kept in mind that *Judaism is not the religion of the Old Testament, though obviously rooted in it*. To describe Judaism within the framework of the Old Testament is as misleading as constructing a picture of American life in terms of the Constitution, which is, to be sure, the basic law of the land but far from coextensive with our present legal and social sys-

tem. Modern Judaism is the product of a long and rich development of biblical thought. It possesses a normative tradition embodied in the Mishnah and the Talmud, as well as the *Responsa* and the Codes of the post-talmudic period. By the side of this dominant strand are the aberrant tendencies, sectarian and heretical, that were never without influence and cannot be ignored. These include the apocryphal and pseudepigraphical literature, recently enriched—and complicated—by the sensational discovery of the Dead Sea Scrolls. The Middle Ages, building upon their biblical and talmudic antecedents, created the strands of philosophy, mysticism, legalism, and messianism, all of which contributed to the character of modern Judaism. In the modern era, as every informed observer knows, the various schools, conventionally subsumed under the headings of Orthodoxy, Conservatism, and Reform, do not begin to exhaust the variety of religious experience and approach which are competing for attention in the market place of ideas in the Jewish community.

5. Finally, it is necessary for modern Jews to rise above the heavy burden of historical memories which have made it difficult for them to achieve any real understanding, let alone an appreciation, of Christianity. It is not easy to wipe out the memories of centuries of persecution and massacre, all too often dedicated to the advancement of the cause of the Prince of Peace.

Theological discussions inevitably raise the ghosts of the compulsory religious disputations so beloved of the medieval church. In these debates, the Christian defender was often a convert from Judaism, deeply hostile to his ancestral faith, and generally ignorant of its contents. Eager to display the proverbial zeal of the neophyte, he attacked Judaism with all the weapons of malice and ignorance at his disposal. The Jewish protagonists, on the other hand, were often re-

warded with exile or other punishment for statements that
could be construed as critical of Christianity.

More than medieval memories enter into this heritage.
The extermination of six million out of the seven million
Jews living on the European continent was actively carried
out by Hitler, but the process was not actively opposed by
the free nations of the world who fought him in the name
of Christianity and the ideals of Western civilization. Moreover, there are cynics who maintain that anti-Semitism is not
yet totally dead in the free world almost two decades after
Hitler. It is therefore no easy task for Jews to divest themselves of the heavy burden of group memories from the
past, which are unfortunately reinforced all too often by
personal experiences in the present.

Nevertheless, the effort must be made, if men are to
emerge from the dark heritage of religious hatred which has
embittered their mutual relationships for twenty centuries.
There is need for Jews to surrender the stereotype of Christianity as being monolithic and unchanging and to recognize
the ramifications of viewpoint and emphasis that constitute
the multicolored spectrum of contemporary Christianity.

Christian dogmatics are perhaps at the furthest possible
remove from the viewpoint of Jewish tradition and are
totally unacceptable to the committed devotee of Judaism.
Yet the Jew should see in Christian doctrine an effort to
apprehend the nature of the divine that is worthy of respect
and understanding. Moreover, he should recognize that the
dogmas of the Christian church have expressed this vision of
God in terms that have proved meaningful to Christian believers through the centuries. These have ranged from the
most simple-minded to the most profound, and each has
found it possible to find his spiritual home within the framework of Christian thought.

The Jew will not surrender the conviction that the emphasis upon the Unity and Incorporeality of God which is

basic to Judaism must ultimately prevail. At the same time, he should seek to understand the complexities of life and human destiny which have led Christianity to evolve such doctrines as the Virgin Birth, the Incarnation, the Passion, and the Resurrection. The Jewish alternatives cannot fairly be presented to the world unless the Christian understanding of the human situation is fairly grasped. It should be added that the full Christian tradition, like its Jewish counterpart, includes those whom the church stigmatizes as heretics and not merely those who are glorified as its heroes.

Moreover, there are basic emphases in Christianity that can perform a highly useful function for Judaism. For they compel a perpetual re-examination of the content of Judaism and an unending vigilance against the perils that are inherent in its world view, as in any other. The dialogue between the two faiths might well address itself to the tension between law and freedom, the relationship of the material and the spiritual, or the dichotomy between the letter and the spirit, issues with regard to which there is a difference of emphasis in Judaism and in Christianity.

The Christian doctrine of Original Sin, particularly as reinterpreted by such contemporary thinkers as Reinhold Niebuhr, has already influenced the thought of many exponents of Judaism. It has served to reveal the dark depths within the human soul, which an easy and superficial optimism has tended to overlook. In the area of human relationships, the Christian stress upon universalism vis-à-vis particularism, or the ethics of self-abnegation as against the ethics of self-fulfilment, which will be discussed below, can contribute significantly to the spiritual health of Judaism by helping to guard it against the exaggerations which threaten every valid human insight. Contrariwise, the Jewish approach to these issues, as the present work seeks to make clear, can be of inestimable value to the Western world, the roots of which are Christian and, by that token, Hebraic in substantial degree.

Thus a rational dialogue conducted on the basis of knowledge and mutual respect between the two components of the religio-ethical tradition of the Western world can prove a blessing to our age.

But the dialogue can be fruitful only if it is fair. It is true that if we reckon with the full dimensions of Judaism and Christianity, the substance of the dialogue between the two faiths is immeasurably complicated. Yet without such an understanding the enterprise is stultifying. Men were not promised that the truth would be simple—only that the truth would make them free.

# 5

## THE CHURCH, THE STATE, AND THE WILL OF GOD

Without our entering into the rather threadbare controversy as to the reality and depth of the so-called "revival of religion" in America today, it is clear that the churches are reaching out for a larger measure of authority and influence on the contemporary scene. Equally significant is the fact that more and more Americans are disposed to grant them a greater voice in several crucial areas. A growing number, though still not a majority, are willing to entertain the idea of religious instruction in the public schools. Many Catholics, as well as some Protestants and Jews, favor government support for church-governed schools in principle, even if they are not yet ready to press for this demand in practice. These issues will engage our attention below.

While all groups continue to do obeisance to the historic American doctrine of the separation of church and state, it has in recent years been interpreted in increasingly restricted terms, both in several important decisions of the United States Supreme Court as well as elsewhere. This attitude stems from the conviction expressed by Justice William O. Douglas in his now famous dictum delivered in the *Zorach* case in 1952: "We are a religious people whose institutions presuppose a Supreme Being."

Is that dictum historically true? Even if the answer is in

the affirmative, is the connection between religion and democracy necessary and therefore indispensable in the future? What is the meaning of "institutions" and "Supreme Being" in this context? And, finally, what are the implications of the dictum, properly understood, for the future of American democracy?

Obviously, not all the institutions in American life "presuppose a Supreme Being" to the same extent. If the judgment be true, it must refer primarily to the agencies of government that embody the common will of the people; secondarily to the other organized functions of society, notably education; and in lesser degree to the social and the economic order. Justice Douglas' dictum to the contrary notwithstanding, countless efforts have been made to validate the democratic way of life on purely secular grounds. Some type of philosophic, non-theistic justification for democracy is perhaps possible, though I must confess that in every attempt of this nature, I have discovered, at least to my own satisfaction, that somewhere an "undemonstrable" act of faith becomes necessary to the demonstration.

How are we to account for the untold numbers of dedicated believers in democracy who are committed to a secularist world view and whose passionate devotion to the ideals of freedom, in practice as well as in theory, often puts conventional religious believers to shame? The answer, I believe, is that the standards of personal conduct and group behavior by which these high-minded men and women live are derived from the religious tradition which they no longer accept, but which has been mediated to them either by their own forebears or by the society in which they were reared. Like stars already extinct in the heavens, from which light is still traveling toward the earth, these secular idealists shine with the light of assumptions and behavior patterns that they have inherited from the past. But what of tomorrow? Where will the generation growing up today, without the climate of faith, find the basis for their commitment to the democratic way of life?

Whether or not a secularist ethic is philosophically viable, this much seems clear: for most men the religious motivation for a democratic faith is the most compelling, both theoretically and practically. Moreover, it is a matter of historical record that American democracy consciously related itself to this faith in a Supreme Being. The Declaration of Independence explicitly affirms that "all men are created equal and have been endowed *by their Creator* with certain inalienable rights."

This much the Founding Fathers of the republic found "self-evident," which is to say, generally agreed upon among them. But there was no unanimity as to the specific kind of religion that would foster faith in a Creator. Quite the contrary. As is well known, the signers of the Declaration of Independence included fervent believers in specific creeds, as well as men whose adherence to established churches was largely formal. In their ranks were Catholics, sundry varieties of Protestants, and a goodly number of deists. Many of them might today be described as secularists.

The men who fathered the Declaration of Independence were also the prime movers of the Bill of Rights. For the Founding Fathers, the Declaration and the Bill of Rights constituted the obverse and the reverse of a single coin, two organically related elements of their philosophy of democracy. For all of them, traditional believer and non-traditionalist alike, the two basic articles of faith were (*a*) the rights with which all men are endowed by virtue of their human character, rights that are not the attribute of birth or the gift of government; and (*b*) the equality of all men— obviously not in their physical or intellectual endowment, but in their right to the fullest measure of protection under the law and to the maximum of self-fulfilment in society, consistent with the rights and privileges of others.

The motivations for these articles of faith differed then as they differ now. For the religious believer, this doctrine is a direct corollary of the faith that every human being is a child of God, created in God's image and therefore endowed with equal rights in the universe which he has created according to his will. For the secularist, the doctrine of human equality may derive from the consideration that basically all men are similar in nature and destiny, encountering the identical pattern of experience of life, consciousness, and death. Or he may accept the principle of equality merely as a working arrangement, best calculated to further the stability of society and the welfare of its members. But whether the equality of man is an article of faith, a secular myth, or an operating principle, its acceptance is basic to the existence and persistence of a democratic society.

Among these rights, none is more fundamental than freedom of religion, the right of all men to the expression of their specific views on the meaning of life and man's relationship to the universe. This includes the unhindered propagation of these doctrines through education and public discussion and the free performance of the rites in which that faith is expressed. The safeguarding of the right of freedom of religion, aside from the need to buttress the stability of society, constitutes the *raison d'être* of the First Amendment, which enunciates the doctrine of the separation of church and state.

In the laudable effort to strengthen the religious foundations of the democratic ideal, it has been suggested that the American theory of separation of church and state derives from, or at least has its analogue in, the theological doctrine of two orders of existence, the temporal and the spiritual. Yet in spite of the superficial similarities, these two political and theological concepts have little or nothing in common.

This fundamental distinction in Christian thought may perhaps be traced back to the New Testament: "Render unto Caesar the things that are Caesar's, and unto God the things that are God's" (Matthew 22:21). It may also have been nurtured by the Paulinian dichotomy between body and soul, as representing the two disparate and mutually opposed elements in the nature of man. The conception of two orders of government, however, did not receive its classic formulation until the year 494, in the message that Pope Gelasius I sent to the Byzantine Emperor Anastasius I: "Two there are, august Emperor, by which this world is ruled on title of original and sovereign right—the consecrated authority of the priesthood and the royal power."

It is clear that the doctrine was enunciated in response to specific historical conditions. In the face of the absolute power of the Roman emperors and their later royal successors in Europe, it was felt necessary to demarcate some area where the aspirations and institutions of the Roman Catholic church would be secure against encroachment by the state.

There is, however, little evidence from history to support the idea that the doctrine was an instrument for protecting the freedom of the individual from the tyranny of the state, except in such greatly limited areas as the right of asylum or the benefit of clergy. On the contrary, it seems clear that the church and (to the far slighter degree that it was organized and powerful) the synagogue, as institutions, did *not* do battle for the freedom of men either in the areas of government, in the social and economic order, or in the fields of scientific research or philosophic thought. On the contrary, organized religion generally took its stand with the status quo against the challenge of the new. That this conservative stance was at times justified does not change the historical fact that organized religion per se has rarely been the defender of freedom.

On the other hand, it is equally true that religion has frequently supplied the dynamic for the protagonists of freedom. The Bible has proved a great source of inspiration for many who have fought against tyranny, exploitation, and war. The vision of a better world has been nurtured for many a reformer, rebel, and revolutionary by the prophets and legislators of Scripture.

In sum, there are substantial entries on both the credit and debit sides of the ledger. This evidence the writer has sought to summarize elsewhere.[1] The resolution of the paradox is of far more than historical importance, for it goes to the very heart of our issue. Religion itself is ambivalent, being embodied both in institutions and in ideals. Religion as an ideal has often been the inspiration in the struggle for liberty; religion as an institution has generally been the conservator of accepted values and the instrument for their transmission, and by that token the foe of the innovator and the rebel.

True progress depends upon the creative tension between the ideal and the institution, the interplay between the forces of progress and the agencies for conservation. Without the ideal there would be stagnation; without the institution there would be chaos. The passionate rebel, the glowing creative spirit, are essential—but so are the cool conservator, the skeptical critic, if society is to be marked by orderly growth and stability. Religion in the Western world has attained its lofty position because it is the resultant of both factors in its history: the interaction of the prophet, the sage, and the martyr, who enlarged the boundaries of the religious ideal, with the priest, the officiant, and the teacher, who stood guard over the annexed territory.

The ambivalent role of religion in history offers little support to the view, urged in some quarters, that human liberty will be secure only if we accept the principle of the supremacy of the spiritual over the temporal order. As a matter of

---

[1] Cf. *A Faith for Moderns* (New York, 1960), chap. ii, "The Sins of Religion."

fact, the church itself did not consistently maintain the theory of the distinction between these orders, even after it enunciated the doctrine. Whenever and wherever circumstances permitted, the church, until our own day, continued to maintain its claim to temporal power in the government of lands and peoples. How a theory operates in practice is far from irrelevant to its meaning.

It is, however, important to consider the doctrine in its essential character as well. It has been justly emphasized that the Gelasian theory, "two there are," stands in sharpest contrast to the doctrine of a monolithic state, which exalts the temporal order and subjugates the spiritual order where it does not annihilate it. But we are not compelled to choose between totalitarian statism and the concept of a dual order. There is a "third way" for preserving both the vitality of religion and the rights of men in a free society, suggested by some insights derived from the older component of the Judeo-Christian tradition.

Perhaps the fundamental trait of Hebraism is its emphasis upon unity as the underlying characteristic of the world. It insists upon the all-pervasive, unqualified unity of God and therefore rejects the polytheism of the pagan world, the dualism of Zoroastrianism, and all other attempts to achieve an intermediate position between unity and plurality. The classic Jewish tradition is equally opposed to modern secular humanism, which divides the universe into two segments: the non-human sphere, which at best is indifferent and at worst is hostile to moral ends; and the human sphere, where alone morality has its genesis and significance. The Book of Job maintains the faith that there can be no dichotomy between the natural and the moral order, and it insists, the manifold difficulties notwithstanding, that both have their origin in God.

This conviction has its counterpart in the Hebraic conception of the unity underlying human nature and experience. The entire universe being the handiwork of God, all phases of life are sacred. Since history is a manifestation of God, the redeemer of society, biblical faith admitted no line of demarcation between the temporal and the spiritual orders. On the contrary, during the period of Hebrew political independence the prophets insisted that there was only one order, the kingdom of God, to which all men owed unqualified allegiance. Centuries later Josephus, writing in Greek for the Hellenistic-Roman world, created a neologism, "theocracy," to describe this ideal polity. In modern usage "theocracy" tends to be used as equivalent to "hierocracy," a government under ecclesiastical authority, but that is not what Josephus meant:

> Now there are innumerable differences in the particular customs and laws that are among all mankind, which a man may briefly reduce under the following heads: Some legislators have permitted their governments to be under monarchies, others put them under oligarchies, and others under a republican form; but our legislator had no regard to any of these forms: but he ordained our government to be what, by a strained expression, may be termed a *Theocracy*, by ascribing the authority and the power to God, and by persuading all the people to have a regard to Him as the author of all the good things that were enjoyed either in common by all mankind, or by each one in particular, and of all that they themselves obtained, by praying to Him in their greatest difficulties [*Contra Apionem*, II, 16].

Now what is significant for this *concept of theocracy*, or the *kingdom of God*, as enunciated by the prophets, is that *it is fully embodied neither in the state nor in the church.* The reason is not far to seek. Both state and church, irrespective of their origins, are governed and directed by human beings, who suffer from two drawbacks. The intellectual limitations of human nature make it impossible for men fully to comprehend the will of God in all its implications.

In fact, the more loudly they protest that they are proclaiming his authentic will, the more skeptically should the claim be examined. And, what is perhaps even more important, the moral weakness of men makes them unable or unwilling to fulfil the divine imperatives which they accept in principle. To the extent that the state makes accessible to men the blessings of life, the "good things," as Josephus calls them, the state is in conformity with God's will; to the degree that the church keeps men conscious of God as their author, it is doing his work. But neither is the ultimate seat of authority.

Nor is primacy to be granted to the popular will. The Hebrew prophets would never have agreed with Hesiod's dictum, which in its Latin form, "Vox populi vox Dei," Pope Sylvester II attributed to the Bible. They never equated the voice of the people with the voice of God. With equal force they would have rejected the dictum that "the king can do no wrong" or the definition of patriotism which declares "my country, right or wrong." Samuel and Elijah, Amos and Hosea, Isaiah and Jeremiah, all vigorously denounced the royal rulers and the priests, as well as the masses of the people, for being derelict in their allegiance to the only true government, the kingdom of God.

This independent position vis-à-vis organized religion as well as the state is one of the most valuable aspects of the biblical legacy. It has its origin in the fact that the Hebrew Bible is pre-eminently the work of the rebels, the non-conformists among the prophets who did not hesitate to stigmatize the respectable and recognized "oracles of God" of the day as "false prophets."

This tendency was intensified, as we have seen, by the historic role of Ezra at the reconstitution of the Second Commonwealth after the Babylonian exile. In intrusting spiritual leadership to the scribes and scholars in the synagogue and schoolhouses rather than to the priests in the Temple, he strengthened the non-ecclesiastical character of traditional Judaism.

Throughout the talmudic period (200–500 c.e.), as well as the succeeding Saboraic (500–540 c.e.) and Gaonic ages (589–1038 c.e.), the rabbinate remained an avocation in the great centers of Babylonia and Palestine. Only the officially appointed judges were paid for their work, which was primarily a governmental function rather than a spiritual activity. Certain special privileges were accorded scholars by law, such as the remission of taxes, preference in the market place, and other marks of social deference. But the rabbinate did not become a profession until the Middle Ages. As compact Jewish communities, isolated from the general population, increasingly came into being, there was a growing need of a permanent functionary to supervise the life of the congregation, to be available for religious guidance, and to exercise a judicial role in the civil suits among members of the community.

The payment of a salary to a rabbi, however, posed a grave problem from the standpoint of Jewish law. The tradition was clear—the teaching of Torah was a religious duty from which no material gain might be derived. "As I have taught thee freely, so teach thou freely," God said to Moses, according to an old legend. This warning against "making the Torah a hatchet to chop with or a crown to glorify one's self with" was taken very seriously. Medieval rabbis in Spain supported themselves by trade, crafts, investments, or moneylending, while a very considerable proportion earned their livelihood as physicians.

In a characteristically vigorous statement, Maimonides declared that, though he knew that not all the scholars would agree with him, it was best for practitioners of Torah not to be supported by public funds.

With the deterioration of the economic position of Jews in the later Middle Ages, it became ever harder for rabbis to support themselves by some other livelihood, and so salaries came into vogue. The imperious demands of life met the

challenge of the Law by defining the salary of the rabbi as
*sekhar battalah*, "compensation for being prevented from
engaging in a gainful occupation," just as the theory was
that teachers were being paid *sekhar shimmur*, "payment for
taking care of the children consigned to their care"—a
glorified anticipation of the modern occupation of baby-
sitting! Yet, as late as the fifteenth century, Rabbi Simon
Duran, who was, incidentally, not "the first Spanish rabbi
to take pay," felt constrained to offer a public apology for
accepting a salary for his services. From the fifteenth century onward, salaries for rabbis were all but universal,
though they remained minimal until modern times.

Nevertheless, the old tradition retained much of its vitality. The great nineteenth-century Hungarian Rabbi Akiba
Eger, toward the end of his distinguished career, it is reported, wrote to a relative in another city, "I understand
that the position of bath-house keeper is now open in your
town. Please propose my name for the post. I should like to
end my days earning an honest livelihood." To use the
crown of learning for material gain was at best a painful
necessity, from which one sought to escape.

The professionalization of religious leadership in modern
times was undoubtedly inevitable and is probably irrevers-
ible. But in its refusal to glorify an ecclesiastical structure
and in its suspicions regarding an institutionized clergy, traditional Judaism continues to make a significant contribution to vital religion. For it keeps alive the spirit of the Bible,
which is the creation of the amateurs in both senses of the
term, the non-professional devotee and the lover of God
who seeks to obey his will.

If the institutions of the state and of the church do not
fully represent the will of God, where is it to be found
among men? The answer is implicit in biblical thought: It
resides only in the conscience of the individual, in the moral
will and the intellectual judgment of each human being be-

fore his God. This conclusion holds true not only for those religious groups that emphasize the authority of "private judgment," as in Protestantism, but also for the more group-oriented religious viewpoints. For when a Roman Catholic recognizes the authority of the church in his life, or a Jew accepts the Torah as his guide to conduct, and henceforth looks to the one or to the other for guidance in performing God's will, his basic act of acceptance and allegiance represents a function of his moral will and intellectual judgment no less than in the case of the Protestant who at each juncture in life turns for guidance to his Bible as the Word of God. A man may take this step just once, and the entire pattern of lifelong religious commitment will flow from it. Or his life may be marked by countless acts of decision in specific cases. In either event, it is the conscience of the individual that is sovereign.

This is true with regard both to the church and to the state. In the last analysis, it is always the individual conscience which validates the claim of these religious institutions to loyalty or which inspires men to rebel against them when they demand acts or attitudes which the conscience finds inconsistent with the will of God. The church may stigmatize these rebels as heretics, and they may in truth be committing tragic blunders on which they gamble their lives, honor, and salvation. It is with agony and trembling that the religious reformer and revolutionary breaks with the hallowed community of believers to which he belonged yesterday, but he has no alternative. In Luther's words, "Here I stand, I can do no other."

Similarly, it is the individual conscience which counsels men to accept the authority of the state and obey its laws or which impels them to oppose its laws and even to revolt against them if it finds that they violate the will of God. Lincoln's words remain basic: "If by the mere force of numbers a majority should deprive a minority of any clearly written constitutional right, it might, in a moral point of view, justify revolution—certainly would, if such a right were a vital one." Nonetheless, no one in his right mind would undertake a far-reaching rebellion unless the evils of the state transcended the good which it renders. One does not start a revolution because of a misplaced traffic light. But it is the individual conscience that must, in spite of all its weaknesses, be the ultimate arbiter of the claims of the state and of the church to obedience.

Since the individual conscience is notoriously individual, and since society needs a basic consensus in order to function, democracy has accorded hegemony to the majority; that is to say, to the greatest number of individual consciences, who determine the policies of government to be pursued. But centuries of tragic experience have demonstrated the unique and abiding importance of the individual, standing out against the masses of his fellows. History has shown that the suppression of the rights of the minority is fatal to the long-term interest of the majority in the preservation of freedom. The democratic way of life rests upon the twin pillars of the power of the majority and the right of the minority, both of which must be safeguarded in every area of life. In this necessary and creative tension between the individual and society, both the church and the state must play important roles.

If this analysis is sound, it follows that the state and the church represent invaluable agencies for the functioning of society and that neither has an inherent, universal claim to priority over the other. The religious consciousness sees in both institutions tragically imperfect yet eternally indispensable instruments for advancing the reign of the kingdom of God. For each is perpetually exposed to the danger of falling prey to the lust for power which is so easily rationalized as loyalty to the truth. No easy a priori formula can answer in advance the agonizing question that arises in a conflict between church and state. Whether it is the one or the other, or neither, that can legitimately claim the allegiance of conscience depends upon the particular issue. The church has often served as the defender of freedom against the tyranny of the mass, whether embodied in the law of the state or in the savagery of the mob. Contrariwise, the state has frequently been a bulwark against the ravages of intolerance and bigotry spawned by the representatives or the institutions of organized religion.

There have been cases where the state, in order to safeguard the health and welfare of society, has overridden the contentions of certain religious sects that "faith and morals" are involved. On a given issue, the state may be in closer conformity with the will of God than the church or the synagogue that speaks in his name. Not the least of the services which the state can render to vital religion is its recognition that, while each church may legitimately propagate its conviction of its superior validity, it is necessary for the stability and progress of a free society that all belief and disbelief in religion be accorded an equal hearing and equal treatment.

In recent years, as thoughtful exponents of democracy have sought to create an ideological basis for the free way of life, two alternative proposals have been advanced. One suggestion that will be discussed in detail below is to abstract the "common core" of the great religious faiths of the Western world and seek to inculcate these common elements through the public schools, thus buttressing loyalty to the American way. It is not merely that insuperable administrative problems and new tensions in society have been created by such relatively minor efforts as the introduction of a "non-denominational" Ten Commandments or the recitation of a "non-sectarian" grace at meals in the public schools. Even more perilous is the threat that the "common core" approach poses to the vitality of living religion. The various forms of Judaism and Christianity are embodied in specific traditions, each possessing its own individuality, without which its devotees would find their religion unrecognizable. The particularity of religion is the essence of its personality.

The other proposal is to create a religion out of democracy itself, equipping it with scriptures, creeds, and sacred rites. It, too, must fail. The democratic way of life derives largely from the Judeo-Christian tradition, to be sure, but also, even if in lesser degree, from the secular humanism of the eighteenth century. For the spiritual underpinning of democracy, all that is required is a recognition of a supreme being, the creator of the world and of men and therefore the source of men's equal rights to justice and freedom in the world. But for any of the great formulations of the Judeo-Christian tradition, such a faith is far from enough. The "democratic faith" is inadequate as a world view because of its paucity in the area of religious doctrine, which each church will elaborate in accordance with its own insights and attitudes, as it seeks to deal adequately with the human situation in all its grandeur and misery. The "democratic faith" is inadequate as a way of life, because it is totally unconcerned with the area of religious living, as embodied in the variegated patterns of rites and institutions of the various communions.

It is therefore clear that the state may foster in society a climate favorable for the ideals of religion, but it should not devote its resources of influence and substance to the support of the institutions of religion. To do less means to undermine the foundations of democracy; to do more is to render a grave disservice to religion as well. For the church must strive to win men's loyalties in an atmosphere of freedom, if it is not to gain the whole world and lose its own soul.

# 6

# RELIGION AND THE
# FREE SOCIETY

More than once we have had occasion to advert to the idea
that biblical ideals have served as a pillar of the democratic
way of life. Certainly the Founding Fathers of the United
States were very conscious of their roots in the biblical tradition. The classic thesis of the Declaration of Independence, which loses none of its power by dint of constant
repetition, is deeply suffused by the spirit of biblical faith,
refracted by the rationalist liberalism of John Locke: "We
hold these truths to be self-evident that all men have been
*created equal* and have been endowed by their *Creator* with
certain inalienable rights, among which are life, liberty and
the pursuit of happiness."

When the Continental Congress asked a committee consisting of Benjamin Franklin, John Adams, and Thomas
Jefferson to propose a Great Seal for the United States, they
suggested the scene of the Israelites crossing the Red Sea.
To accompany the picture, they proposed the Puritan
apothegm, which likewise derived from the authentic Hebrew tradition, "Rebellion to tyrants means obedience to
God." During the dark days of the American Revolution
the sermons that were preached in American pulpits found
both analogy and hope in the biblical narrative of the enslavement in Egypt and the Exodus from bondage. George

III was Pharaoh, George Washington was Moses, the American colonists were the Israelites, the Atlantic Ocean was the Red Sea, and Independence was the Promised Land.

Not all the Founding Fathers were believers in traditional religion, some of the most distinguished being deists. Yet even they were deeply rooted in biblical thought. Thomas Jefferson prepared a special text of the New Testament for his own use in which he excluded miracles and other supernatural elements and preserved the ethical content of Jesus' utterances. The great pamphleteer of the American Revolution, Thomas Paine, who was called "a filthy little atheist" by Theodore Roosevelt, was neither filthy nor little nor an atheist. On the contrary, Paine was deeply concerned with a religious faith that would not do violence to his ethical convictions.

In any summation of the spiritual sources of the American Revolution, Lecky's words are often quoted, "Hebraic mortar cemented the foundations of American democracy." Hence the frequently repeated assertion that the Bible is the source of democracy is true. But it is not the whole truth—and that on two counts. On the one hand it fails to reckon with the full complexity of biblical thought, and on the other it ignores the varied influences that helped shape the democratic ideal. To argue for a single line of descent from the Bible to democracy is an oversimplification which becomes a distortion.

According to an old saying, the Devil can quote Scriptures for his own purpose. This is an oblique way of stating the truth that within the Bible we may find every shade of opinion, radical, moderate and conservative, on the basic questions of life and thought. This is entirely to be expected, since, as we have seen, the Hebrew Bible is not the work of a political sect or of a religious denomination but the distillation of the experience of an entire people.

For this reason, it has been possible for some readers to

find a few passages in the Bible on the basis of which they have branded it as reactionary. The author of the statement in Proverbs: "My son, fear God and king, and meddle not with those who seek change" (24:21), was scarcely an apostle of the revolution! The common biblical phrase, "the anointed of God" (I Samuel 24:7), by which the king is described, was utilized for centuries as a basis for the doctrine of the divine right of kings, a theory which is totally rejected today by all democratic countries, monarchical and republican alike. Similarly, the existence of biblical laws regulating slavery was used by apologists until the days of the Civil War in order to justify the institution. Passages of this type led a critic like Leonard Woolf to make the statement that "Democracy is essentially anti-religious and anti-Christian." He might have found support for his view in the words of the first-century Alexandrian Jewish philosopher, Philo, who declared: "God is one—a principle which opposes the polytheists, who are not ashamed to transfer the worst possible type of government, that of mob-rule, from earth to heaven."

Nonetheless, this conclusion is mistaken, being based upon an inadequate and faulty reading of the text. The Hebrew Bible, like Judaism as a whole, is a mighty river with many currents and eddies besides the main stream, and these variations must be clearly told apart, their relative importance being carefully gauged. He who reads the Bible with understanding and sympathy will recognize that the passages which we have cited do not represent the main stream of thought in biblical religion. The phrase "the anointed of God" was an old idiom, which the Hebrew thinkers of old never used to justify the doctrine that the king or the dictator can do no wrong. On the contrary, the biblical historians and prophets were overwhelmingly convinced that the kings rarely did anything else. Samuel's scathing attack on the institution of the monarchy is well known. It may be that Hosea, who lived three centuries later, during the last days of the Northern Kingdom, also opposed the kingship in principle. So much for the theory. In practice, virtually all the prophets found the royal rulers an affront to God and morality.

All in all, John Wycliffe was not far from the mark when, in the Preface to his translation of the Scriptures, he stated that the Bible believes in "government of the people, by the people, and for the people," a phrase which was destined to echo down the centuries.

Undoubtedly other factors, both theoretical and practical, played their part in the emergence of democracy. The rationalist thought of Hume and Locke gave the eighteenth century an intellectual basis for retaining the biblical faith in the equal rights of man. The rise of individualism was a consequence of the Industrial Revolution which required the breakdown of feudal distinctions and long-established vested rights and restrictions. The growing recognition that each man counted, or, in Robert Burns's words, "A man's a man for a that," became a dominant factor in many humanitarian movements, as the abuses of the Industrial Revolution created widespread hardship and human degradation.

Yet the religious tradition of the Western world remained a significant source for the democratic vision not only for traditional believers but for deists, both official and unofficial. This was particularly true in the Anglo-Saxon world. Elsewhere in the West, as in France, subterranean biblical influences may have operated, but on the conscious level there was a strong anticlerical bias, often outspokenly antireligious. The French Revolution opposed both the power and the outlook of the Catholic church and in its early, most confident days, sought to replace it by the "religion of reason" with its own temples, festivals, and rituals. While both the American and the French revolutions produced classic statements of principles, the American Declaration of Independence was far more deeply rooted in traditional religious thought than the French Declaration of the Rights of Man.

When due allowance, however, is made for all the secular factors, it still remains true that religion is a basic element in the world view underlying democracy. It may or may not be theoretically possible to validate democracy without a religious foundation. What is certain is that these non-religious philosophies rarely possess the emotional drive, the power of conviction to fire the generality of men with the passion to defend liberty and equality.

In the twentieth century, another test, tragically prag-matic, has emerged which highlights the nexus between faith and freedom. Every form of tyranny in our age has been marked by hostility to religion. All brands of totalitari-anism, brown, black, and red, have made it a prime objective to destroy the church as a vital institution for worship, edu-cation, and standards of conduct. Moreover, in the heyday of naziism, all the institutions of a liberal society became silent and inactive and only the voice of religion was heard in protest against the new resurgence of bestiality. Albert Einstein, surely no apologist for traditional religion, has borne testimony to this phenomenon of our day:

> Only the church stood squarely across the path of Hitler's campaign for suppressing the truth. I never had any special interest in the church before, but now I feel a great affection and admiration, because the church alone has had the courage and persistence to stand for intel-lectual truth and moral freedom. I am forced to confess that what I once despised I now praise unreservedly.

It should be noted, however, that this debt which democ-racy owes to religion has, in large measure, been repaid by the beneficent influence which the democratic way of life has exerted upon the content of religion. The American republic, in particular, has contributed a significant pattern for the relationship of religion to a free society. If the American way cannot serve as a blueprint, it may nevertheless be useful as an ideal norm for the world community of tomorrow. When this new world emerges, it will necessarily be rooted in the realities of the present. It will therefore be inherently and incurably pluralist, reflecting the variety of national loyalties, racial differences, and religious divergences that mark the contemporary scene.

Moreover, in the world community of tomorrow there will be many more faiths to be reckoned with than are comprehended in the Judeo-Christian tradition. The religions of the West, Judaism and Christianity, to which Islam may be added, have so much in common that to a Far Eastern observer they may well seem to be variants of the same faith. There is no common background of history or outlook linking the Judeo-Christian tradition to Buddhism, Hinduism, Confucianism, or the various religions of Africa. Even more far-reaching would be the chasm separating the way of life of the religiously oriented peoples of the East and the West from the militantly secularist and antireligious outlook of the nations in the Communist orbit. Even if communism were ultimately to be modified or even discarded, the antireligious bias would be too deeply ingrained to disappear quickly or easily.

In the face of this bewildering plethora of religions, including atheism, there would be an ineluctable need to construct a common language of discourse for the emerging world community. A pattern would be required which would permit the free expression of divergent religious loyalties, side by side with an overarching sense of unity binding all nations together. Here the unique pattern of the separation of church and state, as it has taken shape in America, would be of the highest significance. It is true that in other democratic lands the church-state relationship takes on forms different from that prevailing in the United States. Yet I submit that the American principle of separation is bound to prove far more useful for the world than the varying forms of union or support between the church and state that exist elsewhere.

It is worth recalling that the American experience in this area is unique not only in its character but in its durability. The American republic is the oldest continuously functioning democracy in the world. Only Great Britain has an older democratic tradition, and there religion occupies an altogether different position in the structure of the state. The American way therefore possesses far more than local significance.

The importance attached by the Founding Fathers of the American republic to the status of religion in a free society is underscored by the fact that it is the subject matter of the First Amendment to the Bill of Rights: "Congress shall make no law respecting an establishment of religion, or prohibiting the free exercise thereof. . . ." A vast literature of interpretation on these fifteen words has grown up during the century and three-quarters of the life of the republic. It is embodied in Supreme Court decisions, in the discussion of legal theorists, and in the debates of the advocates of religion and of its opponents.

Like the Constitution as a whole, the First Amendment has been subjected both to a "broad" and a "narrow" construction, the detailed history of which does not concern us now. In essence, the "broad" interpretation of the amendment was understood to prohibit all governmental aid to religion, whether preferential or non-preferential. To be sure, there were some contradictions in practice, but they were ignored or were regarded as minor and in any case held to be incapable of subverting the general principle. The "limited" view sees the Constitution as forbidding only preferential treatment for one religion but not as excluding aid to all on an equal or largely equal basis.

The classic enunciation of the "broad" interpretation of the amendment is to be found in the frequently quoted words of Justice Hugo Black in the *Everson* case: "The 'establishment of religion' clause of the First Amendment means at least this: Neither a state nor the Federal Government can set up a church. Neither can pass laws which aid one religion, aid all religions, or prefer one religion over another." The "limited" construction found expression in Justice Douglas' utterance in the *Zorach* case in which he declared:

> The First Amendment within the scope of its coverage permits no exception; the prohibition is absolute. The First Amendment, however, does not say that in every and all respects there shall be a separation of church and state. Rather, it studiously defines the manner, the specific ways, in which there shall be no concert or union or dependency one on the other. That is the common sense of the matter. Otherwise the state and religion would be aliens to each other—hostile, suspicious, and even unfriendly.

In the face of such august, if divided authority, it is clear that there must be substantial legal and constitutional authority on both sides. That both Jefferson and Madison, who were leading forces in fashioning the Bill of Rights, clearly interpreted the First Amendment to mean a "wall of separation" is certain. Yet their opinion has no binding or legal force, though it is certainly highly significant for establishing the climate of opinion under which the Bill of Rights came into being.

Moreover, the oral tradition, to borrow a phrase from Jewish religious experience, has considerable weight in establishing the meaning of the written Constitution. Thus it is noteworthy that while the phrase "the separation of church and state" does not occur in the Constitution, the First Amendment has always been recognized as a statement of this principle, both in popular American thought, as well as in the more precise formulation of American legal and judicial opinion.

The analysis of legal distinctions and the investigation of the original intent of the Founding Fathers are interesting enterprises. There is, however, another test, far more significant for the future of democracy, both within the confines of the United States and within the as yet unmarked territory of the world community of tomorrow. An examination of the record makes it clear that this peculiarly American doctrine of separation of church and state has been highly beneficial to both parties. Undoubtedly, the principle was originally adopted in order to safeguard the stability of the state and protect it against the divisiveness of sectarian strife, which is written large in the religious wars, controversies, and persecutions of Europe. This conscious purpose of the Founding Fathers has been achieved to a very high degree—America has largely been spared the ravages of a *Kulturkampf* between the religious and non-religious elements in society. As a result, we have been free both from the clerical political parties common on the European continent and from the violent anticlerical movements which flowered into the Nazi, Fascist, and Communist dictatorships. Moreover, the differences among the various sects, Protestant, Catholic, and Jewish, have rarely been exacerbated to the point of violent conflict in America. The effort to raise the ghost of Catholic-Protestant antagonism in the 1960 presidential campaign proved a failure, in large measure because it was disavowed by both parties and by their standard-bearers, so that it remained principally the province of the lunatic fringe among the bigots.

Scarcely less important has been the contribution of the First Amendment to the vitality of religion as a whole. The centrality of this principle in the development of our country has been well set forth by H. Richard Niebuhr: "What democracy and free land have meant for the political and economic development of America the separation of church and state has meant for its religious development."[1]

Long before the present, much discussed revival of religion, or revival of interest in religion—it matters little here whether we write these phrases with or without quotation marks—the percentage of church affiliation in the United States was far higher than abroad. The phenomenon had already attracted the attention of the sociologist Max Weber.[2] He sought to explain the facts on the ground that economic sanctions for church adherence have here taken the place of the political sanctions of European countries. There is some degree of truth undoubtedly inherent in his interpretation, but it is far from an adequate explanation. In Richard Niebuhr's words, "The very lack of any sort of compulsion has placed the responsibility for its maintenance upon the church itself and has invigorated it, as no reliance upon political agencies could have done." As a completely voluntary agency in American life, organized religion has attained a position of influence and prestige, outstripping by far its status in lands where the alliance of church and state is the norm.

The steadily rising percentage of the total population which is affiliated with a church, the level of development and prestige which religious education has reached, the range and extent of other church-related activities, and, by no means least, the attitude of respect, or at least of non-hostility, on the part of the non-affiliated that religion enjoys in the United States—all these phenomena testify to a position attained by religion without parallel anywhere else in the world.

Frequently observers of religion on the current American scene criticize the current religiosity on the score of its superficiality and vagueness. Though there is substantial

---

[1] Cf. his *Social Sources of Denominationalism*, p. 201.

[2] Max Weber, *Aufsätze zur Religionssoziologie*, I, 207 ff.

justice in the complaint, the criticism may be swallowed too uncritically! One often has the feeling that the critics are objecting to the fact that the masses of Americans do not seem to be interested in the niceties of the theological distinctions to which they, the critics, are committed. But the so-called "undenominational religion" of most Americans today, while undoubtedly suffering from many defects, deserves more of a defense than it has yet received. The proverbial "man in the street" would define his religion as love of God and faith in him, though he might be unable to present a thoroughly elaborated theological position. He would insist that the love of one's fellow man expressed in decent human relations is the essence of obedience to the divine will, no matter what other creedal and ritual demands the specific tradition may make. If the unsophisticated advocates of such a religion possessed the requisite learning, they could easily buttress their position by citing chapter and verse from the prophets and sages of Judaism and from Jesus and the saints of Christianity. The Rabbis did not hesitate to declare that God himself mused, "Would that men forsook Me, but kept My law"—adding the afterthought, to be sure, "because the light within it would bring them near to Me" (*Jerusalem Talmud, Hagigah* 1:7, reading *ma'or* with all authorities).

It is true, as one observer points out, that "classrooms filled with eager students taking courses in religion and public forums on the same subject are a far cry from betokening a sense of personal commitment to religion." But it should be noted that even this type of superficial interest in religion is rarely to be met with in Germany, France, Italy, or the Scandinavian countries, either among the youth or in the academic world. This in spite of the fact that in many of these countries the relationship of church and state is organic and formal religious training is a compulsory element in the school system.

If the strict separation of church and state is as fundamental and beneficial as we have argued, how are such apparent deviations as free textbooks and bus transportation for parochial school pupils to be understood? A study of the various instances involved suggests that the American people is unwilling to surrender its allegiance to the principle of separation of church and state, even if it does not always adhere to it in practice. In other words, the deviations are to be regarded as exceptions to the rule, not as its abrogation.

These deviations fall into several categories. Such practices as the opening of Congress with prayer, the swearing in of government officials on the Bible or its use in court oaths, and references to the Deity in Thanksgiving proclamations are sufficiently general in character and minor in scope as to offend neither the rights nor the sensibilities of the overwhelming majority of Americans.

Much more substantial acts, such as the establishment and support of chaplaincies in the armed forces and in government prisons, are also justifiable. They are based on the recognition that men who are in service or behind bars have been forcibly removed from their usual environment by the state. The government therefore may be legitimately called upon to replace such facilities as they enjoyed while at liberty or in civilian society. These include various kinds of entertainment, access to books and music, exercise, and sport. Obviously a very high priority among these facilities is occupied by the ministrations of religion.

Still more far-reaching is the tax exemption accorded houses of worship and religious schools. It obviously presupposes a belief in the beneficial character of religion in the life of the citizenry and is parallel to the tax exemption granted other institutions like museums, hospitals, universities, and other specialized schools. While each of them serves only a fraction of the population, their functioning is regarded as beneficial to the body politic as a whole.

Because these deviations from the separation of church and state have been utilized in some quarters to justify direct government aid to religion, some high leaders in American Protestantism have called for the churches voluntarily to surrender their tax-exempt status, even though it might be theoretically defensible and is not currently being challenged. Whether such an act of voluntary self-abnegation on a large scale is likely to take place is open to doubt. The churches are finding fund-raising a painful and soul-shattering enterprise, even without the necessity of paying taxes.

In sum, all these instances of relationship between the state and the church—whether they be regarded as justifiable deviations or as inconsistent violations of the First Amendment—have not affected the basic ideal of separation which most Americans continue to regard as inviolate.

However, the penetration of organized religion into society is not limited to the areas of government. Nor are the means being employed always restricted to the arts of persuasion and discussion, which religion has both a right and a duty to use in furthering its ideals. Instances are multiplying of sectarian groups seeking to impose their specific religious and ethical views on the general public by bringing pressures to bear, either overtly or subtly, on government officials and other policy-making organs. The struggle affects such areas as legislation concerning marriage, divorce, and planned parenthood, the operation of government hospitals, and the censorship of books, plays, and films. Where the law proves inadequate to enforce submission to a sectarian viewpoint, recourse is had at times to administrative fiat and the threat of economic boycott. It is clear that the role of religion in a democratic society constitutes a growing tension-area in our day.

Far more acute and momentous than any of these problems in the field of church-state relationships in the United States is the issue of religion in education. Because of its importance and complexity, the subject deserves separate consideration.

# 7

# RELIGION IN EDUCATION

Education constitutes the major battleground in the field of church-state relations in America today. This is not at all astonishing, since the school is the matrix of the future and what is at stake is nothing less than the destiny of the nation.

Though presumably dedicated to wisdom, the American public school did not appear full grown, like Pallas Athene springing from the brow of Zeus. The system of free, public, and compulsory education represents a painful and faltering evolution from the elementary schools originally sponsored by churches and church-related groups, principally Protestant. As a result, from their inception the public schools have maintained various forms of religious activity and holiday celebrations in their programs. By and large, these practices have the weight of tradition behind them, and the patterns originally established have survived into the present as part of the natural order of things.

It is therefore obvious that these practices are not likely to be eliminated in the foreseeable future. On the contrary, new features of sectarian belief and practice are being introduced. Efforts to oppose this trend are arousing such violent reactions that the month of December, traditionally the season of good will, is fast becoming the most tension-laden in the American school year. In this climate of clashing opinions and charged emotions, minority groups may well feel it wiser to desist from all-out active opposition to the

dominant pattern. Instead they may seek to safeguard, as
well as they can, the rights and sensibilities of their own
children. This may indeed be the course of prudence, at
least for the present, but it is difficult to see how these sectarian practices, however widespread and well-intentioned,
can be justified in principle.

A striking analogy is at hand in the issue of "racial integration," to which we shall turn later in this book. Here the
decision of the Supreme Court is of far greater scope and
has aroused correspondingly greater hostility than the issue
of religious observances in the public schools. Here too, as
in the case of religion in the schools, there is a clear-cut
moral and legal principle being challenged by a host of
many-faceted and deep-seated violations in practice. Whether the American people embarks upon a program of very
"deliberate speed" or whether it proceeds with racial integration at a more rapid tempo will depend upon a variety
of pragmatic considerations. But to maintain that the present
practice takes precedence over the principle is to undermine
and ultimately to annihilate the principle.

Many of those who favor religious observances in the
public schools and urge government support of religion in
the area of education are well aware that these procedures
pose potential perils to the freedom of religion and the cohesion of American society. What impels them, nevertheless,
to adopt these positions? It is their deep-seated conviction
that religion is a basic enterprise in the life of the human
spirit which cannot be eliminated from the educational
process. The corollary is then added that the American
public-school system, as constituted at present, from which
formal religious teaching is excluded, does not adequately
fulfil the task of fashioning human personality.

How is the problem to be met? Here there is a divergence
of opinion among the protagonists of religion in the school
system. There are those who believe that the public school,

being by its very nature a non-sectarian or even multi-sectarian institution, suffers from incurable ills and that only a religiously permeated, church-controlled school system can be regarded as ideal. Others are convinced that the situation can be remedied by introducing the teaching of religion into the public-school curriculum.

These two proposed solutions to the problem of religion in education are far more fundamental than the presence of religious or quasi-religious practices in the public schools, which, however widespread they may be, remain peripheral to the educational enterprise. Both issues merit careful analysis by all who are concerned with the future of democracy or of religion.

That there should be a growing demand for the governmental support of parochial schools is quite understandable. In the past half-century, parochial education has grown into an extensive and imposing system with millions of students on the elementary, intermediate, and university levels. The process of growth has been tremendously accelerated by the decision of the American Catholic hierarchy that all Catholic children must be educated in parochial schools, unless there be exceptional overriding considerations to the contrary.

The maintenance of this far-flung educational system imposes heavy economic burdens upon loyal Catholics who represent every economic level in society. Hence the effort is being made to justify the use of public funds for parochial schools, most of which are Catholic, but which also include Lutheran, Episcopalian, and Jewish institutions, and probably schools of other sects as well.

In the realm of theory, two principal contentions are advanced. It is maintained (a) that no one but the parent has a "natural right" to determine the education of his children and that this right is prior to all other claims in this area, and (b) that the state in the field of education is merely acting as surrogate for the parent, making it possible for him to exercise his right through the collection of taxes by the state from all residents for a general education fund.

Several types of schools, the argument continues, are equally entitled to support from this fund. The first is the public school, which may be defined as the instrumentality created for such parents as do not wish any religious instruction for their children in the school, whether or not they favor religious education in general. The other is the parochial school, which is the institution available to those parents for whom education implies a religious orientation organically related to the entire curriculum. In sum, the secular school and the religious school are equally "public" and hence are equally deserving of their proportionate share from the public-education fund to which all residents have contributed.

As evidence that the democratic spirit is compatible with government support of parochial schools, the example of Holland is frequently invoked. Here government support is provided for the secular public schools, as well as for Catholic parochial schools and other private schools.

Thus the broad outlines of the argument. How decisive should they be? With all genuine sympathy for the practical problem confronting the parochial school, the theoretic contentions which are advanced do not prove convincing. In addition there are other aspects of the role of the school in democratic society, all too often overlooked, which must be taken into consideration. Let us deal with these issues in order.

The conception of the state as being merely the administrator of a public-education fund to which each individual contributes and from which he is free to withdraw his "share" at will is a vast oversimplification. It is totally unrealistic to regard the government as merely an agency for collecting the funds required to carry out these purposes.

Nor is it logical to conclude that the individual or a group is therefore free to secede from the collective enterprise at will.

Conscientious objectors must pay their taxes to the federal government, most of which are allocated today to military purposes. A group of citizens may feel that the sanitation system in their community is inadequate or even hazardous to health. They cannot withhold their share of municipal taxes, in order to create their own system of garbage removal. There is nothing to prevent them from arranging for a private carting service to supplement the public sanitation department. Various groups and associations may need special libraries; they are not on that account free to avoid library taxes. A business concern or an individual may feel the need for more protection of property and life than the police department affords. He would not be permitted, however, to retain part of his taxes in order to pay for a burglar-alarm system, a private police force, or a bodyguard. In the field of education, the role of the state is far more central and inclusive than merely to serve as the repository of a public-education pool.

Moreover, it may well be denied that the school is merely a surrogate for the parent, for its functions are both more and less extensive than the parental obligation. They are less, because important elements of the child's education, such as religious doctrine and practice, ethical standards of behavior, etiquette, and other aspects of personal conduct, are not intrusted to the school but are, and should be, the functions of the home and the church. They are more, because the school is concerned with the transmission of group values which society regards as essential for its survival and unity and which are not the primary concern of the parent.

In addition, the assumption of a primal and prior right of the parents with regard to the education of their children seems highly questionable on two grounds: the order of the alleged priorities and, consequently, the nature of the relationships involved. It is obvious that man is not merely a biological creature but a social being, and it is this second characteristic which sets him apart from the lower animals. *Hence a child possesses concurrent and parallel relationships both with his parents and with society, and both are equally rooted in his nature.*

Finally, one may argue on the grounds both of religion and of logic that the nature of these relationships is to be subsumed under the category of *duty* rather than of *right*, since the newborn child finds himself born into a family and a society not of his own choosing.

It is noteworthy that biblical thought regards the education of the young basically as an obligation of parents rather than as their right: "Thou shalt teach them diligently unto thy children" (Deuteronomy 6:7).

Rabbinic thought, with its penchant for spelling out the implications of biblical teaching, sets forth the duties of a father toward his son in these terms:

> Our Sages have taught, "A father is obligated to circumcise his son, to redeem him (if he be taken captive), to teach him Torah, to train him in an occupation, and to marry him off." Some say, "He should also teach him to swim." Rabbi Judah said, "Whoever does not teach his son an occupation is virtually teaching him robbery." Rabbi Judah the Patriarch said, "He must also teach him civilized conduct. Whatever is the father's duty toward his son, if left unfulfilled by the father, must be performed by the son for himself" (B. *Kiddushin* 29a–30b; *Mekilta, Bo*, ed. Lauterbach, Sec. 18).

The details reflect the mores of an earlier and simpler era, but the principle is clear—primarily parents have duties, not rights, with regard to the education of their offspring.

To sum up, both the parents and the state have *concurrent obligations* to prepare the young for life in the environment in which they find themselves, by training them to be useful, respected, and self-fulfilling members of society and by transmitting to them the necessary tools for making a living and for being at home in the world.

Not the least of these obligations, both of the parents and of society, is to recognize the child as an independent personality. Though procreated by his parents and nurtured by society, the child is not a creature of either. Nor is he required to be a facsimile of the one or a robot in the other. Safeguarding the child's individuality and affording him the opportunity for free self-development constitute ethical imperatives of the highest order, to which a free society must always be dedicated. The process of growth is frequently charged with pain and peril, as both parents and society can testify out of their experience, but it is an inevitable feature of the human situation.

Obviously, this parallel duty of the parents and of the state gives rise to corresponding rights. Parents have the right to inculcate in the young the ideals by which the family lives and maintains its character. Society has the right to transmit the values needed for the civic good. It is not reasonable to expect that either the family or the social order should be burdened with obligations toward the younger generation and at the same time be denied the power to help assure its own preservation.

The stability of society and the unity of its citizens under freedom constitute indispensable goals of the democratic social order. To achieve these goals, the school tax is imposed on all Americans equally, including those who have no children or who are non-believers, in order to meet the cost of these objectives, which all Americans share in common.

To further these ends, the public school teaches not merely spelling and arithmetic, as well as vocational arts and skills, but the English language, American literature, and American history. It utilizes these elements of the curric-

ulum in order to imbue the coming generation with a sense
of communal unity and national loyalty.

Similarly, parents have a right to transmit to their children
the religious and ethical values they regard as precious and
life-giving. For some parents, supplemental religious instruction after public-school hours may appear adequate, whether
in Sunday schools or in afternoon schools. For others, religion is too important to be relegated to a subordinate position
and religious culture is too extensive to be adequately taught
in the interstices of a child's leisure hours. Such parents will
necessarily seek to satisfy their needs through a parochial
school, in which religion and secular studies are integrated.
Parents have a right to establish such schools, but they have
no right to claim the help of the state in maintaining them.

Moreover, the proponents of governmental support for
parochial schools seem to have committed the error of the
undivided middle. Since parochial schools are not conducted
for private gain, it is insisted that they are "public schools."
Actually, communal institutions fall into three—not two—
principal categories:

1. *Public institutions,* which are tax-supported, being directed, controlled, and staffed by the government—like the
public schools, municipal and state hospitals, and local, state,
and national museums and parks. It is not merely a theoretical procedure that dictates that these activities supported
by public funds be under the supervision of the government.
A government agency is the instrumentality created by the
citizens for achieving those socially desirable ends they all
share in common.

2. *Private institutions,* conducted for profit, such as pri-
vately owned hospitals, commercial museums, private business and vocational schools, which are subject to governmental taxation, like all business enterprises.

3. *Non-public, voluntary institutions,* created by free
associations of individuals who alone are responsible for

their program and functioning. The role of the state here is essentially negative and regulatory, to make sure that minimal standards of competence, safety, and sanitation are maintained. Within this category fall the voluntary community hospitals, homes for the aged and infirm, child-shelter and family guidance agencies, specialized museums like the Museum of Modern Art, and musical organizations like the New York Philharmonic. That institutions in this third category should be exempted from the burden of taxation is fair and just, in recognition of the values they contribute to society, but, being free from governmental control, they cannot expect maintenance from public funds.

The economist may argue that exemption from taxation is no less a subvention than a direct grant. This is undoubtedly true in theory, but life has a logic of its own and recognizes a distinction between the two procedures. The existence of institutions in this third, intermediate category is paralleled by the presence of a third, intermediate position with regard to public funds—no direct allocation, but no tax obligation.

Obviously, the driving factor behind the endeavor to create the theoretical basis for government support of parochial schools derives out of very genuine practical considerations. One can well understand why many Catholic Americans feel that they are being subjected to the injustice of "double-taxation."

This double burden, however, is inherent in the larger sphere of loyalties to which an American Catholic gives his allegiance and which includes both his devotion to his church and his loyalty to the American community of which he is a citizen. The nature of this double obligation, which falls upon all Americans who are strongly committed to a given creed, is often misunderstood or overlooked. So, too, the full contribution of the public-school system to the American way of life needs to be appreciated.

The past one hundred years, which coincide with the history of the American public school, have witnessed the emergence of the American nation as a living entity. It was during this time that the overwhelmingly white, Protestant, Anglo-Saxon character of the American nation underwent its most far-reaching and potentially critical transformation. The small island of Anglo-Saxon Americans was inundated by successive waves of immigration, consisting of untold ethnic groups, notably the Irish, Scandinavian, German, Slavic, and Italian, and including substantial numbers of Catholics and Jews. Their impact subjected the American body politic to substantial strains, which are far from spent even today. Yet, by and large, the nation fulfilled its originally projected goal of *e pluribus unum*. In the space of a generation or two, an overwhelming sense of unity, beyond the prevalent ethnic and religious diversity, was engendered among the old and the new Americans. The three major wars in which the United States was involved in the twentieth century underlined this unity in blood, but it had come into being long before the outbreak of hostilities.

This achievement is all the more remarkable when we recall the long record of religious, ethnic, and social conflict which disfigured European history for nearly twenty centuries, a heritage which these immigrants brought to America as part of their backgrounds. Nonetheless, these hostilities were largely dissipated both for these immigrants and, above all, for their children, by the public school, which created a basis for American unity and loyalty by teaching its pupils to live together not merely as neighbors but as fellow citizens of the republic.

The home and the church taught the beliefs and the practices that were to serve as the firm foundations of the child's personality. The public school completed the ethical training of the youth by inculcating a respect for the right of others to differ with him, as well as a feeling of friendship and camaraderie with those of other races and creeds.

Those who stigmatize the public school as godless would do well to remember that no school has ever been intrusted successfully with the task of being the sole character-building agency. Always the home and the church have central roles to play, and when these fail, no school, no matter how efficient in operation or dogmatic in theory, can hope to succeed.

The personal meeting, in the classroom and outside, of children and teachers coming from varied religious, cultural, and ethnic backgrounds has proved far more efficacious in creating the *homo Americanus* than the abstract preaching of brotherhood in the pulpit or the school assembly. In the give-and-take of daily life, the pupil developed a recognition of the truth that intelligent and well-meaning men and women might well differ among themselves on many issues, cherishing their specific viewpoints, yet finding it entirely possible to live and function in co-operation, harmony, and mutual respect with one another. One does not exaggerate the merits of the public school to see in it a unique laboratory for the democratic process. Martin Buber has eloquently reminded our age that it is the personal confrontation of human beings that is decisive in building their relationships and not the forensic or written word, however elevated in sentiment.

Nor does this task belong only to the past. Unlike the racially more homogeneous nations of western Europe, America is, in Walt Whitman's words, "a nation of nations, a people of peoples." This cultural and ethnic diversity may not remain a feature of the American landscape forever, but its disappearance is still a long way off. Besides, religious pluralism is recognized by nearly all Americans as a good, worthy of permanent preservation. If there is to be a maximum degree of freedom in American society, it must be counterbalanced by an equally powerful instrument for building unity and mutual fellowship. The need for this balance was recognized by the Hebrew prophet when he cited the ancient wisdom of the tent-maker: "Lengthen thy cords and strengthen thy stakes" (Isaiah 54:2). Longer cords of liberty require stronger stakes of unity. There is no other institution in American life that can rival the public school in fulfilling this indispensable function for the present and the future.

The living tension between the two poles of unity and diversity is the measure of the vitality of the democratic way of life. If either principle is submerged, true freedom is imperiled. Hence, when the Supreme Court in the *Pierce* case affirmed the legitimacy of parochial schools, and, more recently, when California voters rejected the attempt to void tax-exemptions for parochial schools, Americans were defending one of the two indispensable elements of a free society. At the same time, it should be recognized that the destruction of the public-school system or even its attenuation would seriously affect the moral and social values of national unity. The weakening of the social fabric would ultimately undermine the religious and cultural diversity of the American way.

The example of Holland, often advanced as an instance of a democratic government which supports all types of schools, is not altogether reassuring in this respect. In 1948, the so-called "public-school system" numbered only about 27 per cent of the school population (328,000), while the Catholic parochial schools contained 43 per cent (525,000) and "other private schools" 29 per cent (349,000). This stratification has apparently become permanent. In 1955, according to the Ministry of Education of the Netherlands, of the 1,413,402 children of elementary-school age, 28 per cent attended the "public schools" (407,034), 27 per cent were pupils of Protestant schools (387,318), 41 per cent were enrolled in the Catholic schools (592,356), and 1 per cent attended "other schools" (26,694). A school system which included only one child out of four can be called "public" only by courtesy. One may anticipate that the absence of a fund of shared experience and common living for Dutch youth is bound to affect the sense of unity in the Dutch people as time goes on. Be this as it may, the Dutch, like most other west European nations, are ethnically homogeneous. Perhaps the problem is not so acute for the Netherlands because the task of creating a nation out of disparate elements no longer confronts the Dutch as it does the American people.

One can scarcely expect American society to help underwrite the cost of parochial education, the merits of which may be freely granted, but one of the results of which may well be the destruction of the public-school system. This is not merely a matter of group strategy or expediency but of basic principle. Parents whose loyalty to their church leads them to send their children to parochial schools are not on that account freed from the obligation to support the public schools, an obligation which they share with all other Americans, including those who have no children or who send their children to private schools. For the public school remains the basic agency for building mutuality of relationship among the children of various faiths and backgrounds who are the citizens of tomorrow. Nor is this duty obviated by attacks upon the "irreligious" character of the public schools, which have always been friendly to religion and which have contributed to the character-building of at least four generations of Americans with gratifying success.

Throughout our discussion thus far, a theory with regard to the nature of the parochial-school program has been taken for granted. The implication has been that a parochial school gives the pupils what is essentially a secular education, to which religious studies have been added. The truth is, however, that no religious educator, Catholic, Lutheran, or Jewish, would be willing to define his educational philosophy in such terms. For him, religion should permeate every course in the curriculum, in greater or lesser degree, so that no aspect of culture would be exempt from the influence. This applies not only to literature, history, and music, but also to language, geography, and even arithmetic, at least as far as the form in which problems are formulated. Many religious educators would go further and wish to have the children's entire lives spent in an atmosphere created and informed by their specific tradition and way of life. Often it is the desire to create this pervasive religious spirit rather than the wish to impart specific religious knowledge to the children that is the driving force behind the creation of parochial schools.

From this underlying philosophy of education, however, flow constitutional consequences which cannot fairly be evaded. Since all parochial education is religious in character and intent, it follows that governmental support of schools would represent aid to religion, direct, concrete, and substantial, and thus run counter to the "non-establishment" clause of the First Amendment.

American Catholics possess a deep dedication to their faith and a zeal for their children's education that cannot be too highly praised. The American Catholic school system is unequaled in extent and prestige anywhere else in the world, including "Catholic" countries. The full significance of this fact should not be lost sight of. It is one more sign of the strength of religion when it relies upon its own inner resources in a free society rather than upon the compulsive power of the state. The record of history, both past and present, demonstrates that wherever the state buttresses the church, the results are often an external, soulless conformity at best and a violent antagonism at worst. Rarely do men give the free allegiance of their spirit to God, which is the essence of true religion.

In the area of education, as in others, the highest interests of religion are in harmony with the basic needs of a free society. Only shortsightedness can see these two objectives as contradictory. It is essential to recognize the legitimacy of both ideals, the tension between which can be resolved only by a painful and partial process of accommodation.

The same problem, on a lesser scale, confronts the Jewish community in America. The difficulties of transmitting the rich and complex content of Jewish culture and inculcating the values and practices of the Jewish religion are tremendous, particularly in an open society in which Judaism is the heritage of a minority group.

To fulfil this task, American Jews have created a vast array of supplementary schools, some meeting on Sunday mornings and others on weekday afternoons after public-school hours. Because of limitations in the child's time and energy after a full school day, these supplementary schools cannot satisfy those parents and educators who are committed to an intensive Jewish religious education. As a result, Jewish day schools have been rapidly increasing in number, although they include only a small minority of the Jewish school population in America.

Most Jewish educators are profoundly conscious of the human and ethical values imbedded in the American public-school system. Hence most of those leaders who are devoted to the day-school idea do not look forward to having all, or even most, Jewish children enrolled in these private schools. Their goal is the creation of a corps of Jewish men and women in the coming generation who, possessing a more extensive knowledge of Judaism and a correspondingly deeper sense of personal commitment, will supply the professional and lay leadership for the Jewish community and the creative scholars, artists, and writers to further its spiritual life.

In deepening the content of Jewish life, these educators feel that they will be contributing to the benefit of America as a whole. They understand that some lesser, though worthwhile, objectives, such as some of the day-by-day relationships with children whose religious background is Catholic, Protestant, or humanist, have had to be surrendered in the case of children enrolled in a Jewish day school. They recognize the value of the American public school as "the potter's house where the soul of the nation is fashioned." By and large, American Jews believe that it is in the public school that most Jewish children should continue to receive their general education, supplemented by the training supplied by the religious school.

Undoubtedly, the problem is felt more intensely by Catholics, but the difference is one of degree, not of kind—the reconciliation of the basic needs of the American people as a whole with the equally legitimate requirements of religious education. It is far better that both goals be met, albeit in part, than that either be totally ignored. We believe that both ideals—concern for national unity and zeal for religious commitment—receive their optimum fulfilment under the present arrangement, which grants tax-exemption to parochial schools without giving them tax support. The "middle way" is the best for America as a whole and for the various faiths which undergird its way of life.

The parochial school represents one effort to counter the "secularism" of the public school, by establishing an alternative religious school system. The other approach seeks to remedy the condition by introducing religion into the public-school curriculum itself. Such responsible agencies as the American Council on Education, the Religious Education Association, and other educational and religious bodies have explored possible avenues of solution and have shed considerable light on the issue.

That the widespread "religious illiteracy" of our day poses a problem for contemporary education is universally conceded. Religion has been one of the most potent factors in human history, and its influence is written large in literature, music, and art, as well as in politics and morals. It follows that some knowledge of the scriptures, beliefs, rites, history, and heroes of the great religious traditions of the world is indispensable to a truly educated person.

Thus far the problem. With regard to the solution, too, there are substantial areas of agreement. It is generally felt that there are many advantages and few drawbacks to the teaching of religion on the college level. On the other hand, it is widely agreed that there are many pitfalls in undertaking the teaching of religion in the elementary school, particularly in the lower grades.

The problem becomes acute with regard to the secondary school and the upper grades of the elementary school. It is not difficult to make out a convincing case for objective teaching *about* religion, its institutions, tenets, and practices, as a part of history or civics in the high-school curriculum. Churches constitute an important part of the social scene, no less than the institutions of government, culture, education, and recreation. To ignore the religious life of the community means to create a vast lacuna in the children's understanding of the society in which they live and function.

The truth of this position is incontrovertible. Yet the diagnosis is far easier to come by than the remedy. There are major difficulties involved in implementing such a plan which cannot be glossed over. Thus it has been proposed that the public high schools offer "teaching *about* religion" and avoid "the teaching *of* religion." But the history of recent events gives ground for feeling that here the danger of the "camel's head in the tent" is not imaginary. It cannot be denied that there are those who would regard "teaching *about* religion" merely as the entering wedge for the "teaching *of* religion" along denominational lines within the public-school curriculum, or at least with the authority and prestige of the state behind it. The good faith of most advocates of the introduction of the teaching *about* religion in the school system is not in question. But they are not representative of those who want to see outright religious instruction in the schools.

Even where bona fide programs in "teaching about religion" have been experimented with, important practical problems have come to light. The study materials thus far produced in this area leave much to be desired from the standpoint of objectivity and content and raise the serious question whether adequate material can be prepared to meet this need. The growing shortage of personnel in the teaching profession as a whole would be aggravated by this new and delicate assignment, which would necessitate special training in the untried art of teaching about religion. It is also difficult to see how the introduction of such an arrangement could be prevented from leading to a "religious test" for teachers in the school system, in fact if not in law, particularly in view of the mounting pressures by church groups for "positive" religious values in the schools. Besides, it is highly doubtful whether most Catholics, Protestants, or Jews would be willing to have their tenets and rites presented to their children by those outside their respective traditions.

Difficulties such as these have led to another approach to the problem. It has been suggested that the teaching about religion be given by the priests, ministers, and rabbis in the community, whose houses of worship would be visited by the classes as part of the course in civics, similar to trips taken to other institutions. To be sure, this procedure would relieve the present school staffs of most of the burdens mentioned above, but it would create new problems of major proportions. It is doubtful whether most ministers of religion, who are trained to be devoted advocates of their respective faiths, would be willing or able to give objective instruction on religion, overcoming their natural and legitimate impulse to "win souls" for the convictions they hold sacred.

Moreover, the multiplicity of denominations in Protestantism, as well as the variety of viewpoints in Judaism, would necessarily mean the elimination of most sects and the favored treatment of a few. It would hardly be practical for high-school students in a given community to visit five or more Protestant churches, three Jewish synagogues, in addition to the Catholic church, in order to cover the major traditions. There would still remain such groups as Unitarianism, Ethical Culture, Christian Science, Jehovah's Witnesses, and Theosophy, which would presumably be ignored. In addition, it is certain that many denominations would not sanction their children's visiting other houses of worship and studying alien doctrines from their ministers. Whether such attitudes are justifiable or not is totally irrelevant; they need to be reckoned with. Given these circumstances, however, it seems clear that the comprehensiveness and impartiality of the program would be gravely compromised.

Besides, if the "teaching about religion" were successfully introduced into the public high schools and all these problems were overcome, it might prove a Pyrrhic victory for the cause of religion. If this type of teaching became widespread, many parents might regard it as an adequate substitute for religious education in church schools, which requires the expenditure of additional time, energy, and substance. Thus the fabric of the traditional religious school would be weakened still further and the difficult struggle now being waged to give religious education greater breadth and depth might well receive the kiss of death.

Finally, the objective presentation of religious beliefs and practices, with a scrupulous avoidance of any effort to secure the pupil's commitment to the faith under discussion, would seem to many, if not to most, religiously minded people to be highly objectionable. Such teaching of religion would be playing Hamlet without the Prince of Denmark, or, if we may heap Pelion on Ossa, keeping the bath while throwing the baby out. There would be the very real danger that the position of objectivity of the teacher would be translated by the pupil into an attitude of indifference to all genuine religious commitment.

In sum, the problem of religious illiteracy is genuine but so are the drawbacks confronting the various proposals advanced for the teaching of religion in the public schools. What would therefore seem to be indicated is the need for further concentrated study of the question, to be followed by experimentation in selected areas, through adequate teacher-training, the preparation of proper curriculum material, and the careful orientation of the community in question to the program. Perhaps many of the difficulties envisaged in advance might be dissipated in the bright sunlight of reality; conversely, new and unanticipated problems might well arise.

Until such programs for "teaching about religion" in the public-school system are tried and found thoroughly feasible, we would do well to recall some basic truths about religion and life. In spite of the inbred American propensity for panaceas, the truth remains that the total education of the child as a human being, as a citizen, and as a child of God cannot be intrusted to any single agency. The home, the public school, the religious school, the church, and, by no means least, "the street," all play their part in molding the personality of the child and the youth. Never in American history, even before the emergence of the secular public school, was the school expected to assume the full burden of educating a generation that would be loyal to religious and ethical values. The home and the church never abdicated their roles in this complex undertaking.

It is understandable why some religious leaders and institutions, their energies already taxed to the full, are tempted to seek the power and prestige of the state to help them in the grueling task of religious education. Yet there is no escaping the law that water cannot rise higher than its source; it is an illusion to imagine that the United States can be made "religious" in spite of itself. If the public-school system were to be saddled with the tasks that should be borne by other agencies, we might well develop a religion-by-rote which would spell the decay of religious vitality.

Religious education has been compulsory in many parts of Europe, and the full power of the state has been placed behind it on the Continent. Yet it was here that the principal versions of totalitarianism, communism, fascism, and naziism arose. Among the features that these systems hold in common is a violent hostility to religion in all its forms. With the overthrow of naziism and fascism in Europe, religious education under state auspices has been restored in most west European countries. Yet observers are generally agreed that this universal exposure to religious education has not halted, let alone reversed, the widespread decline of religious loyalty among the youth and their elders.

If America is to make its full contribution to the world community, it must strive to safeguard its double heritage of religion within the context of freedom and freedom in the area of religion.

# 8

# RACE AND THE RELIGIOUS
# TRADITION

The tensions among religious groups, though often marked by misunderstanding and hostility, rarely erupt into violence in our day. The age of religious wars—or wars waged in the name of religion—seems to be over. It has been our contention of the preceding pages that in the realm of interreligious relationships, the American experience has something both distinctive and valuable to contribute to the world. The unique doctrine of the separation of church and state offers a pattern for conserving the vitality of religion as expressed in its diversity, while safeguarding the unity of society on a foundation of freedom.

No such high claim can be made for the American treatment of the problem of race. If the entire sorry record in this area could be expunged, there would be little to regret. To be sure, the initial tragedy and sin of chattel slavery came to an end with the Emancipation Proclamation of 1863. Yet even today, the United States has not solved what Gunnar Myrdal has acutely called "the American dilemma," the contradiction between the traditional ideal of "liberty and justice for all" and the widespread practice of discrimination against Negro citizens in the fields of political rights, economic opportunity, education, housing, and social acceptance.

In the century since the bloody expiation of the Civil War, the Negro has made substantial progress in all these areas. Because war, for all its destructiveness, is a dynamic factor of extraordinary range and power, it is a fact that the major turning points in the Negro position in the twentieth century have come in the wake of the First and the Second World Wars, and the Korean conflict. Each war was a tide propelling the Negro to new positions of equality; the ebb, which succeeded the flow, was powerless to carry him all the way back to his original position.

The "cold war" now being waged has led to perhaps the most far-reaching advance. The Supreme Court decision of 1954 overturning the hoary doctrine of "separate but equal" schools for whites and Negroes stamped segregation as unconstitutional. The "sit-in" demonstrators and the Freedom Riders have sought through non-violent methods to accelerate the process of desegregation. Progress both in the schools and in southern life as a whole has been slow but perceptible. What is most significant is that both the advocates and the opponents of Negro rights recognize that segregation is doomed. The destination is certain—only the timetable can be manipulated and not very much at that.

Another element in the struggle for racial equality in the United States transcends the domestic scene. The inherent logic of world events, notably the violent upsurge of African and Asian nationalism, has made it crystal clear that segregation is not only morally unjust and economically unsound, but, vis-à-vis a world in ferment, politically suicidal for America. All observers are agreed that the Negro problem is of crucial significance in the war for the world being waged by the democracies against the encroaching tide of communism. The uncommitted nations of the world are almost all dark-skinned. They constitute a tremendous bloc of votes in the United Nations. In addition, they possess great strategic importance, while much of the raw materials still to be found in the world lies in their territories. It is not the industrial efficiency of private enterprise or even the intellectual joys of free speech and parliamentary elections which will win them for the West. Even the promise of better food, shelter, health, and education, which Communist propaganda holds out and which is considerably easier for them to comprehend than our abstract "freedoms," will not be the determining factor. The choice between democracy and communism is likely to be made on the basis of which system offers the African and Asian a deeper sense of human dignity and equality.

It is unfortunately true that in this world-wide campaign powerful and skilful forces of propaganda are ranged against us. Every success that America achieves in its progress toward racial equality and justice is likely to be minimized, and every failure is sure to be exaggerated as it is trumpeted over the world. This cannot be helped, but it adds a special sense of urgency to the struggle for racial justice at home.

Has the biblically rooted religious tradition any significant role to play in this battle? Perhaps the most important contribution it can make is to supply the right motive for the right action. If we urge justice to the American Negro simply in terms of our international needs, we are not likely to succeed at home or to win friends abroad. Acting purely in terms of the Dale Carnegie gospel of "winning friends and influencing people" is a sure way to lose friends and alienate people. Our approach to the complex and deep-seated issue of the Negro and his position in the United States must flow out of an integrated world view, a deeply rooted conception of man and society. Not expediency but principle must be its foundation.

Yet even here there is a danger that must be guarded against. It would be totally self-defeating for religion to adopt an attitude of self-righteousness on the racial problem.

Let it be remembered that for many thousands of years organized religion found it perfectly compatible with its teaching of the dignity of man to support the institution of slavery. This was true not only in the Christian churches but also in the Jewish community. In the fateful decade before the outbreak of the American Civil War, two of the best-known rabbis in the United States publicly debated slavery. Rabbi Morris J. Raphall was able to point to the various biblical ordinances regarding slavery as evidence that the institution did not run counter to biblical teaching. Rabbi David Einhorn, on the other hand, who opposed slavery and termed it "the greatest possible crime against God," had, in purely scholarly terms, the weaker side of the argument. It is no accident that both in the United States and in the Union of South Africa extreme pietism and racial discrimination occupy the same territory. The Ku Klux Klan is able to speak in the name of Christian virtue, and there is no diminution in the sense of piety or self-righteousness which characterizes the apostles of segregation and racial discrimination today.

The fundamental error of Rabbi Raphall's reading of the biblical record, an error repeated again and again to the present, lay in his approaching the Bible statically instead of dynamically. The sacred text must be seen against the background of ancient society in which extensive free labor was an economic impossibility, because of the primitive and unproductive techniques of labor then available. Thus Plato, in his *Republic*, in depicting the ideal society of the future, regarded both slavery and war as inevitable and made provision both for a slave class and an army to keep the "barbarians" perpetually at bay. So too Aristotle held that slavery of the many was necessary in order to provide the leisure required for the fullest development of an elite few. Moses would have agreed wholeheartedly with Aristotle that leisure is essential for the full unfolding of human personality. From this premise, Aristotle justified slavery, but Moses established the Sabbath. Hence the Fourth Commandment in the Decalogue:

Six days mayest thou labor,
And do all thy work.
But the seventh day is the Sabbath of the Lord thy God:
In it thou shalt not do any work,
Thou, nor thy son, nor thy daughter,
Nor thy manservant, nor thy maidservant,
Nor thine ox, nor thine ass, nor any of thy cattle,
Nor thy stranger that is within thy gates;
That thy manservant and thy maidservant
May rest as well as thou.
And remember that thou wast a slave in the land of Egypt,
And that the Lord thy God brought thee out thence
Through a mighty hand by an outstretched arm:
Therefore the Lord thy God commanded thee
To keep the Sabbath day [Deuteronomy 5:14–15].

Moreover, the entire institution of Hebrew slavery was virtually abolished in Israel by limiting service to a six-year period (Exodus 21:2). As for the non-Hebrew slave, biblical law established countless other safeguards for his physical safety and human dignity as well.

When the United States Congress passed a law in 1854 making it mandatory for American citizens to restore any fugitive slave to his master, high-minded and law-abiding Americans throughout the land called attention to a higher, divine law which took precedence:

Thou shalt not deliver unto his master the slave
Which is escaped from his master unto thee:
He shall dwell with thee, even among you,
In that place which he shall choose in one of thy gates,
Where it liketh him best:
Thou shall not oppress him [Deuteronomy 23:15–16].

Thus the Bible made it unmistakably clear that its sympathies were ranged on the side of liberty and not slavery.

As in many other instances, the doctrine that all men have an inalienable right to freedom was carried further and deepened in post-biblical Judaism. According to the Bible, if a slave at the end of the six-year period refused to go free, he was brought to the gate of the city and there his ear was bored through (Exodus 21:5–6). The great sage Johanan ben Zakkai, who lived in the first century c.e., gave a profoundly ethical interpretation to this peculiar form of branding. According to Jewish tradition, all the unborn generations of Israel stood at the foot of Sinai and took a vow of allegiance to the Torah. Hence this slave, too, was a party to the pact, and his ears had heard God proclaim: "Unto Me shall the children of Israel be slaves, not slaves unto slaves." Since he is prepared to accept human bondage in spite of the divine proclamation, he deserves to have his ear bored through as a punishment! (B. *Kiddushin*, 22*b*.) Thus, the entire tenor and direction of biblical and post-biblical thought was firmly set against slavery. It sought to mitigate its worst abuses, only because it could not abolish it *in toto*.

What is the biblical attitude toward the Negro? In answering this question, one is reminded of a well-known, possibly apocryphal incident in the life of Samuel Johnson. When still a lad, he was asked to write a theme on a subject of his own choosing. Being congenitally indolent, he chose as his subject "Snakes in Ireland," and his essay ran as follows: "There are no snakes in Ireland." Religion, a striking phrase has it, is color-blind. It therefore draws no distinctions on the basis of race or color and is aware only of men, stripped of these differences.

The epigram, however, is ambiguous. If it is taken to mean that religion refuses to admit that the existence of the various colors of skin justifies setting up distinctions in men's obligations, rights, and privileges, the phrase is true. But, if it is understood to imply that religion can continue to ignore

the problems which the various hues of men create in contemporary society and blandly keep on preaching human
brotherhood in the abstract, as it has done in the past, the
phrase is downright dangerous.

The classic texts of both Judaism and Christianity make
little mention of Negroes as such, probably because there
were few contacts between the ancient Hebrews and the
darker races.

A passage frequently invoked by the apostles of Negro
inferiority is the incident narrated in Genesis (9:20–27).
After the Flood, the Bible tells, Noah planted a vineyard,
drank of its fruit, and became drunk, stripping himself of
his clothes in his tent. Noah's son Ham, who was the father
of Canaan, saw his father's nakedness and reported the fact
to his brothers, Shem and Japheth. The two brothers took
their garment, placed it on their backs, and walking back-
wards, covered their father's nakedness without putting him
to shame. When Noah awoke from his wine, he knew what
Ham had done and declared:

> Cursed be Canaan;
> A servant of servants shall he be unto his brethren.
> And he said, Blessed be the Lord God of Shem;
> And Canaan shall be his servant.
> God shall enlarge Japheth,
> And he shall dwell in the tents of Shem;
> And Canaan shall be his servant [Genesis 9:25–27].

Why is Canaan, who is entirely guiltless, cursed with
slavery, rather than Ham, who failed in filial piety? The
answer is that the Bible, which depicts the historical destiny of the Hebrew people, is interested in Canaan and not
in Ham, who is the traditional ancestor of the darker races,
such as Ethiopia, Egypt, and Put (Genesis, chap. 10). The
incident with Noah is designed to justify the ultimate sub-
jugation of the Canaanites at the hands of the Hebrews. It
is therefore an egregious misreading of the biblical narrative,

even on the most literal terms, to derive from it any warrant for the notion of Negro inferiority. There is no curse of slavery or inferiority placed upon Ham.

A more significant reference, which is directly relevant to our theme, occurs in the life of Moses:

> Miriam and Aaron spoke against Moses
> Because of the Ethiopian woman whom he had married:
> (For he had married an Ethiopian woman).
> And they said, Has the Lord spoken only to Moses?
> Has he not spoken to us as well?
> And the Lord heard it.
> (Now the man Moses was very humble,
> Above all the men upon the face of the earth.)
> And the Lord spoke suddenly unto Moses,
> And unto Aaron, and unto Miriam, . . .
> And he said, Hear now my words:
> If there be a prophet among you,
> I the Lord will make myself known to him in visions,
> And will speak to him in dreams.
> Not so with My servant Moses, faithful in all My house.
> With him I speak directly,
> Clearly, and not in dark sayings.
> And he sees the very image of the Lord.
> Why then were you not afraid to speak
> Against my servant Moses?
> And the anger of the Lord was kindled against them;
> And he departed [Numbers 12:1–9].

The Bible goes on to tell how Miriam is punished by being stricken with leprosy. Aaron pleads for her forgiveness with Moses, who prays to the Lord on her behalf. After seven days, Miriam is healed of her disease and the Israelites proceed on their journey.

The incident obviously reflects the existence of a bias in ancient Israel against the darker-skinned peoples. Prejudice, which has been rather summarily described as the dislike of the unlike, would naturally fasten upon so obvious a difference as the color of the skin. However, the biblical standpoint is clear—Aaron and Miriam have been guilty of folly and sin. In no uncertain terms God castigates them for their action and vindicates Moses' action in taking an Ethiopian woman for a wife, using the occasion to extol his unique relationship with God as the prophet par excellence.

The prophet Amos used this widespread state of mind—or mindlessness—which looked down upon the darker-skinned people, as the point of departure for his ringing declaration on the equality of all races and nations. In his day, the Hebrews, like all nations, ancient and modern alike, held to the comfortable doctrine that they were the chosen people of God. As proof of their favored status, they were wont to adduce their miraculous exodus from Egypt. Against this national exclusivism, the prophet declares that God directs the migrations of all nations in history. He then caps the climax by comparing the elect people of God to the Negroes:

> Are ye not as children of the Ethiopians unto me,
> O children of Israel? saith the Lord.
> Have not I brought up Israel out of the land of Egypt?
> And the Philistines from Caphtor,
> And the Syrians from Kir? [Amos 9:7].

This insistence upon the equality of all men and races became basic to post-biblical Judaism and to Christianity which derived from it. It must be conceded that Christian calls for racial equality were frequently motivated by a concern for winning converts. In Judaism, the stress upon human equality remained free from the motive of proselytization. Thus, the second-century scholar and martyr Rabbi Akiba declared that the Golden Rule enunciated in Leviticus 19:18, which is, incidentally, pointed specifically toward aliens in verse 34, was the greatest principle in Scripture. His contemporary, Ben Azzai, argued that a more fundamental principle was to be found in the passage in Genesis (5 :1):

> This is the book of the generations of Adam,
> In the day that God Created man.
> In the likeness of God made he him.

In this verse, he discerned the two doctrines of the unity of mankind and the dignity of all men (*Midrash, Sifra* on *Lev.* 19:18). The religious protest against notions of group superiority is strikingly expressed in the talmudic statement, "All men are descended from a single human being, Adam, so that no man may say, 'my ancestor is greater than yours' " (*Mishnah, Sanhedrin* 4:5). One recalls the moving words of Buddha:

> There is no caste in blood, which runneth of one hue;
> Nor caste in tears, which trickle salt withal.

Even in the vast reaches of rabbinic literature, specific references to the Negro are scarce, again due to the limited number of Jewish contacts with Negroes during the Roman period and the succeeding medieval era. An early medieval homily or *Midrash* on Isaiah (66:19) contains what is probably the only extant reference to Negroes.[1] The passage seems almost prophetic as a protest against the arrant and bloody nonsense of racialism which arose in Nazi Germany: "Said the Prophet Isaiah, In the days to come, a German will come and take hold of the hand of a Negro, and a Negro will take hold of the hand of a German, and arm in arm they will walk together and will proclaim among the nations the miracles and wonders of God."

It is undeniable that contemporary religious teachers have been right in regarding the Negro problem as requiring for

---

[1] I am indebted for this reference to my colleague, Dean Saul Lieberman, professor of Talmud at the Jewish Theological Seminary, who generously placed his vast erudition at my service. The text is to be found in *Ginze Schechter*, Part I, p. 86.

its solution the application of the fundamental Judeo-Christian doctrines of the brotherhood of man rooted in the Fatherhood of God. It is clear, however, that they cannot content themselves merely with the repetition of resounding generalities. Religious leadership cannot ignore the complex issues that are involved in the various aspects of the racial situation or avoid coming to grips with the specific proposals that have been advanced to meet them. There is great wisdom in the insistence of Judaism that the Law takes precedence even over the Prophets. Ideals must be concretized in law and in life.

Aside from co-operating with other agencies, organized religion has its own special contribution to make to the solution of this critical problem. Basically, the function of religion in the area of Negro-white relationships lies in the field of moral education. The synagogue and the church have an unequaled opportunity as well as an ineluctable obligation to set forth their ideal vision for mankind and to spell out its implications for the social realities of the present, utilizing all the means available to them for this purpose: the sermon, the adult class, the youth discussion group, the religious school, and the various auxiliary groups.

When religious leaders emphasize the right of the Negro, not to sympathy, tolerance, or kindness, but to equality and dignity as a basic imperative of vital religion, they bring aid and comfort to the small, active minority in contemporary American society which is fighting the Negro's cause. In supplying a rationale in the battle for racial justice, religion offers the double support of morality and morale for a difficult struggle. It also does more. It foments an inner discomfort in the inert majority who would prefer to be "let alone" and continue to ignore the implications of the faith they profess for the world in which they live. With regard to the racial situation, religion has too long been comforting the afflicted. The hour has struck for afflicting the comfortable.

Traditionally, the religious and ethical teacher has always condemned a man's hatred of his neighbor in individual terms. But when this hatred is generalized against a group and a "philosophy" is generated in order to justify the prejudice, the duty of religion is equally clear, even if rendered more difficult. Religion must continue to proclaim the truth that group hatred does not differ in essence from individual hatred and is equally to be condemned, and that prejudice, operating through stereotypes, discriminatory laws, and generalized attitudes, constitutes a cardinal sin. Herman Bahr, the German Social Democrat, declared, "Anti-semitism is the morphine of the small people." Anti-Negro prejudice may be described as the anti-Semitism of the white race, who, to quote Herman Bahr again, "since they cannot attain the ecstasy of love, seek the ecstasy of hatred."

From the standpoint of religious faith, prejudice is not merely a major sin against man but an offense against God, since it is an expression of the sin of blasphemy. It is, in Haselden's words, "the latest and most virulent form of man's ancient urge for self-exaltation, [the sin] which the Bible condemned in the ancient narrative of the Tower of Babel. It is one of man's several neurotic and perverted expressions of his will to be God."

Sir William Temple has delineated prejudice in theological terms in these words:

> When we open our eyes as babies we see the world stretching out around us; we are in the middle of it. . . . I am the center of the world I see; where the horizon is depends on where I stand. Now just the same thing is true at first of our mental and spiritual vision. . . . So each of us takes his place in the center of his own world. But I am not the center of the world, or the standard of reference as between good and bad; I am not, and God is. In other words, from the beginning I put myself in God's place. This is my original sin. I was doing it before I could speak, and everyone else has been doing it from early infancy.

In the war against prejudice, vital religion can draw powerful weapons from the arsenal of contemporary science. All competent sociologists and psychologists are agreed that prejudice is not inherent but acquired, that it is a coefficient of Western culture, particularly of Anglo-Saxon society, and is not rooted in the universal human situation. Once a child is imbued with it, its eradication becomes difficult, for he begins to display all the characteristics of psychotic behavior. A prejudiced individual is all but immune against any assaults from the domain of reason. His attitude flows around and bypasses the facts, disregarding all logical discussions and factual demonstrations as though they did not exist.

The religious school, to which children are sent at their most tender and impressionable years, therefore has a high responsibility, all too often neglected, to deal concretely with the disease of prejudice and seek to immunize its wards against its virulence. For virtually all social scientists would indorse the view that prejudice is not innate but is inculcated early in life, before the child is six, seven, or eight. The complexities of racial prejudice must continue to be brought to the attention of teen-age and adolescent groups affiliated with the church and the synagogue. The pulpit must deal not only with the broad lines of biblical teaching on the subject of race and brotherhood but apply them to the various concrete developments in the local and the general community and interpret them in the light of the noblest insights of the Judeo-Christian tradition. It must constantly underscore the etiology of prejudice and remind its devotees that "every 'in-group' has an 'out-group' upon which it projects all that is by its standards abhorrent and in which by contrast it sees its own glorification reflected."

It is also necessary to deal realistically with some of the roadblocks toward understanding and mutual respect. It is a basic insight of religion that the practice of evil not only perverts the soul of the perpetrator but warps the spirit of the victim. It would be difficult to deny that in the present period of stress and strain, many antisocial manifestations may be found among Negroes as well as among the whites. Lawrence Hogben has well pointed out that "prejudice does not make men attractive. This is one of the best arguments against prejudice." It is the duty of the enlightened conscience to follow the wise counsel of Goethe, "If we take people as they are, we make them worse. If we treat them as if they were what they ought to be, we help them to become what they are capable of becoming."

The evidence is accumulating, through hundreds of thousands of cases, that where the Negro is given the sense of a stake in the social order, he responds, as do all human beings, by manifesting a feeling of responsibility. In modern housing developments, under decent employment opportunities, in education—wherever Negroes are offered the opportunity of participating in life on a level of equality—they reflect the same range of reactions and attitudes as their white fellow citizens.

In sum, the most fundamental service that religion can render lies in the field of education, where no other agency can approach it either in the authority of its pronouncements or in the legitimacy of its attitudes. Even the most rabid defender of Negro inferiority cannot hurl the charge of communism against the doctrine of human brotherhood rooted in Holy Writ!

In addition to this special role in moral education, religious leaders have an obligation to participate with other sectors of society in the far-flung battle for Negro rights. Here two principal weapons are available, legal action and economic pressure, both non-violent in character.

It is sometimes argued that legislation for the benefit of Negroes is largely self-defeating because "you cannot make people moral through laws." The statement misses the point entirely, for the purpose of legislation is not to make bad people good but to make innocent people safe. No one intends to endow men with righteousness by means of racial legislation, the use of economic power, or the practice of sit-in demonstrations. These tactics are designed to grant the Negro his due as a man and as a citizen. In fighting to advance their legitimate interests and buttress their inherent rights, Negroes are not only within their rights but are fulfilling their American and human duty.

These rights fall under several principal categories: the right to vote, to equal and unsegregated education, to equal employment opportunities, and to adequate housing. In all these areas, many agencies and groups can make their influence felt, and religion should be one of them.

All these aspects of the struggle for equality, political, educational, and economic, are preliminary to the most far-reaching battle of all, *the war against social discrimination.* Here vital religion has a distinctive contribution to make on the ethical frontier, still far in advance of the prevailing standards of our society. Haselden has defined discrimination as "the unjust separation of people from things and circumstances" and segregation as "the immoral separation of people from people." It cannot be too strongly stressed that in this struggle against social discrimination Negroes, like all minorities, must be freely granted the *right of spiritual self-determination,* without which freedom is a mockery. Some persons containing varying proportions of Negro blood may wish to integrate completely with their white fellow men. Many will wish merely to associate themselves with the cultural, social, and political life of the larger community. Others may feel impelled to strengthen their racial and cultural distinctiveness. In James Weldon Johnson's words, "There should be nothing in law or public opinion to prevent persons of like interest and congenial tastes from associating together, if they mutually desire to do so." Negroes should be free to choose whatever approach they prefer, as free men and women, created in God's image and endowed with his spirit.

That there are many thousands of Negroes who have "passed" into the white community is a commonplace in our social experience. If any stigma attaches to this practice, it is not so much because of any inherent immorality involved in the act but primarily because the Negro who passes into the white community deprives his race of an important effective in its struggle for equality. "Passing" may therefore be deplored by certain groups, because it represents the impoverishment of he Negro community by the loss of some of its most creative and valuable elements, whose leadership and participation it desperately needs in order to achieve its due rights. If, therefore, there be any hesitation with regard to the morality of "passing," the fault lies squarely at the door of the white race which practices discrimination rather than with the Negroes who are its victims.

This right to spiritual self-determination comes upon the obstacle of Negro stereotypes. The social evils that flow from men's universal penchant for stereotyping their fellows are self-evident. But there is a profound religious sin involved in group stereotypes. It is highlighted by Berdyaev's profound analysis of the unrepeatability of personality. The dignity of man as taught by religion expresses the mystery and the grandeur, the peril and the sacredness, of each human personality. Herein lies the particular worth which God has set upon each of his individual children. Stereotyping men denies this essential attribute of human personality— its particularity.

The process takes on various forms. The most common is a direct effort to debase the Negro by picturing him as deficient in intelligence or in character, or in both. Almost equally harmful is the romanticizing of the Negro, the defensive posture according to which the Negro is responsible for no errors or weaknesses charged to him. What the Negro has a right to ask is that he be regarded neither as an angel nor as subhuman, but rather as a man, unique like every other, with his individual complement of virtues and vices, strengths and weaknesses.

The resistance to the social integration of Negroes and whites stems from a widespread fear of racial intermarriage. Whenever the evils of social discrimination against Negroes are discussed, the rhetorical question is sure to be asked ultimately, "Do you want to marry a Negro?" To this triumphant query designed to silence the opposition, Lincoln responded in his famous debates with Stephen A. Douglas, "Now I protest against the counterfeit logic which concludes that because I do not want a black woman for a slave, I must necessarily want her for a wife. I need not have her for either, I can just leave her alone."

This answer, sensible and balanced as it is, cannot fully satisfy the religious conscience. The truth is that no great religious tradition in the Western world, Christian, Jewish, or Islamic, sees any inherent objection to racial intermarriage. The biblical incident in the life of Moses is a classic prototype of the reaction of high religion to the promptings of racial prejudice. Father John La Farge sets forth the doctrine of his own church in these words:

> The Catholic Church does not impose any impediment upon racial intermarriages, in spite of the Church's great care to preserve in its utmost purity the integrity of the marriage bond. And she safeguards the right of persons to choose their own marriage partners, so long as they observe the laws that the Church considers essential to the integrity of the sacrament of matrimony. However, from a purely prudential standpoint, serious reasons can militate against entering into such a marriage, where—as is very apt to be the case—there is a wide difference between the parties as to their social background or social environ-

ment. This is particularly the case in sections of the country where racial differences have become rigidly crystallized by custom and tradition.[2]

To be sure, there are laws against the marriage of whites and non-whites, so-called "racial miscegenation," in twenty-nine states of the Union. As a civil officer, the minister of religion in those states will not violate the law by solemnizing interracial marriages. Yet from the standpoint of ethical religion, not to speak of authoritative science, there is no basis whatever for those restrictions. It is not altogether pointless to note that the word "miscegenation" is commonly used in this connection, perhaps because it suggests an erroneous and terror-laden etymology. The first syllable is often taken by the uninstructed as meaning "wrong," as in "mistake," or "misstep." Actually, the word is derived from the Latin *misceo*, "to mix," and *gigno* (perfect stem *gen*), "to beget," and hence means only "mixed marriage," with no negative connotation.

It is true that Jewish religious tradition, like that of Catholicism, is strongly opposed to religious intermarriage and seeks to minimize it to the best of its ability. The reason lies in its concern for the preservation of the authenticity and vigor of its own religio-cultural tradition, which tends to be diluted, if not totally destroyed, when a mixed marriage takes place and religious loyalties dissolve into an atmosphere of indifference and lack of commitment. The opposition to religious intermarriage, therefore, has deep meaning for all those who seek to perpetuate the values inherent in a given religious tradition.

This is emphatically not the case with racial intermarriage. The American Negro may cultivate, quite properly, a special interest in African culture, particularly its music or

---

[2] John La Farge, *The Catholic Viewpoint on Race Relations* (New York, 1956), 128–29.

its art, but in this respect he is no different from other Americans. Actually, as Father La Farge has reminded us, outside of the aboriginal American Indian, the Negro is "the only American who has no hyphen background, no traditions of a mother country across the seas. In this respect he is like the Indian, the only American who knows no other cultural tradition than the American way of life."[3] In theory, therefore, an authentic religious tradition, be it Jewish or Christian, can impose no objection to racial intermarriage.

The religious teacher, however, must necessarily be conscious of the stark realities of the racial situation in America today. He will therefore tend to urge caution before two young people of different races embark on matrimony. He will point out the hazards of prejudice to which they and any children born to them are likely to be exposed in the United States. He will suggest that they will be complicating the normal problems of marital adjustment because the disparate racial backgrounds of the two partners will add special difficulties with regard to housing, education, and social life in our all-too-imperfect world. Since these considerations are not ethical and universal but purely the counsels of expediency, they are limited in scope. They would not apply to areas where racial prejudice is less deep-seated, as in France, the West Indies, or South America. Having pointed out these problems, the religious leader would have no reason for opposing interracial marriage if the partners were so minded.

For historical reasons, the Jewish community has had little opportunity to demonstrate the extent of its loyalty to the high doctrine of racial equality which is clearly taught in its tradition. It is only in recent years that the color problem has become a reality for modern Jews. In the State of Israel, many of the Yemenite Jews who were transported from

---

[3] John La Farge, *op. cit.*, p. 43.

Arabia on the air lift called the "Magic Carpet" during the first decade of Israeli independence are of darker hue and constitute a kind of "colored" group in Israel. Other darker-skinned Jews have come from Iraq and Morocco to the Promised Land. In part because of the difference of pigmentation and in part because of their relative unfamiliarity with Western standards and the amenities of technical civilization, these oriental Jews have tended to occupy the lower sectors in the economy, roughly analogous to the position of the Negro in the United States.

According to some reports, prejudice has made itself felt among certain elements of the population in Israel, and the orientals have complained of various types of discrimination practiced against them. Here the response, both of the government and of all influential segments of public opinion, has been refreshingly clear and unequivocal—prejudice against any human being on the basis of his color is totally repugnant to the Jewish conscience and Israeli law. Important government officials, as well as leaders in the arts and sciences and the commercial and industrial life of the country, have done more than oppose color prejudice in words. They have exhibited their loyalty to the principle of equality through encouraging—and in their own families as well—the growing number of marriages between European and oriental Jews.

Another authentic Jewish Negro community, rich in romance and tragedy, is that of the Falashas in Abyssinia. For many hundreds of years, going back to the early centuries of the Christian period, there has been a large isolated community of Negroes there practicing Judaism as they had been taught. They held on tenaciously to their faith in the face of continual efforts to persuade or force them to accept the religion of the majority. These Falashas were rediscovered by scholars in the nineteenth century, and the antique form of Jewish tradition by which they lived has been

highly interesting to scholars, who have sought to recon-
struct the historical development of Jewish tradition. Unfortunately, the ranks of the Falashas have been decimated
in recent years by a variety of factors. Calls have been issued
to Jews throughout the world for support of the communal
institutions and the amelioration of the economic lot of their
black brethren in Africa.

Perhaps the most enigmatic element in the problem of
Negro-Jewish relations is that of the black Jews of Harlem.
In this, the largest Negro community north of the Mason-
Dixon Line, there is an organized congregation of Negroes
called "Keepers of the Ancient Covenant." Their synagogue,
ritual, and way of life follow the basic pattern of traditional
Judaism, but there are some practices that point to the
Christian origin of the members of the group. By and large,
the accredited Jewish religious leadership in the United
States has tended to doubt the authentic Jewishness of these
black Jews in Harlem. According to reports, there are other
Negro Jewish congregations in New York, as well. The
relationship of these black Jews to Judaism is therefore not a
racial but a religious issue and it will ultimately need to be
resolved in these terms.

At the same time, there have been instances of individual
Negro families professing Judaism. They have been admitted to the synagogue and their children have been enrolled in Jewish religious schools, some of them distinguish-
ing themselves in their studies. Marriages of Negroes and
white Jewish young people also take place at intervals and,
at times, the non-Jewish partner is converted to the Jewish
religion. When a Negro accepts Judaism and fulfils the traditional requirements of a proselyte, his position is exactly
the same as that of a white convert—he is a child of the
covenant, a descendant of the patriarch Abraham.

Interesting as these "problem islands" of the Falashas in
Africa and of the Negro Jews in the United States may

be, they are minor. Far more basic is the role which the Jewish tradition can play in helping inspire the American people in general and the Jewish community in particular to a greater sensitivity and a more active role in the struggle of their Negro fellow citizens not merely for their legal rights but also for the attainment of their human dignity as brothers under God.

# 9

# POLITICS AND HUMAN NATURE

That American democracy is confronted by complex and even grave problems with regard to group relations at home cannot be denied. Yet it is clear that the truly critical area, fraught with life and death both for the free world and for its adversaries, lies in the field of international relations. What guidance can the West find in the ethical content of the Judeo-Christian heritage to which it formally gives its allegiance? Is there any relevance in the insights and ideals of biblical thought for the complicated and perilous issues confronting man today?

There are at least three basic positions held on this issue today. The oldest and most widely practiced is the one least often articulated. This is the cynical theory of politics associated with Machiavelli, though his own teaching was far less extreme than the popular image conjured up by his name. This viewpoint finds its classic expression in Machiavelli's *The Prince*, which seeks to train the ruler to manipulate public affairs in accordance with the practical needs of the hour. Centuries later, Karl Marx, who defined religion as the opiate of the people, together with his associate, Friedrich Engels, sought to buttress the view that ethical standards are an instrument created by the dominant classes in order to win obedience to the status quo from the

137

oppressed groups in society. It therefore follows that ethical doctrine, like religious belief, is merely a façade or a tool, possessing no genuine validity of its own.

Hence, the double talk of communism, which employs such terms as "democracy," "freedom," and "peace" in its vocabulary as conscious instruments for achieving non-moral ends. And if a philosophy of ethics is desiderated, "the good" is defined in a dictatorship as whatever advances the interest of the state, the race, or the party.

In democratic lands, like our own, cynicism with regard to politics is widespread among the citizenry. Politicians do little to counteract the notion that there is no connection between ethical ideals and political affairs. Cynicism is painfully evident in municipal political machines, in national party conventions, and in the negotiation, if that be the word, of international relations. It may be added that the "men of affairs" involved in these various enterprises are rarely concerned with finding a rationale for their conduct. Whenever they reflect on the process in which they are engaged, they remind us, first, that politics is the art of the possible and, second, that in our grossly imperfect world, the possible is almost always evil.

At the opposite pole from this cynical approach is the naïve idealism of the liberal during the pre-World War II period. There is a current tendency, which must be guarded against, to oversimplify the liberal position and to exaggerate its naïveté. Yet it remains true that fundamentally this attitude derived from a strong optimism with regard to human nature and its capacities. Its corollary was a belief in virtually automatic progress in history, its moving inevitably toward greater justice and peace in international affairs. Hence the liberal placed great reliance upon treaties and covenants openly arrived at, labored for international agreements for limited or total disarmament, and greeted with enthusiasm

the establishment of the United Nations as the practical instrument for an effective international order.

The ideological sources of the liberal faith are to be found
in eighteenth-century secular humanism. It is expressed, for
example, in Rousseau's faith in the fundamental goodness of
man, which has been corrupted by the artificialities of civilization, and in Condorcet's doctrine of the perfectibility of
human nature. This interpretation of man and of history
was reinforced for religious believers by the liberal interpretation of the Judeo-Christian Scriptures. The prophetic
concept of history was utilized to suggest that the events of
human experience are no meaningless succession of accidental occurrences, no mere aggregation of physical forces
and material powers, but the reflection of God's will, utilizing men and nations for the consummation of his purpose. A
figure as distant from the philosophers of the Age of Reason
as Hegel declared that *Weltgeschichte ist Weltgericht*,
"world history is world judgment." When the kingdom of
God was interpreted in purely secular terms, the harmoniza-
tion of the rational humanism of the eighteenth century and
of the religious idealism of the Scriptures seemed complete.

The idealism of the political liberal, whether derived from
secular or from religious sources, suffered major setbacks in
the mid-twentieth century. The century was ushered in
with high hopes for an era of expanding plenty, freedom,
and peace. The comfortable optimism of the early twentieth
century found theoretical expression in the easy meliorism
of a liberal theology, which stressed the potentialities for
perfection in man, or at least for his perpetual and consistent
improvement.

Within a few decades, however, these hopes were virtually annihilated by virtue of two successive world wars and
the wholesale extermination of millions of men, women, and
children. The "war to end war" and "make the world safe
for democracy" succeeded in neither objective. The Second

World War marked a desperate attempt by the free nations
to destroy the manifestations of bestiality deeply rooted in
human nature, which, according to liberal optimism, had
ceased to exist long before.

The Fascist and Nazi varieties of totalitarianism were
overthrown, but many of their features were absorbed into
the Communist state systems. These have proved at least as
aggressive as, and far more successful than, Hitler and Mussolini in effectively destroying the hopes of achieving freedom for an ever increasing segment of the world population, at least for the present and foreseeable future.

Confronted by the collapse of the liberal vision, many of
its former devotees have relapsed into cynical disillusion.
Another alternative has, however, found a wide response—
that of the "realists" in politics. Many of them are deeply
religious spirits and find in the Bible the source both of their
ethical standards and of their conception of human nature.
Basing themselves on the doctrine of "original sin," they declare that man's weaknesses are the fundamental constituents
of his nature, so that all his activities are at worst evil and at
best morally ambiguous.

The most influential exponent of this point of view in our
age has been Reinhold Niebuhr. The incredible depth of his
insight into human nature, the sophistication of his analysis
of the political process, and the breadth of his religious and
philosophic ideas are qualities which set him above most of
his contemporaries. His basic thesis of moral man in an immoral society, of men who will the good but are powerless
to achieve it in the context of group life, is a modern reinterpretation of Paul's lament, "The good I would, I do not, but
the evil which I would not, that I do" (Romans 7:19).
Niebuhr buttresses his approach by reflecting upon the ambiguous character of power as including the evils of coer-
cion and self-interest. Since politics cannot function without
power, politics must be inherently immoral, or at best an

amoral instrument for achieving purposes that may be good, bad, or indifferent. Yet even these purposes, when basically good, are not free from the taint of aggression, violence, and self-seeking.

Hence politics cannot be reasonably expected to obey the dictates of ethics; the best that can be hoped for is the choice of the least evil of alternatives. Any effort to invoke moral principles in politics must lead to defeat, if not to disaster, because the nature of reality does not conform to the demand of the ethical conscience. Thus Ernest Lefever, in his illuminating volume, *Ethics and United States Foreign Policy*, begins with an illustration to which he returns several times:

> If December 7, 1941, will live on in American history as a "day of infamy," November 2, 1956, may well be remembered as a day of irony. On that day our government joined with its arch enemy, the Soviet Union, and Egypt, her willing tool in the Middle East, in condemning our two closest and staunchest allies, Great Britain and France. This act, which helped to destroy the moral and political position of Britain and France in the Mediterranean World, was done in the name of morality. Herein lies its irony.

Obviously, the "realist's" position is far superior to the approach of the unabashed cynic, who begins by surrendering all ethical ideals and thus helps make of human society a perilous jungle in which dangerously armed wild beasts are loose. This "realist" approach is superior, too, to that of the naïve idealist, who helps make democracy an easy prey to its undemocratic enemies and unconsciously furthers the destruction of the ideals which he cherishes.

The world view of the "realist" is compounded in large measure of the attitudes of crisis theology and of the temper of existentialism. In emphasizing the limitations of reason, the reality of sin, and the ambiguities of human motives, and in rejecting the superficial notion of automatic progress in society, these contemporary schools have performed an exceedingly important function. But, like most reactions, this reaction to "liberal theology" has gone too far. Reinhold Niebuhr's personal and intellectual integrity has led him to admit that "he has tended to overestimate the frustration which sin imposes and to underestimate the creative possibilities for man in a world which is still God's world, despite the sin and ambiguity of life lived within it." It should also be kept in mind that, this theory apart, Niebuhr's entire public activity, his political liberalism, and his lifelong concern with social justice are based on the assumption that somehow ethics must determine the character of politics. There are many other religiously oriented political and social liberals who theoretically maintain the principle of the amorality of politics and then proceed to belie it by their own public activities. At the same time, many social and political thinkers continue to advocate the "realist" position and deny the possibility of any other approach.

Those who seek biblical warrant for their views take it for granted that the concept of "original sin" is the hallmark of biblical religion and of the Judeo-Christian heritage. Now while this doctrine is eloquently expounded in the Epistles of Paul, it is by no means identical with the biblical view of man as expounded in the Hebrew Bible. As a matter of fact, it does not appear in the Gospels. Modern Judaism and, it may be added, substantial groups in Protestant Christianity as well, find no warrant either in the intent of the biblical text or in the realities of human nature for the doctrine of an ineradicable taint of evil in mankind. As for Catholicism, its official theology views "original sin" in far more moderate terms, as representing the loss of the supernatural "state of grace" with which man was originally endowed by his Maker.

Nonetheless, the doctrine of original sin in its more extreme form, when reinterpreted by "neo-orthodox theology" and "realist politics," continues to have a powerful appeal for many spirits in our time. The reason is not difficult to understand. The "idealist" of yesterday turned "realist" today has developed a deep-seated despair with regard to the future of society and a profound disillusion with regard to the capacities of human nature. Both these attitudes, the realist now insists, are not temporary phases characteristic of an age in travail but permanent and ineradicable features of the human condition.

Actually, we are not compelled to adopt either the naïvely optimistic or the grimly realistic concept of human nature. The proof may be found in the outlook of normative Judaism, which developed the theory of human nature as consisting of "two Yetzers," the good impulse and the evil impulse. Rabbinic thought, which yielded to no one in its recognition of the elements of imperfection in man, conceived of man's native endowment as neutral, regarding his instinctual drives neither as good nor as evil per se and passing ultimate judgment upon them only within the context of the uses to which they are put. Essentially, Judaism regards it as fruitful to pass judgment, not upon man's *nature*, but upon his *actions*.

In this world view, man is a battleground for the lifelong struggle between these two impulses, the good (*yetzer hatobh*) and the evil (*yetzer hara*). There is no disposition in Judaism to underestimate the power of the evil impulse in its manifold forms, notably envy, lust, and the desire for glory. Man's instinctual equipment is referred to by the rabbis by the term, "the evil *yetzer*," because they are conscious how frequently it leads men to violate the dictates of reason and the canons of morality. It is, however, a mistake of overliteralism to fail to realize that the term *yetzer hara* in talmudic literature frequently has no negative connotation, as in the classic passage: "Thou shalt love the Lord thy

God with all thy soul—with both *yetzers,* the good impulse
and the evil" (*Berakhot* 61*a*). This passage recognizes that
even "the evil impulse" can be an instrument for the service
of God. Anticipating Freud on several counts, the talmudic
sages are fully aware of the power of sexual desire in human
life and of its capacity for working havoc with men's lives.
But they also express the insight that without "the evil impulse," most of man's functions, such as his creative activity,
family life, and economic pursuits, would cease. Thus the
rabbis declare several times, "Were it not for the sexual impulse [literally, the evil impulse], no man would build a
house or marry a woman or engage in an occupation"
(*Genesis Rabbah,* Sec. 9; *Koheleth Rabbah* 3:11). According to this approach, *human nature is plastic, and any ethical
judgment upon its character must follow, not precede, its
manifestations in human life.*

Moreover, the Judaic world view emphasizes its conviction that man is morally free and by that token responsible
for his actions. Judaism rejected the pagan conception,
which reached its most moving expression in the classic
Greek drama, that saw man as a pawn of destiny, a play-
thing of the caprice of the gods or the helpless victim of an
impersonal and implacable *fatum.* With equal vigor it denies
the pseudo-Darwinian contention that man is merely a biological creature, who needs obey only the jungle law of the
survival of the fittest. Similarly, it opposes the Marxian (or
pseudo-Marxian) theory of economic determinism as super-
seding all ethical standards. It rejects the conception that
morality is merely the cultural compulsive of capitalist society. So, too, it has no traffic with the cloudy notion, so beloved of dictators and their apologists, that there is a "wave
of the future" upon which men and nations are carried along
like flotsam and jetsam and which cannot be resisted.

For Judaism, man is not an object in the universe but a
subject, who is described in the Bible as being fashioned "in

the image of God," because he possesses *in parvo* the qualities which exist in God in infinite degree, and these include
not only the gift of reason but also the power of creativity.
Man is alone among all living creatures in not being at the
mercy of his environment but, on the contrary, able to bend
it to his will.

Vital religion is grateful to the disciplines of biology, sociology, economics, and psychology for the light they shed
upon the factors that *condition* man's activity, but it denies
that they can *determine* his nature, absolve him from his
duty, or fashion his fate. Boldly affirming both elements of
the immemorial paradox, the Talmud declares, "Everything
is foreseen [by God], but freedom is given [to man]" (*Mishnah Abot* 3:15). Or, in another formulation, "Everything is
in the hands of God except the fear of God" (B. *Berakot*
33*b*). What appears as man's reason in the intellectual sphere
is freedom of choice in the moral realm and responsibility
within the context of society. The biblical call is repeated
three times in the Book of Deuteronomy: "Life and death
have I placed before thee this day, the blessing and the curse.
Thou shalt choose life, so that thou mayest live, thou and
thy seed" (Deuteronomy 30:19; cf. also 11:26; 30:15). The
freedom and the responsibility which are the hallmark of
human nature apply both to men and to nations.

# 10

# ETHICS AND THE
# POLITICAL PROCESS

It is no accident that so many sensitive and idealistic men in our day have decided that politics and ethics are two disparate worlds. That the temper of the age has been crucial in this regard has already been indicated. But the attitude also derives in large measure from our faulty understanding of the character and limits of biblical ethics itself. In seeking to bring the insights of the Bible to bear on the contemporary world, the West has erred both in including and in excluding too much of its biblical heritage. On the one hand, there are resources within biblical ethics that have remained untapped, while on the other there are elements within the tradition that have been called upon to do service where they are irrelevant and meaningless and therefore misleading.

The mood of the hour, or of the moment, in contemporary religious thought and biblical scholarship is one of disdain for "historicism" and the analysis of sources. What is in favor today is the synthetic approach, the sloughing-over of differences within the tradition for the sake of a unitary pattern. Undoubtedly, the reaction against the narrow and painful atomization of the biblical text and the violence done to biblical thought by extreme historical criticism was overdue. But it has swung too far in the opposite direction and has thus obliterated features of the landscape that can serve as landmarks and without which we are likely to lose our way.

Actually, two major conceptions of ethics may be distinguished within the Judeo-Christian heritage. They may be called the *ethics of self-abnegation* and the *ethics of self-fulfilment*. It cannot be stressed too strongly that it is an error to equate the ethics of self-fulfilment with the Old Testament and label it the Jewish component and to identify the ethics of self-abnegation with the New Testament and describe it as the Christian element within the Judeo-Christian tradition. Actually, *both concepts of ethics exist in each tradition*, though by and large what is dominant in one tends to be secondary in the other.

I believe it a highly useful contribution to analyze the value and relevance of both elements of the Judeo-Christian tradition for contemporary politics. It should be stressed that in rethinking its relationship to biblical ethics, the Christian world is not being called upon to go outside its own authentic tradition. The Western world has only to avail itself fully of the resources already available to it in its religious background in order to establish a viable ethical system by which to mold its future.

To turn to the first of the two concepts, the *ethics of self-abnegation* is often, though inaccurately, described as "the ethics of absolute love." It is characterized by several basic features:

1. It makes extreme demands upon human nature, including the total surrender of self-interest, as in the famous injunction, "Love your enemies" (Matthew 5:44). It should, however, be added that this exalted imperative is contrasted with a norm of behavior never taught in the tradition:

> Ye have heard that it hath been said,
> Thou shalt love thy neighbour, and hate thine enemy
> [Matthew 5:43].

No scholar has ever been able to cite a passage in normative Jewish sources that preaches or even condones hating one's enemy. The classic teaching is of quite the opposite tenor, as will be noted below.

2. It expresses itself in terms of emotional attitudes, extolling virtues like love and charity, rather than the promulgation of specific norms of conduct through a system of law. In fact, it tends to decry such efforts as legalism, as an impersonal and heartless approach to the problems of human relationships. Its antinomian bias, as Paul indicates, is directed not merely against the ritual elements of the law but against ethical enactments as well: "The letter killeth, but the spirit giveth life" (II Corinthians 3:6).

3. The ethics of self-abnegation has also been the source of the doctrine of non-resistance to evil. It may, incidentally, be pointed out—a fact little known—that the New Testament teaching of "turning the other cheek" (Matthew 5:39) is derived from the Old Testament:

> It is good for a man that he bear the yoke in his youth. Let him put his mouth in the dust; if so be, there may be hope. Let him give his cheek to him that smiteth him [Lamentations 3:27, 29–30].

In the Hebrew Bible, however, this behavior is described as a tragic necessity of the human situation, not as an intrinsic ideal. To be sure, non-resistance to evil has never been widely practiced, except as the policy of homogeneous and small religious minorities. Yet it must be conceded that it has been regarded by many as representing the highest ethical good. Thus it became part of the system of values of a considerable section of the Western world.

The ethics of self-abnegation counsels submission to political tyranny:

> Let every soul be subject unto the higher powers.
> For there is no power but of God;
> The powers that be are ordained of God.
> Whosoever therefore resisteth the power,

Resisteth the ordinance of God;
And they that resist shall receive to themselves damnation.
For rulers are not a terror to good works, but to the evil.
Wilt thou then not be afraid of the power?
Do that which is good and thou shalt have praise of the
    same;
For he is the minister of God to thee for good.
But if thou do that which is evil, be afraid;
For he beareth not the sword in vain;
For he is the minister of God,
A revenger to execute wrath upon him that doeth evil.
Wherefore ye must needs be subject, not only for wrath,
But also for conscience sake.
For for this cause pay ye tribute also;
For they are God's ministers,
Attending continually upon this very thing.
Render therefore to all their dues;
Tribute to whom tribute is due; custom to whom custom;
Fear to whom fear; honour to whom honour.
Owe no man any thing, but to love one another;
For he that loveth another hath fulfilled the law [Romans
    13:1-8].

The classic utterance of Jesus, "Render unto Caesar the things that are Caesar's and unto God the things that are God's" (Matthew 22:21; Mark 12:17; Luke 20:25), has been subjected to a vast amount of interpretation. It is generally taken by Christian thinkers to be normative for the relationship of church and state or, alternatively, of religion and society. Whatever other levels of meaning may be found in it, this utterance seems to be in conformity with Paul's elaboration in Romans, cited above, and would seem to express a willingness to accept political tyranny. It is, of course, entirely possible, indeed probable, that this was a counsel for the moment, an act of expediency dictated by the necessity of proceeding with the greater concerns which Jesus had at the fateful Passover season in Jerusalem.

The ethics of self-abnegation also urges submission to social inequality, including slavery:

> Submit yourselves to every ordinance of man for the Lord's sake, whether it be to the king, as supreme; or unto governors, as unto them that are sent by him for the punishment of evil-doers, and for the praise of them that do well. . . . Honour all men. Love the brotherhood. Fear God. Honour the king. Servants, be subject to your masters with all fear; not only to the good and gentle, but also to the froward. For this is thankworthy, if a man for conscience toward God endure grief, suffering wrongfully. For what glory is it, if, when ye be buffeted for your faults, ye shall take it patiently? but if, when ye do well, and suffer for it, ye take it patiently, this is acceptable with God [I Peter 2:13–14, 17–18, 19–20].

Whether the counsel for wives falls under the same category may perhaps be left undecided:

> Likewise, ye wives, be in subjection to your own husbands [I Peter 3:1].

4. The ethics of self-abnegation is basically individualistic and focuses upon the individual human soul, while group relations are ignored either as artificial or as unimportant. The abiding value of this approach lies in its stress upon the dignity of each individual soul in the presence of God, irrespective of the accidents of time, space, and circumstance. Its weakness inheres in its failure to recognize that the national, social, economic, cultural, and racial characteristics of men are inherent elements of their personalities which cannot be ignored if we are to address ourselves to the whole man and the total human situation.

To disregard these relationships simply means to leave large areas, including those that are of critical concern today, untouched by the ethical impulse. The general failure of the church to transform the attitude of its communicants with regard to minority groups, as in the ubiquitous presence of anti-Semitism in Western society and in the tension-laden area of Negro-white relations in all parts of the United States, will be generally admitted. It stems in large measure from the age-old emphasis of the church upon the individual in the abstract and from its failure to grapple with his group characteristics in the concrete.

5. The ascetic impulse in Paul's teaching is strikingly manifest in his negative attitude toward family relations. Many factors entered into his outlook, such as his conception, derived from the Greeks, of the dichotomy of body and soul, and his theological doctrine of the Fall of Man, which he found in the Genesis narrative of the Garden of Eden. Yet it should be noted that the demand for the suppression of the sexual impulse whenever possible is thoroughly congruent with the ethics of self-abnegation:

> Now concerning the things whereof ye wrote unto me: It is good for a man not to touch a woman. Nevertheless, to avoid fornication, let every man have his own wife, and let every woman have her own husband.
>
> For I would that all men were even as I myself. But every man hath his proper gift of God, one after this manner, and another after that. I say therefore to the unmarried and widows, it is good for them if they abide even as I. But if they cannot contain, let them marry; for it is better to marry than to burn.
>
> He that is unmarried careth for the things that belong to the Lord, how he may please the Lord. But he that is married careth for the things that are of the world, how he may please his wife . . . [I Corinthians 7:1-2, 7-9, 32-33].

Paul's opposition to divorce undoubtedly derives from more than one element in his theological outlook. Yet it is clear that the ascetic strain in Paul's thought played a significant role in his prohibition of divorce, as is indicated by the fact that it is imbedded in the same major pronouncement on marriage (I Corinthians 7 : 10-14, 27). In this regard, he was repeating the attitude attributed in the Gospels to Jesus, who opposed divorce and extolled celibacy (Matthew 19:3-12). It is noteworthy that in the parallel passage in Mark (10:1-

12), the praise of celibacy, which constitutes the closing section of Jesus' utterance in Matthew, is lacking.

6. Economic issues are beyond the purview of man's highest concern. Particularly significant for understanding the ethics of self-abnegation is the counsel given to the young man who claims to have observed all the major injunctions of the Decalogue and asks how he may inherit the kingdom of heaven: "Sell all thou hast and give to the poor" (Matthew 19:21; Mark 10:21; Luke 18:22. See also Luke 12:33, "Fear not . . . sell your possessions and give alms"). From the standpoint of any long-range view, such a course would simply add him to the ranks of the poor, so that he would need to become a recipient of charity himself and no benefit would accrue to society. This consideration explains the contrasting talmudic dictum, "He who wishes to dispense his wealth to charity should not dispose of more than one-fifth of his possessions" (B. *Kethubbot* 50a).

The key to these various characteristics of the ethics of self-abnegation lies in the saying of Jesus cited in Luke 9:59 ff.:

> And he said unto another, Follow me.
> But he said, Lord, suffer me first to go and bury my
>     father.
> Jesus said unto him, Let the dead bury their dead;
> But go thou and preach the kingdom of God.
> And another also said, Lord, I will follow thee;
> But let me first go and bid them farewell,
> Which are at home at my house.
> And Jesus said unto him, No man, having put his hand
>     to the plow, and looking back, is fit for the kingdom of
>     God [Luke 9:59–62].

Early Christianity was permeated by a sense of imminent eschatology, the conviction that an apocalyptic disaster was about to take place. This cataclysm would usher in the kingdom of God and therefore, quite logically, all normal, long-range human concerns became nugatory. Only an interim ethic, concerned with bringing the individual human soul into a state of perfect virtue ("if ye would be perfect"), made sense in these pregnant hours before the great Judgment was about to become manifest.

This faith in an apocalyptic revolution derived from an unshakable conviction in the power and justice of God when confronted by the implacable power of Roman tyranny. Only a supernatural intervention from on high could avail to destroy the forces of evil. Every political crisis in the state was therefore seized upon by fervent believers as evidence that the dissolution of Roman tyranny was at hand. Nor was it a purely political upheaval or a national liberation that they envisaged, for they were acutely aware of social injustice and personal immorality. What they anticipated was a miraculous transformation of the world and the establishment of a new heaven and a new earth.

This faith was not limited to the young Christian community in Palestine. It was shared by elements among the Pharisees and by several of the other Jewish sects. It was the motive power of the Essenes, who, as we now know from the *Manual of Discipline* and the other scrolls found in the Dead Sea area, constituted not a single sect, but a constellation of semimonastic, mystical groups. By an intensive regimen of self-purification and abstinence from ordinary human concerns, the Dead Sea sectarians were actively preparing themselves for the ushering in of the kingdom of God. The scroll of *The War between the Children of Light and the Children of Darkness* is a military manual describing the tactics to be employed in the imminent war in which victory would fluctuate between the forces of good and the forces of evil until the ultimate triumph of God's cause.

Briefly, the ethics of self-abnegation arose out of an eschatological vision at a given moment in history within a group destined to exert tremendous influence upon humanity. In such a regimen, the ethics of self-abnegation can quite

properly demand of its devotees the ultimate, which is a total sacrifice of self for the sake of others. Given the brief but
decisive hour in history to which it is applicable, it offers a
consistent and even rational course of action for the individual. Yet the ethics of self-abnegation, be it noted, does not
deny that life is a supreme good, or, in Jesus' words, "that
men might have life and that they might have it more
abundantly" (John 10:10).

On the other hand, to apply the interim ethics of an eschatological vision to the permanent structure of an enduring society, or even to use it as a measuring rod of political
and social action, is self-defeating. It is analogous to the
practice of some isolationist groups in America today who
find their warrant in Washington's Farewell Address, in
which he urged the thirteen new struggling states on the
Atlantic seaboard, clinging precariously to their newborn
independence, to avoid entangling alliances with foreign nations.

A distinguished contemporary theologian was recently
asked, "What has contemporary politics to do with the Sermon on the Mount?" To this he replied, and with perfect
justice, "Nothing, and it shouldn't." The same categorical
negative could not, I believe, have been given to the question, "What has practical politics to do with the Ten Commandments?" For the Decalogue was proclaimed at the beginning of history; the Sermon on the Mount was believed
to usher in the end of history. The former inaugurated the
commencement of the significant moral activity of the
people of God; the latter announced the conclusion of its
group experience in the context of the natural order.

The question of the compatibility of ethics and politics
can therefore not be resolved by juxtaposing the activities
and achievements of the political order and passing judgment upon them in terms of the ethical teaching to be found
in the Gospels or in the Epistles of Paul or, for that matter,

in the writings of certain medieval Jewish moralists. Yet even in these sources of the Western religio-ethical tradition, be it noted, the doctrine of renunciation is nowhere expounded in as uncompromising a form as in the Bhagavad-Gita and the other Hindu scriptures.

There are those who are disposed to insist that the ethics of self-abnegation represents a higher level of aspiration than any alternative approach. The literature of apologetics both in Christianity and in Judaism is replete with such comparisons and contrasts, which are generally neither illuminating nor true. All that may be said is that the various ethical approaches are different, each with its own canons of meaning and its own field of relevance to the good life.

In sum, the ethics of self-abnegation cannot be fruitfully or legitimately applied to the problems confronting a viable and enduring social order. It is noteworthy that when the Christian church turned to the task of building an ethical system to serve the needs of a permanent society, or at least one with a long-term life expectancy, it did not adopt the ethics of self-sacrifice or self-abnegation as its basis. Instead, the Catholic church created its elaborate system of "natural law" which is based upon another approach. Its guiding principle, as we shall see, also has a basis in the biblical tradition and therefore is equally congenial to the Christian ethos. This concept may be called the ethics of responsibility or, as we prefer, the *ethics of self-fulfilment.*

At the very outset, two caveats are in order. One must guard against the widespread error of equating the ethics of self-fulfilment with "the ethics of justice," unless it is recognized that justice stands in a dialectic relationship with love, as will be noted below.

Moreover, one must avoid identifying self-fulfilment with self-interest or selfishness. What is crucial is the concept of man's selfhood, which is not exhausted by the boundaries of his physical organism, its needs and appetites. Basic to the ethics of self-fulfilment is the emphasis upon the total human personality, which has a thousand invisible strands linking it to other human beings in the family, the community, the nation, the religious group, and the human race. We may leave out of account here, since our present concern is with ethics, the relationship of the individual human soul to God, which for all religious believers both undergirds these relationships and constitutes their capstone.

The ethics of self-fulfilment regards it not only as natural and permissible but also as obligatory for every living organism to strive to maintain its life and function and to seek the maximum expression of its individuality, so long as it does not vitiate or destroy the equal and similar right of other living creatures of the same order of being. The biblical passage, "Ye shall take good heed of yourselves" (Deuteronomy 4:15), is interpreted in rabbinic tradition as a divine injunction to protect one's life and well-being.

Obviously, there is no "iron curtain" separating the two types of ethical attitude. As a contemporary religious thinker has noted, "There is no self-fulfillment without self-abnegation and, in turn, self-abnegation is not an end in itself but must be viewed as an organic part of an ultimate life-affirming concept of man and of his existence."

Nonetheless, the difference between the two types of ethical systems is real. We may cite in this connection the statement of Francis Bacon which he proposed in praise of the new dispensation: "Prosperity is the blessing of the Old Testament, adversity of the New." The record will demonstrate that the deprivations of the submerged groups in society were more than once justified by spokesmen of religion and of the status quo on the ground that deprivations were good for their souls.

In 1829, Charles Cotesworth Pinckney, nephew of the Founding Father of the same name, vigorously urged a campaign for the evangelization of the Negro in an address before the Agricultural Society of South Carolina. He based his plea on two grounds, of which the first was the criticism leveled by the "northern brethren" against the southern slaveholders who had failed to give their chattels "religious instruction." The second argument would have brought savage delight to Karl Marx's heart. Pinckney suggested that the imparting of Christianity to the Negro would tend to make a more docile, obedient, and tractable slave, adding moral suasion to statute and the lash as a control over the Negro. In this regard, he said: "Nothing is better calculated to render man satisfied with his destiny in this world than a conviction that its hardships and trials are as transitory as its honors and enjoyments; and that good conduct, founded on Christian principles, will ensure superior rewards in that which is future and eternal." Of more recent vintage is the bitterly sardonic chant of the now defunct I.W.W.: "You'll eat pie, in the sky, bye and bye." On the other hand, a Hasidic teacher was accustomed to say: "Why do you worry about my soul and your own body? Worry about my body and your own soul!"

The ethics of self-fulfilment is the source for a basic principle of rabbinic law which declares that all the commandments may be set aside in order to save a human life, except three: the prohibitions of murder, idolatry, and sexual immorality.

The two types of ethics which we have delineated are juxtaposed in an interesting passage in the Talmud. The hypothetical case is advanced of two men in a desert with a flask of water belonging to one of them and adequate to sustain one human life. One otherwise little-known sage, Ben Patura, suggests that they share the bottle of water so that neither may look upon his companion dying before his eyes. The famous sage Rabbi Akiba disagrees. He cites the biblical verse: "Thy brother shall live *with thee*" (Leviticus 25:36), from which he deduces that "thy life takes precedence over the life of thy neighbor" (B. *Baba Mezia 62a*). Akiba declares that in such a tragic circumstance the owner would be morally justified in drinking the water himself, thus preserving at least one human life instead of having both of them die out of a sentimental impulse. It goes without saying that he would be free to give his bottle to his companion, out of love for him or out of the conviction that there was a greater gain in preserving the life of his companion than his own. *What Akiba rejects is the idea that both lives ought to be lost, when one can be saved.*

On the other hand, the Talmud insists, if A threatens to kill B unless B kills C, B is forbidden to murder C in order to save his own life. He must be prepared to die at the hand of A, since in either event one innocent human life would be lost and B would thus keep himself free from the crime of murder: "Who is prepared to say that your blood is redder than that of your proposed victim?" (B. *Pesahim 25b*).

To evaluate fairly the impact on life of the ethics of self-fulfilment, it is worth recalling that Akiba himself died a martyr's death during the Hadrianic persecutions. What is perhaps even more to the point, rabbinic law declares that if a man sees his neighbor drowning in the river or being dragged off by a wild animal or being attacked by bandits, he is obligated to save him. In this connection, the biblical command (Leviticus 19:16), which I regard as one of the most far-reaching principles of biblical ethics, is adduced, "Thou shalt not stand idly by the blood of thy fellow man" (B. *Sanhedrin 73a*). In the eighteen centuries since Akiba, untold men and women, seeking to live by the ethics of self-fulfilment, have died for other human beings or for the advancement of an ideal.

In sum, the ethics of self-fulfilment regards the preservation of life, which is the gift of God, as the highest good, so long as it is not achieved by the destruction of other life

which is equally the creation of God and has an equal right
to survival.

We are now in a position to relate the practice of martyrdom to these two conceptions of ethics. At first blush, martyrdom would seem to be consistent only with the ethics of
self-abnegation, of which it would be the highest manifestation. But while the martyr may indeed be actuated by this
ideal, the justification for his act is to be sought in the
ethics of self-fulfilment. For it flows out of the individual's
conviction that his self-sacrifice will ultimately redound to
the enhancement of life for the commonalty. The martyr,
as its Greek etymology indicates, is a witness. By his heroic
action, he hopes to testify to the truth by which he lives, or
help advance the cause to which he is dedicated, or express
his love for a being outside of himself, be it on earth or in
heaven. In a word, he loses his life to save what is for him
the quintessence of life.

Hence, the lofty ideal of individual martyrdom cannot
be transposed into a justification for the voluntary self-
immolation of a nation. It is at the furthest possible remove
from genocide, the forcible liquidation of an entire society,
because such an act of mass destruction could have no
beneficial effect upon the remainder of humanity. Quite the
contrary, it would impoverish the survivors of the human
race and brutalize the perpetrators.

The ethics of self-fulfilment is marked by several other
outstanding characteristics:

1. It favors the formulation of concrete principles of conduct rather than of abstract emotional attitudes:

> If thou meet thine enemy's ox or his ass going astray,
> Thou shalt surely bring it back to him again.
> If thou see the ass of him that hateth thee lying under its
> burden,
> Thou shalt forbear to pass by him; thou shalt surely re-
> lease it with him [Exodus 23:4–5].

and

> Thou shalt not hate thy brother in thy heart;
> Thou shalt surely rebuke thy neighbor. . . .
> Thou shalt not take vengeance, nor bear any grudge
>     against the children of thy people,
> But thou shalt love thy neighbor as thyself;
> I am the Lord [Leviticus 19:17–18].

and

> If thine enemy be hungry, give him bread to eat,
> If he be thirsty, give him water to drink;
> For thou wilt heap coals of fire on his head;
> And the Lord will reward thee [Proverbs 25:21–22].

The Golden Rule, enunciated in the Holiness Code in Leviticus (19:18) and cited by Jesus as well as by Akiba as the highest ethical commandment, has overshadowed two other imperatives in the same chapter which are perhaps ethically more fruitful because they are concrete in their application.

The first is concerned with the protection of the weaker groups in society, who differ from the dominant majority and who in the ancient world were even more defenseless than are aliens in the contemporary world:

> And if a stranger sojourn with thee in your land,
> Ye shall not vex him.
> But the stranger that dwelleth with you
> Shall be unto you as one born among you,
> And thou shalt love him as thyself;
> For ye were strangers in the land of Egypt;
> I am the Lord your God [Leviticus 19:33–34].

As for the second, Scott Buchanan has stressed the truth that each individual is directly responsible for injustice anywhere in the universe, and traced this teaching to Tolstoi, Dostoevski, and Gandhi. He could have cited it from Leviticus 19:16, a passage which we have already quoted: "Thou shalt not stand idly by the blood of thy fellow man." Here the sin of permission is placed on a par with the sins of commission and omission that are set forth in the Holiness Code, the Decalogue, and elsewhere in biblical ethics.

2. The ethics of self-fulfilment also stresses the importance of the act rather than the motive. Conscious though it be that motives constitute the matrix of deeds, it is unwilling to regard intention as more important than execution. It believes that the right act will ultimately engender the right attitude, a kind of unsophisticated version of the James-Lange theory of the emotions. The talmudic principle is, "A man should perform a righteous deed, even if he does so only for ulterior motives, because he will thus learn to do the right for its own sake (*lishmah*)" (B. *Pesahim* 50*b*).

3. Because of its concern with a perdurable society, rather than with a brief interim period, this ethical approach is conscious of the obligations owing to all men everywhere and not merely to those with whom the individual comes into direct contact. Hence, the ethics of self-fulfilment tends to stress justice rather than love as the basic attitude in human relations.

Yet it is far from ignoring love as the highest motive in human conduct. On the contrary, love is an integral element in the ethics of self-fulfilment. But ethics should be viewed not as a point but as an arc, the lower end of which is justice, representing the minimum standards in man's relationship to his fellows, and the upper end of which is love, the ideal goal toward which men are to strive. Yet, like most analogies, this is not completely satisfactory, because the relationship of justice to love is not quantitative, a matter of less and more, but dialectic. Justice and love are perpetually in tension with one another, each virtue safeguarding the other by preventing it from degenerating into its counterfeit, a peril to which it is liable if held in isolation. For justice without love is vengefulness; love without justice, sentimentality. Justice without love denies the principle of moral freedom by robbing men of the capacity for regeneration; love without justice negates the principle of law in the world by pretending that men can escape the consequences of their actions. Thus both justice and love, standing in creative tension with each other, are essential to human ethics. The conviction of religion that they are rooted in the universe is dramatically expressed by the rabbinic tradition that God possesses two thrones, the seat of justice and the seat of mercy, which he occupies when he judges his creatures.

Contrary to a general impression, the Golden Rule does not express the teaching of self-abnegation but the doctrine of self-fulfilment. As some ethical teachers have acutely noted, it does not command, "Thou shalt love thy neighbor *more* than thyself," but presupposes the love of one's self as a prerequisite and as a standard for the love of one's neighbor. Erich Fromm emphasized the error involved in equating love of self with selfishness:

> The assumption . . . is that to love others is a virtue, to love oneself is a sin. Furthermore, love for others and love for oneself are mutually exclusive. Theoretically, we meet here with a fallacy concerning the nature of love. Love is not primarily "caused" by a specific object, but is a lingering quality in a person which is only actualized by a certain object. . . . From this it follows that my own self, in principle, is as much an object of my love as another person. The affirmation of my own life, happiness, growth, freedom, is rooted in the presence of the basic readiness and ability for such an affirmation. If an individual has this readiness, he has it also toward himself; if he can only "love" others, he cannot love at all. . . . Selfishness is rooted in this very lack of fondness for oneself. The person who is not fond of himself, who does not approve of himself, is in constant anxiety concerning his own self.

This insight of a modern psychologist was anticipated by the intuition of the fifteenth-century mystic Nicholas of Cusa: "I love my life supremely, because Thou art my life's sweetness. For if I ought to love myself in Thee who art my likeness, I am most especially constrained thereto, when I see that Thou lovest me as Thy creature and Thine image."

4. The ethics of self-fulfilment, being concerned with the total human personality in the context of a functioning society, is acutely conscious of the group relations of men. It is not satisfied to urge love of one's fellow men in the abstract but demands justice before the law and compassion beyond the law for the underprivileged and the unprotected, the widow, the orphan, the alien, and the landless sharecropper. It is concerned with the legitimacy of other national groups, a principle which it keeps in creative tension with its universalistic bias, which flows out of its preoccupation or, if you will, its obsession, with the principle of unity.

5. Moreover, only the ethics of self-fulfilment, which is life-affirming, affords a rational basis for regarding oppression as immoral. Political tyranny and economic exploitation, physical and intellectual slavery are all instruments for suppressing or minimizing the selfhood of their victims and for depriving them of their share of the blessings of this world. Obviously, these manifestations are evil only if we believe that the preservation of the self and the fullest expression of human personality, including the enjoyment of the world, are ultimate goods.

6. The biblical ethics of self-fulfilment seeks everywhere the principle of unity which derives from the passionate Hebraic commitment to the uncompromising unity of God.

Perhaps the most concrete embodiment of this principle lies in the doctrine of the unity and equality of mankind, which was first explicitly proclaimed by Amos, though it is implicit in Genesis. We have already cited in another connection the discussion reported in the Midrash as to the most fundamental passage in Scripture. While Rabbi Akiba cited the Golden Rule in Leviticus (19:18), Ben Azzai quoted Genesis 5:1: "This is the book of the generations of Adam, in the day that God created man, in the likeness of God made He him," a passage which emphasizes the unity of all men who share a common origin, as well as their equal dignity as fashioned in the divine image (*Sifra, Kedoshim* 4:15).

The Book of Job gives cosmic expression to another aspect of this quest for unity. It believes that there can be no dichotomy between the natural and the moral orders, because the moral order is rooted in the universe and the natural order is the matrix of morality. This conviction of the Hebraic tradition has consequences both for the world and for man. First, it implies that ours is a law-abiding universe, not merely with regard to the physical laws disclosed by science but also with regard to the law of righteousness which the prophets saw as operating in the world and validated by the realities of existence. Second, morality does not mean "doing what comes naturally." It means that obedience to the moral law does not require doing violence to human nature by suppressing human impulses or appetites; it requires, rather, that men discipline and channel their impulses and make them instruments for the service of God, sanctifying them through obedience to the divine imperative.

This leads directly to the Hebraic conception of the unity underlying all elements of human experience. John MacMurray has written: "The Hebrew form of thought rebels against the very idea of a distinction between the secular and the religious aspects of life." This acute observation does not go far enough. Authentic Hebrew thought does not merely rebel against the dichotomy; it does not recognize its existence.

Hence, the ethics of self-fulfilment finds no inherent line of demarcation between the material and the spiritual needs of man's nature and, consequently, between a temporal and a spiritual order in society, as we have seen.

Nor need we accept the contention that one system of ethics is applicable to the life of the individual, while another is valid for the behavior of nations and states. It is understandable that such a dichotomy will be proposed by those who are seeking some area of practical relevance for what we have called the ethics of self-abnegation. Those who recognize the historical situation in which this approach to ethics arose and are conscious of the radically different circumstances of modern life will find this distinction both unnecessary and untenable, unless they are committed to it on theological grounds. They will see no basis for establishing a wall of separation between "individual" ethics and "collective" ethics. On the contrary, they will not lose sight of the fact that ethics always involves a group, be it familial, communal, racial, religious, or national, and that, conversely, every group, be it large or small, intimate or public, is an aggregation of individuals.

Similarly, there is no need or justification for setting up a deep chasm between politics and ethics in theory nor can any be permanently countenanced in practice. The world is the handiwork of a righteous God who is both its creator and governor. What is right must somehow prove practical, and what is practical must conform to the right.

Only the ethics of self-fulfilment, as we have sought to delineate it here, can serve as the basis of a collective ethic, because it alone can serve as a permanent guide for the behavior of the individual. And only this system of ethics can be invoked for creating a moral approach to politics, because it alone can supply a rational basis for conduct vis-à-vis individuals outside the range of one's personal experience, where the minimum norm of justice and not the maximum standard of love can be meaningfully invoked. In the mutual relations of group aggregations, like nations or blocs of nations, only the ethics of self-fulfilment, of self-preservation within the framework of regard for the equal rights of others, can serve the needs of the political process.

This insistence upon the confluence of politics and ethics may seem naïve and highly unrealistic, particularly in an age when *Realpolitik* is practiced on a global scale and is reaching out to cosmic space as well. But such a conclusion is based upon a failure to grasp the full scope of biblical ethics, which is largely derived from the prophets but is not exhausted by them. The biblical canon includes not only Law and Prophecy, but a third current of great importance, Wisdom teaching.

A word is in order with regard to the structure and content of the Hebrew Bible, which is divided into three main sections. The first of these is Torah, generally rendered "The Law," but more accurately rendered "teaching," or "guidance." These Five Books of Moses, containing the most ancient traditions of the Hebrew nation and its basic ritual, civil, criminal, and medical law, constituted the special province of the priests, who were not only the officiants of the Temple and the custodians of its traditions, but also the judges and the medical officers of ancient Israel. Their authority as custodians and interpreters of the Torah derived from the revelation of the Lord to Moses and to the Israelites at Sinai, as in the recurrent formula in the Pentateuch, "And the Lord spoke unto Moses, saying. . . ."

The second element in the tripartite division of Scripture was that of the Prophets, who claimed to be the "spokesmen of God," the recipients of his direct immediate communication, declaring, "Thus saith the Lord." In his name they castigated the evils of their day and held fast to the conviction of a Golden Age which lay not in the distant past, as the ancients believed, but in the future, "the end of days," when the kingdom of God would inevitably be ushered in on earth.

The third current in the spiritual life of ancient Israel was that represented by Wisdom, or *Hokmah*. Biblical *Hokmah* embraced far more than the ultimate wisdom of life. It began on a much less exalted plane, incidentally paralleling that of Hellenic *Sophia*, from which post-Socratic Greek philosophy arose and against which it was a protest. Basically, Hebrew Wisdom, which was a branch of ancient oriental Wisdom, represented all the practical skills and technical arts of civilization. In biblical Hebrew, the term *Hokmah* therefore included the arts of the statesman and the military leader, the artist, the musician and the poet, the singer, the interpreter of dreams, the sailor, the craftsman, the architect, the soothsayer, and, in later Hebrew, the midwife.[1] It also included the inculcation of all the virtues which make for practical success in business affairs, in one's relationship to wife and children, and in the attitude toward one's peers and superiors.

The sages or teachers of Wisdom tended at times to envy the high pretensions of the priests to be the custodians of the Torah revealed to Moses and the even more passionate claims of the prophets to be the immediate recipients of divine communication. Some of the Wisdom writers therefore sought to hypostatize Wisdom into a supernal figure,[2] who guided the creation of the cosmos and was the divine *fons et origo* of their own activity.

Generally, however, Wisdom teachers made no claim to supernatural illumination. Their authority and power to convince derived from the accuracy of their observation of life and from the logical deductions they based upon it. Most of these Wisdom teachers were occupied in applying

[1] See Liddell-Scott, *Greek Lexicon*, s.v. *Sophia, Sophistes*, for the variety of meanings in Greek literature and thought; and Robert Gordis, *Koheleth—the Man and His World* (New York, 1951), chaps. i–iii, for a survey of the content of oriental and Hebrew Wisdom, esp. p. 17 and notes.

[2] Cf. Proverbs 8:21–32; *Ben Sira*, chap. 1:1–18; *Wisdom of Solomon* 7:15–8:1; 10:1 ff.

careful observation and logical deduction to the practical
concerns of life and in teaching the practical virtues that
made for success to the young men who were their pupils
in the academies.

Incidentally, the Wisdom teachers either emanated from
or ministered to the upper classes of society. They therefore
reflected the religious, social, and ethical attitudes and biases
of those who find life tolerable here and now. This background explains why the most conservative utterances in
the Hebrew Bible, though few in number, are largely concentrated in the Wisdom Psalms and the Books of Proverbs
and Job,[3] as, for example:

> My son, fear thou the Lord and the king,
> And meddle not with them that are given to change
>      [24:21].

Among these Wisdom teachers were a few highly sensitive spirits who were concerned with the fundamental issues
of life, the goal of existence, the nature of suffering, the
character of death, the meaning of truth, and God's will for
man. Being accustomed to logical demonstration, they were
congenitally incapable of taking on faith the confident as-
surance either of the prophet that he spoke the will of God
or of the priest who declared that he was interpreting it as
embodied in the Torah of Moses. They preferred to approach these perennial issues with the same instruments of
observation and reason that they utilized in their more mun-
dane activities.

Unfortunately for these Wisdom teachers, these tools did
not succeed in supplying the answers. Some of them ended
in skepticism and despair, notably Ecclesiastes, who found
no other good for man except the enjoyment of life, since
truth, like justice, was forever denied to man. The author

---

[3] For the evidence, both direct and indirect, and its implications, see
R. Gordis, "The Social Background of Wisdom Literature," in *Hebrew
Union College Annual*, XVIII (1944), 77–116.

of Job agonized over the problem of suffering and injustice in a world created by God. He finally achieved a level of faith which is probably the ultimate level of insight possible to man.[4]

To sum up, biblical Wisdom falls into two main categories, which have their parallels, though on a far less profound level, in all branches of oriental wisdom, Sumerian, Babylonian, Egyptian, and Ugaritic:

The lower Wisdom, practical, non-speculative, conventional, was concerned with bringing to its wards the maximum success in their careers in business, society, and the family. Its chief literary deposits are the books of Proverbs and the apocryphal *Ben Sira*.

The higher Wisdom, speculative, unconventional, dealt with the ultimates of human existence. Its major products are the books of Job and Ecclesiastes in the Bible and the *Wisdom of Solomon* in the apocrypha.

Before we revert to our basic theme, it should be pointed out that the three elements of biblical thought, the Law, Prophets, and Wisdom, were by no means hermetically sealed from one another, but on the contrary interacted upon and fructified each other.

Generally, the lower practical Wisdom has been looked upon with varying degrees of condescension as being unduly concerned with material ends of limited value. Hence, its unique contribution to the content of biblical ethics has been overlooked. This contribution lies in its emphasis upon realism as a virtue and upon intelligence as constituting obedience to the will of God. For the Wisdom writers, notably the authors of Proverbs, Ecclesiastes, and *Ben Sira*,

[4] The interested reader may be referred to my monograph, "The Bible as a Cultural Monument," in *The Jews*, ed. Louis Finkelstein (3d ed.; New York, 1960), pp. 783–822. In addition to *Koheleth—the Man and His World*, cited in n. 1, a detailed study of Job, its text, structure, and meaning, is in preparation.

the fool is a sinner and the violation of the moral law is folly as well as transgression. From this identification, two corollaries follow: a course of action, however practical it may seem at the outset, is doomed to failure if it violates the canons of morality; and, conversely, a course of action, however high-minded its aims, is likewise unacceptable if it be impractical, because it, too, cannot genuinely advance human well-being.

Closely related to the quality of intelligence is the virtue of honesty. We should do well to recall Samuel Johnson's demand, "Clear your mind of cant," echoed in Carlyle's warning, "Until cant cease, nothing else can begin." When this insight is kept in mind, it is clear that several of the besetting sources of failure in international affairs, which are frequently cited as proof that ethics is irrelevant to politics, are actually illustrations of the opposite. Thus *legalism*, which Lefever defined as "an approach to politics which invests in legal symbols, documents, and structures a power and authority which they do not in fact possess," does not fail because of an excess of ethics but because of a deficiency in ethics, the lack of intelligence. So, too, *moralism*, the constant invoking of high-sounding principles in carrying out national policy, often fails, but again not because of an excess, but through a deficiency, in morality. To put the matter succinctly, moralism is morality minus intelligence or honesty or both.

Thus, intelligence teaches what experience exemplifies— the human situation will often pose a plurality of opposing goals and ends which need to be adjusted to one another. But the existence of a contradiction between two ideals is not a denial of their inherent validity. Nor is it an inherent "evil" in the world or in human nature that men seek to establish a hierarchy of values among their goals in order to retain as much as possible of each good. To cite one instance from American history: When Abraham Lincoln declared,

"If I can save the Union by abolishing slavery, I shall abolish slavery, but I shall save the Union," there was no ethical flaw in his position merely because he did not seek to achieve all ideal ends simultaneously. The destruction of the federal union, which was already in existence, would have been an ethical retreat; on the other hand, the retention of slavery, which was likewise in existence, would have marked simply the failure or the postponement of an ethical advance. In establishing a scale of priorities in his goals, Lincoln demonstrated that intelligence is one of the most important of ethical virtues.

The same quality of intelligence offers the clue to a distinction all too often ignored in our day—that between expediency and prudence. *Expediency* means the temporary suspension of a moral principle because of the demands of necessity. *Prudence* is the reconciliation of two valid moral principles, which under given circumstances stand in conflict with each other. Both *expediency* and *prudence* have their place in ethically motivated international affairs. It is, however, a fatal flaw to fail to recognize the difference. What is merely *expedient* should be modified as soon as possible. A *prudential* policy may remain valid for a considerable period or even permanently.

One of the most useful insights of religion is the recognition that all human action takes place in a world in which both determinism and free will operate and, indeed, are in perpetual tension with one another. Since this interaction holds true of the individual in his day-to-day activities as well as in the decisions of nations, there is no reason to see in this trait any evidence that individual morality differs from the group activity which is politics. Politics, the art of the possible, can never, or almost never, represent total and uncompromising adherence to ethical standards but must reckon with the stubborn data of the environment, which are determined and beyond the control of the actors.

Yet it does not on that account differ from the application of the principles of morality to the life of the individual.

There were no more uncompromising advocates of the moral law than the Hebrew prophets, yet they would never have said *fiat justitia, ruat caelum*, "Let justice be done, though the heavens fall." On the contrary, they would have maintained, "Let justice be done, *or* the heavens will fall." But biblical ethics is not synonymous with prophetic ethics. It is prophetic morality chastened by the attributes of intelligence and realism, as exemplified by the Hebrew teachers of Wisdom.

William Lee Miller points out that a long catena of observers of American life "from De Tocqueville through Bryce, Siegfried, and others, down to such recent studies as those of Vernon L. Parrington, Margaret Mead, Gunnar Myrdal, and Harold Laski, have agreed on at least one point: Americans tend to 'see the world in moral terms.' " He cites Margaret Mead's comment on the national character of the United States:

> As America has a moral culture—that is, a culture which accepts right and wrong as important—any discussion of Americans must simply bristle with words like *good* and *bad*. Any discussion of Samoans would bristle with terms for awkward and graceful. . . . If I were writing about the way in which the Germans or the Japanese, the Burmese or the Javanese, would have to act if they were to win the war, I would not need to use many moral terms. For none of these peoples think of life in habitually moral terms as do Americans.

The implied criticism leveled against this mode of seeing the world is justified only if we define ethics as "voluntary, individual and moral"—that is to say, in terms of the ethics of self-abnegation, which is irrelevant. When the correct frame of reference of Hebraic ethics is employed, excluding what is irrelevant and including what is essential, there is no better category than that of right and wrong to be applied to the life of the individual or to that of society, whether in domestic affairs or in international politics.

The Suez episode and the American role in the debacle of the Anglo-French *démarche*, to which reference has already been made, are often exhibited as an instance of the incompatibility of ethics and politics. The practical consequences of American intervention were the ascendancy of Nasser and the penetration of Soviet influence into the Middle East, a major setback for Western policy, from which we may never recover. But the high-sounding formulas invoked at the time by Secretary Dulles were not an instance of morality but of moralism, for our approach was lacking in the cardinal virtues of intelligence and honesty. The seizure of the Suez Canal and the confiscation of Israeli or Israel-bound shipping in its area constituted grave, unilateral violations by Egypt of international commitments under the Convention of 1888, which took place prior to the intervention of France, Britain, and Israel. It may be argued plausibly that had the Western powers seized the Suez Canal and then referred its disposition to an international tribunal, not merely politics, but ethics, would have been better served.

In the festering and explosive conflict between Israel and the Arab states, there are tragic issues at stake, and the Arab case certainly possesses substantial elements of justice. It is true that the hundreds of thousands of pitiable Arab refugees who live on the borders of Israel left their homes because of the promise made by the five attacking Arab armies that the new state would quickly be liquidated and that they would gain rich spoils as the Israelis would be driven into the sea. They were therefore in overwhelming measure the architects of their own tragic fate. Yet their sorry lot in the present and the hopelessness of their future are a crying evil which requires a solution, in which the participation of the Israeli government is indispensable.

So, too, many of the spokesmen of the Arab states in the United Nations and elsewhere may well be sincere in voicing their fears that Israel may seek to expand its borders again in the future. In the present atmosphere Israel's repeated denials have not persuaded the Arabs. Israel, on its part, has its own very real grievances against its Arab neighbors. Aside from the fact that only negotiation offers any hope of solving the issues and of dissipating mutual suspicions and fears, these bitter foes do share a substantial common interest. The future of all depends upon the establishment of peace and the reduction of military expenditures, which are draining all these countries, and upon the economic and cultural development of the entire area.

The perilous status quo in the Middle East is a practical threat to the free world and a moral calamity as well. On both grounds, it should have been one of the objectives of Western policy all along to use all possible means not to compel a settlement of the issues, desirable as that might be, but at least to persuade the recalcitrant parties to sit down together and discuss their differences. Instead we have permitted the situation to deteriorate steadily. Though it would have been easier to achieve the goal of peace in the Middle East before Russian penetration into the area, it remains an indispensable objective of Western policy even now.

The conclusion may be set forth briefly. To permit politics and ethics to be divorced from one another is fatal to the future of society. It may simplify the task of the religious believer who wishes to wrap himself in the mantle of piety and mystic contemplation and turn his back on the world. It may ease the task of the cynical manipulator of the political process by freeing him from any moral check or discipline. But the basic insight of the biblical world view remains true—a society divorced from morality must perish. In the words of the Hebrew Bible, "Where there is no vision, the people perish, but he who observes the Law, happy is he" (Proverbs 29:18), and "Righteousness exalts a nation, but sin is the shame of peoples" (Proverbs 14:34). In the words of the New Testament, "The wages of sin is death" (Romans 6:23). Always politics and ethics may seem to diverge, but it is the task of the leaders and the citizenry of the free society to strive perpetually to bring them into harmony. We may find both encouragement and guidance in the words of the Talmud (*Aboth* 2:21), "It is not for you to complete the task, but neither have you the right to desist from it."

# 11

# NATIONALISM AND THE
# WORLD COMMUNITY

The mid-twentieth century may well go down in history as marking the high-water mark of nationalism as a factor in the world. The nineteenth century had seen the rise of national loyalties in Europe, notably among the Greeks, the Italians, and the Germans. In the first decades of the twentieth century, national aspirations swept across the remainder of Europe and led to the creation of a dozen independent states along the Baltic Sea and in the Balkan Peninsula. The middle years of the present century have seen the triumph of nationalism in the Middle East through the creation of Israel and of the Arab states, as well as in the Far East, where India, Pakistan, Indonesia, and China have appeared as independent states in the modern world.

The situation in Asia is far from stable, but the spotlight has now shifted to Africa, where nationalism has erupted in forms that impress the Western powers as violent, irrational, and deeply disturbing. The two mighty aggregations of East and West, arrayed against each other, find in these new and explosive national aspirations of Asia and Africa potential focal points of defense and of attack in their war against each other. All too often the immediate problems that these new states pose to the status quo obscure the long-range significance of their struggle. The far-flung battle of the darker-skinned peoples of the earth for freedom from colonial domination and their ever louder demand for the right to be masters of their own destiny and resources are much more than a succession of unpleasant incidents fomented by subversive forces and paid for by Russian gold. These events must be recognized as part of the trajectory of human liberation, the inevitable process of history, which can be hindered but never permanently halted.

It was the biblical prophets and historians who first enunciated a philosophy of history or, more accurately, developed the insight that history has a meaning. Hegel and Marx, Pareto and Spengler, Toynbee and Voegelin have all presented their own philosophies of history, which are generally poles apart from the prophetic world view. Yet they, like every scholar and philosopher who finds in history, not a meaningless succession of events, but a pattern and direction, owe an incalculable debt to the Hebrew Scriptures. With the biblical authors of Joshua, Judges, Samuel, and Kings, the penning of chronicles became transformed into the writing of history.

Judaism, however, does more than honor the prophets as pioneers in the field of the philosophy of history. It regards the prophetic conception of history as fundamentally valid today. Basic to the prophetic faith in a God of righteousness is the principle of consequence, of moral causation in the world. The prophet Hosea emphasized that this law was rooted in the universe, by expressing it in a metaphor drawn from nature:

> For they sow the wind, and they shall reap the whirl-
>   wind. . . .
> Sow to yourselves in righteousness, reap in mercy,
> Break up the fallow ground,
> For it is time to seek the Lord,
> Till He come and teach you righteousness. . . .
> Ye have plowed wickedness, ye have reaped iniquity,
> Ye have eaten the fruit of lies [Hosea 8:7; 10:12–13].

Hosea's older contemporary, Amos, had applied the same principle of justice as the law of history to contemporary world affairs and had found in it the key to the destiny of all nations and not only of Israel (Amos, chaps. 1–2).

The prophets were, however, too clear-sighted to overlook the vast chasm that loomed between the ideals of justice and peace, which alone could be regarded as the will of a righteous God, and the realities of a world in which poverty, oppression, and war were rampant.

This tragic contradiction they resolved by the concept of God at work in history. They saw human history not as static but as dynamic, as a drama and not a tableau. It is filled with movement and struggle and is destined to flower ultimately in the creation of the kingdom of God, the establishment of freedom and plenty, justice and peace among men. This vision of the kingdom of God which the prophets had before them supplied them with a standard of judgment by which they could, on the one hand, criticize the weaknesses and the sins of their own society and, on the other, enunciate the ideals of the emergent society of the future.

But the present could not be wholly submerged in the vision of the future. How could the spectacle of evil triumphant be reconciled with faith in a just and almighty God? This contradiction the prophet Isaiah met by another profound insight, his concept of "the rod of God's anger." Isaiah saw the proud world conqueror, Assyria, as pitiful in its conceit, for, unbeknown to itself, it was merely an instrument in God's hand for rooting out the evil and ushering in the good. At any given moment in history, the forces of evil, blind and arrogant, may regard themselves as masters of their own destiny. In reality, they serve as unwilling and unwitting instruments for the achievement of God's purposes in his universe. Immorality, whether collective or individual, brings on its inevitable doom. "Should the axe boast itself against him that hews with it? Should the saw magnify itself against him that moves it? It is as if a rod should move him who lifts it up, or as if a staff should raise him that is not wood" (Isaiah 10:15).

It should be clear today that this religio-ethical interpretation of history does not, per se, preclude the various scientific or philosophic approaches to history. Thus, different historians have sought to explain an event like the fall of Rome as the result of climatic, socioeconomic, political, or psychological factors, individually or in combination. This historic catastrophe is attributed to the expropriation of the peasantry, the rise of a class of absentee landlords, the creation of a *Lumpenproletariat* in Rome, and the loss of a sense of a stake in the status quo by the Roman masses. Hence, the Teutonic barbarians at the gates found no effective resistance from the citizens of the Imperial City.

The prophetic view of history would not necessarily deny the validity of these theories—it would insist that these factors needed to be transposed into a moral key as well. The prophets would maintain that the Roman Empire crumbled because, like every civilization before or since, it did not rest upon the only firm foundation in the world, the principles of justice and freedom in the moral universe, which can no more be violated with impunity than the laws of gravitation in the physical world. The prophet Isaiah, confronted by similar socioeconomic phenomena in ancient Israel, castigated the situation as immoral and prophesied the doom of Hebrew society:

> Woe unto them that join house to house, that lay field to field,
> Till there be no room, and ye be made to dwell alone in the midst of the land!
> In mine ears said the Lord of hosts:
> Of a truth many houses shall be desolate, even great and fair, without inhabitant [Isaiah 5:8–9].

To be sure, the consequences of violating the natural laws are much more quickly evident than those that follow the breaking of the moral law. The biblical sage Koheleth called attention to this truth in the life of the individual:

> Because judgment upon an evil is not executed speedily, men's hearts are encouraged to do wrong, for a sinner commits a hundred crimes and God is patient with him [Ecclesiastes 8:11].

This truth is even more applicable in the life of civilizations, which generally take a long time dying. But this time-lag is surely of secondary significance *from the standpoint of God, for whom a thousand years are but a day.* Moreover, *even from the human vantage point,* the process of decay and death for civilization has been tremendously accelerated. Indeed, in this day of atomic bombs and radioactive fall-out, the annihilation of the race may be instantaneous. This suggests that the failure of modern men to recognize the moral governance of the world is perhaps the very heart of the crisis confronting humanity. It may well be that the command of the hour is the application of this prophetic insight concerning the law of righteousness to the historic drama of our time.

Following in the footsteps of the prophets, the Judeo-Christian tradition would insist that our civilization is doomed to destruction unless it bases itself in ever increasing measure upon the principles of justice and freedom for all men and nations. It would find the ethical superiority of democracy over totalitarianism to inhere precisely in this: that democracy offers the best hope for correcting the evils of our society and achieving social justice and individual freedom through the processes of peace and law.

We have noted at the very beginning of this book that an organic bond links the religio-ethical tradition of Judaism to the specific cultural-national group known as the Jewish people. In ancient times, the ethnic character of religion was universal; among the Babylonians, the Egyptians, the Greeks, and the Romans, culture and nationality were united into an organic totality. Today only Judaism among the major world religions retains this organic relationship.

This ethnic character of Judaism has impelled the tradition from its inception to recognize *the legitimacy of national groups* and later to find room for national loyalty in its world view. In one of the most justly famous passages in the Bible, which occurs in Micah (4:1–5) and, with some verbal changes, in the Book of Isaiah (2:1–5), the prophets set forth their vision of the End-Time, the ideal goal toward which history is moving:

> In the end of days it shall come to pass,
> That the mountain of the Lord's house shall be established
>    on the top of the mountains
> And it shall be exalted above the hills.
> People shall flow unto it,
> And many nations shall come and say,
> "Come, let us go up the mountain of the Lord,
> To the house of the God of Jacob;
> So that He will teach us of His ways,
> And we will walk in His paths;
> For from Zion shall go forth the Law,
> And the word of the Lord from Jerusalem."
> And He shall judge among many peoples,
> And rebuke strong nations afar off;
> They shall beat their swords into plowshares
> And their spears into pruning hooks;
> Nation shall not lift up sword against nation,
> Neither shall they learn war any more.
> They shall sit every man under his vine and under his
>    fig-tree;
> And none shall make them afraid;
> For the mouth of the Lord of hosts hath spoken it.
> For as all the peoples walk every one in the name of his
>    god,
> We will walk in the name of the Lord our God forever.

There are several highly significant aspects of this great vision which are not our present interest. We are concerned here with the prophet's concept of nationalism. Within these five short verses, it should be noted, the word for "people" and "nation" occurs no less than seven times—striking testimony of his belief that national groups will remain permanent features of human society even in its ideal phase.

The bearing of Micah's and Isaiah's thought on our age is obvious. For today, nationalism has reached the acme of its power and the nadir of its degradation. It is the basic ill of our age, aside from the economic strife, to which, indeed, it has largely contributed. No greater peril threatens the survival of man than nationalism, men's total absorption in the view that all law emanates from one's own ethnic or political group, that there is no morality beyond it, and that its interests at all costs are the highest good.

It is sufficient to recall the intimate bond between nationalism and Nazi and Fascist dictatorship. But communism, too, which began with the slogan of internationalism and the world proletariat, has adopted with mounting fervor the gospel of the "Communist fatherland," whose "rights" to expansion and to buffer states are indistinguishable from the "legitimate interests" of Czarist Russia forty or fifty years ago, except that they are pursued with greater efficiency and ruthlessness. World War II was the result of unbridled national ambition, which wiped out every vestige of fair play and pity in the hearts of otherwise normal men. Should World War III eventuate, it would be another colossal and horrible burnt offering on the altar of exclusive national loyalty.

What is the remedy? Sickened by the prospect of worldwide catastrophe, some have espoused the ideal of cosmopolitanism, the merging and disappearance of all national groupings. This ideal is, of course, not to be identified with the various concrete proposals for world federation which envisage only the limitation of national sovereignties. Under cosmopolitanism, men would cease to be Frenchmen, Germans, or Americans. One nationality, one language, one culture, and, if religion is to survive at all, one faith—this would constitute the common heritage of mankind.

At first blush, such an ideal has an undeniable grandeur and nobility as the concrete embodiment of the ideal of the unity of mankind. Upon sober examination, however, it becomes clear that if current versions of nationalism are a nightmare, this type of internationalism would prove an impractical dream.

The history of mankind, both recent and remote, discloses no signs that nations are disappearing or are seeking to sink their differences in a common world patriotism. On the contrary, the past half-century has seen the creation of scores of new nations that are struggling desperately for their place in the sun, in Europe, Asia, and Africa. The Soviet absorption of the Baltic and Balkan states into the Communist orbit cannot be regarded as a permanent elimination of their local nationalisms but rather as an effort to exploit their national loyalties for Russian aims. In sum, signs everywhere are pointing not to a diminution of nationalist loyalty but to its intensification, or at least to its retention, for decades to come.

Nationalism will endure, not merely because of propaganda or the innate corruption of man, but because it draws upon deep roots in the soul of man. It is normal that a man should be attached to the soil where he was born and where he spent the pleasant years of his childhood; that he should feel drawn to his own people, with whom he is most familiar. The song one's mother sang, the language she spoke, the festivals of one's childhood—these have an appeal beyond words and beyond reason, an appeal which no reasonable man will lightly dismiss.

The goal of a uniform mass of human beings seems, therefore, to fly in the face of reality. But aside from being impractical, this conception of internationalism would prove disastrous for the human spirit. National loyalty is the matrix in which all culture is formed. Every cultural achievement of which we have record is particularistic in origin, however universal its goal. Culture is always rooted in a given milieu, drawing its substance from a specific tradition, expressing itself in a given language, and deriving its power from a sense of kinship with a definite people. It is true that Hebrew prophecy, Greek art, Italian opera, German poetry, and English drama "belong to the world." But in every instance, they reflect their ethnic sources and their environmental influences, without which they are inconceivable. If, contrary to all indications, national loyalty were to dissolve, it would spell cultural anemia for the world. To borrow a distinction employed by some thinkers, *civilization*, the science and technology of the world, which is impersonal, may be conceivable without nationalism, but not *culture*, which embraces the literature, art, music, and philosophy of the age.

Undoubtedly, the growing scientific progress of the age, particularly noteworthy in the fields of communication and transportation, is extending the common elements of our technological civilization. Yet even with regard to the more technical aspects of culture the process is not unilinear in the direction of greater standardization. The opposite process of growing differentiation, though less obvious, is also taking place and may well prove the more decisive. Thus two distinguished authorities on modern architecture write:

> In so far as architecture is based on reason instead of sentiment, it is not concerned with frontiers. But countries also have their own different temperaments and ideals, and different climates, habits, and raw materials. They also have a past, and the national culture of which their modern architecture is part is not separable from its roots. So, as modern achitecture matures, it tends to dif-

ferentiate itself according to national characteristics—not on the basis of the racial exclusiveness of Nazism, and not so clearly and distinctly as would have been the case before steam, the airplane, the telephone and the radio broke down once and for all many national barriers; but Americanness is a definable quality found in things American, as Frenchness is found in things French [Mock and Richards, *Introduction to Modern Architecture*, p. 96].

This process of "re-nationalization," as the authors call it, is not limited to any one art or technique but is essential to most aspects of a healthy, rooted culture. The uniform pattern of a mechanical civilization which is spreading over the world today is the result of the first flush of technological invention, to which men are still enslaved. Sooner or later, however, when men master the machine, they will rebel against the deadening conformity of a mass-production civilization and will turn once more to the development of a living and creative culture, infinite in its variety, color, and form, rooted in the God-given uniqueness of each individual and group.

We have thus been led to the conclusion that nationalism is natural to society and indeed essential to the growth of culture. On the other hand, it is obvious that it constitutes a major threat to human survival. A tragic dilemma seems to face the human race—either stagnation or death.

Merely to castigate nationalism as the root of all evil may offer some psychological relief but as a practical program it is quixotic and doomed to failure. Another solution, at once more practical and more ideal, is required, and it may be discovered in the prophets of Israel. In the literal sense of the term, the Hebrew prophets were the first true internationalists, believers in the creation of proper relations among nations. Even Plato, perhaps the noblest of the Greeks, looked forward to a perpetual standing army to protect the *polis* of the ideal Republic against the threat of the "barbarians," a term which includes the rest of the human race. The Hebrew prophets, centuries before Plato, saw peace among all nations not merely as possible but as inevitable.

If the Vision of Isaiah and Micah quoted above did no more than enunciate the ideal of peace and express faith in the destined attainment of this goal, it would possess permanent value for the moral education of the race. However, the significance of the Vision is not exhausted by these aspects. The prophet goes on to point out that the road to peace lies in the creation of a binding international law, centered in a recognized authority. He does not depend on good will or on love to guard the peace, nor does he expect that all differences of outlook and self-interest among nations will miraculously disappear in the End-Time. Before peace can be a reality, there must be a law which shall go forth from Zion, which will be accepted as binding among the nations and will be enforced among the peoples.

The prophet would have denied the doctrine of national sovereignty as defined by Stephen Decatur: "My country, may she always be in the right, but my country, right or wrong." He would have subscribed to the reformulation of another American patriot, Carl Schurz, "My country, may she always be in the right, when right, to be kept right, when wrong, to be set right."

If government means an agency capable of imposing its will upon its members, the prophet emphatically believed in world government, the will of God embodied in his law. This idea he expresses by speaking of "judging between nations." Judgment means the enforcement of justice. For the prophet, this law emanated from the God of Jacob, who is the one God of humanity. But irrespective of its source, the character of this international covenant is not legalistic but moral, being rooted in justice and truth and therefore capable of supporting the structure of peace. A talmudic utterance makes this idea explicit: "Upon three things the world rests—upon justice, upon truth, and upon peace. And the three are one, for when justice is done, truth prevails and peace is established" (*Jerusalem Talmud, Taanith* 4:2; *Megillah* 3:5).

The prophetic author of the Vision of the End-Time looked forward, not to the elimination but to the "moralization" of national loyalties. He envisaged the extension to the group of the ethical standards incumbent upon the individual. Just as no man can regard his own desires and interests as overriding all other principles in his relations with his fellows, so nations, whose existence is equally legitimate, cannot make national honor or self-interest or military superiority the ultimate arbiter of their destiny. Unlimited sovereignty is as immoral for nations as for individuals, and far more dangerous. Only freedom under the moral law is justifiable—that is basic to the biblical concept of nationalism.

Deprived of its absolutist character, nationalism must take on the form of loyalty to a common cultural heritage, being embodied in the voluntary association of men and women for the preservation and cultivation of a cherished body of ideals, practices, and values. This ideal of nationalism as exclusively a cultural-ethnic loyalty has scarcely penetrated the thinking of most men, but it offers the only road to survival for mankind.

It is perhaps not altogether irrelevant to note that the only group which embodies this prophetic conception of nationalism, however imperfectly, is the Jewish people, which is united the world over by no central political allegiance, military power, or geographical contiguity. This unique community, possessing an unbroken history of approximately thirty-five centuries, feels itself bound by a sense of kinship from the past, claiming Abraham, Isaac, and Jacob as its ancestors, while welcoming those who voluntarily seek to join its ranks from without. Its members share a common religio-cultural tradition in the present, which they feel free to interpret in accordance with their own attitudes and in-

sights. Finally, they look forward to a common destiny in
the future, however much their status may differ under
varying political, social, and economic conditions across the
globe.

Judaic ethics, in common with all vital religion which
builds upon the insights of the prophets, obviously does not
restrict this concept of national survival to the Jewish group.
The future has room for all other national groups on the
same terms, a *national loyalty cultural in essence and moral
in expression.* In Santayana's words, "A man's feet must be
firmly planted in his own country, but his eyes must survey
the world." The prophets went further: their hearts embraced the world.

In this approach to nationalism, love of one's own people
and loyalty to humanity represent two concentric circles.
The bugbear of "dual allegiance," in which little minds see
a threat to patriotism, would never have troubled them, because for them all loyalties, national as well as international,
should be peaceful in function and subject to the moral law.
Modern thinkers, who deplore nationalism or at best seek to
ignore it or dismiss it as irrelevant to their conception of the
good life of society, would do well to be instructed by the
prophets of Israel. All of them, from Amos and Hosea to
Deutero-Isaiah and Malachi, exemplify both nationalism
and internationalism. For their lives and careers are
grounded on the conviction that nationalism, like all manifestations of the human spirit, is not intrinsically evil, but
neutral, and, what is more, a potential source of spiritual enrichment in the life of man.

The prophet whose words were cited above would have
agreed completely with Amos, who may indeed have been
his contemporary, in demanding the same high standard of
righteousness from Judah as from Moab, from Israel as from
Aram. The conception of an ethical nationalism found its
noblest and most concrete expression in Isaiah. Although he

saw his people being ground to death in the struggle between Egypt and Assyria for world domination, he foresaw the day when Israel would be "the third with Egypt and with Assyria, a blessing in the midst of the earth; for the Lord of hosts has blessed him, saying; 'Blessed be Egypt My people, and Assyria the work of My hands, and Israel My inheritance' " (Isaiah 19:24–25).

We may seem to have wandered far from the realities of the contemporary world with its fierce national hostilities and rivalries in this delineation of the prophet's Utopia, yet that is far from being the case. Man's vision of the future has a basic role to play in fashioning the shape of his present.

# 12

# RELIGION
# AND INTERNATIONAL
# RELATIONS

In exploring the implications of the prophetic concept of the End-Time, we have apparently wandered far away from the morass of perils in which mankind is now sunk. We seem to have sought refuge in Utopia, a never-never land of which men may dream but which they can never hope to attain. Yet when properly utilized, an ideal vision is of incalculable value. For it serves as a standard for evaluating the imperfect reality in which men live, it offers men direction in their day-to-day struggle, and it supplies them with guidance in evaluating the various courses of action open to them.

Thus the conception of nationalism enunciated by the prophets of Israel in their vision of the Messianic Age, their clear recognition of the legitimacy of nationalism and of its moral limits, represents a tremendous debt which we owe to these ancient teachers. But it does not exhaust our debt to them. Their insights also suggest several significant principles and procedures with regard to the conduct of international relations in our imperfect world today.

First is the central importance of the United Nations, which is, to be sure, neither a mere debating society on the one hand nor an international parliament on the other. The

United Nations is an instrument for expressing the opinions and interests of the various governments of the world. When these are democratic in character, they reflect in greater or lesser degree the opinions of the mass of the people. When they are totalitarian or autocratic, they are reflections of the constellations of power of the local ruling groups. The United Nations is a voluntary association of nations that seek to defend their interests without having recourse to the use of force.

The decisions of the United Nations, arrived at by the majority, are therefore of great importance. Unless other factors enter into the picture, the opinion of the majority is likely to be more balanced than that of a minority. A numerical majority, however, is not *ipso facto* universally sacrosanct, as we are discovering to our cost. Soviet Russia and its satellites command many individual votes, but reflect very few individual positions.

Nonetheless, for all its limitations, the United Nations represents unmistakable progress for mankind in the critical race between world order and world catastrophe. The International Court of Justice was established in 1899 at The Hague to arbitrate only such disputes as were put before it by both parties. As a result, its jurisdiction encompassed only relatively minor issues, where neither party was willing or able to use force in order to enforce its will. The League of Nations, created in 1920 but mortally wounded from its inception by the abstention from membership of the United States, was theoretically empowered under its covenant to invoke economic sanctions against aggressors. This crucial step it failed to take for many reasons, in connection with Japan's incursion into Manchuria and Mussolini's adventure into Abyssinia. While the League of Nations continued to make creditable contributions to human welfare in many fields, this failure proved fatal to its principal objective—the attainment of international peace.

A third and more ambitious step was taken in the creation of the United Nations after the Second World War. Its principal drawback, the veto power in the Security Council, is much more than a "constitutional weakness" that can be eliminated by a legal amendment of the Charter. It is an expression of the deep-seated suspicion dividing the adversaries on both sides of the Iron Curtain. It will endure as long as mutual understanding and respect are lacking and as long as the quest for a modus vivendi between East and West continues to be regarded as a kind of "twilight treason" by self-styled "patriots."

Nonetheless, for all its limitations, the United Nations represents substantial progress beyond the League of Nations. The significance of the United Nations lies not only in its considerably expanded roster of membership, in its tremendous value as a forum for world opinion, and in its significant auxiliary services the world over, but pre-eminently in its right to employ military sanctions in order to maintain peace. In the face of great obstacles the United Nations has been able to make great contributions to world order. It has helped to minimize and to contain war in the Middle East and between India and Pakistan. It has succeeded in validating the principle of the sanctity of treaties by the United Nations military action for the preservation of Korean independence. It has struggled with the thorny problem of the Congo and its future.

From the standpoint of ethics, the relationship of an individual state to the collective will of the United Nations is not essentially different from the proper attitude of a citizen to his country. The individual is in duty bound to obey the laws of the state even if he finds himself out of sympathy with them. In the latter event, he has a right and a duty to agitate peacefully for a change in the law. If he finds that the issue is of momentous importance and therefore violates the deepest convictions of his conscience, he has not only, in

Lincoln's words, "the constitutional right to amend the law but the revolutionary right to oppose it even by force of arms." But he must be conscious of the risks in such a step both for society and for himself.

Similarly, in the area of international affairs, each member of the United Nations has a constitutional duty to obey the decisions of the United Nations, but it is not on that account enjoined from exercising its own conscience in dealing with the problems before it. On the contrary, each member has the moral right and duty to think through any given problem and seek to utilize its influence to have its position prevail in the council of nations. A state would have a moral right to contravene the decision of the United Nations only under the gravest provocation, when its right to existence would be in jeopardy, or a fundamental moral principle were being violated.

International relations are, of course, not limited to the halls of the United Nations. On the contrary, most activity in this area is conducted on a bilateral basis. Kenneth W. Thompson wisely called attention to the significance of the expanded diplomatic functions performed by the secretary-general of the United Nations in many tension areas. This relatively new development at present may well prove as important as the theoretical right of the United Nations to apply military sanctions in times of international stress.

Here Judaic ethics would emphasize two truths which have direct bearing on our subject. *The first is the recognition that the world is not the creation of man but the handiwork of God and, by that token, his inalienable possession.* In the psalmist's words, "The earth is the Lord's and the fulness thereof; the world, and they that dwell therein" (Psalm 24:1). Imbedded in the social legislation of the Bible with regard to the jubilee year is a clear-cut expression of this doctrine: "The land shall not be sold in perpetuity; for the land is Mine; for ye are strangers and settlers with Me"

(Leviticus 25:23). Man's temporary possession does not constitute absolute ownership.

Nationalism is legitimate as part of God's plan for mankind, and yet it is subject to God's will as revealed in the moral law. This conception flows clearly from the great "Song of Moses":

> Remember the days of old, consider the years of many generations;
> Ask thy father, and he will declare unto thee, thine elders, and they will tell thee.
> When the Most High gave to the nations their inheritance, when He separated the children of men,
> He set the borders of the peoples according to the number of the children of Israel [Deuteronomy 32:7–8].

There exists a unique relationship between God and the people of Israel who are the custodians of his Torah, but all nations are encompassed in his vision and his concern.

*The second insight is the principle of the interdependence of all mankind and of its destiny.* To recognize this truth in ancient times, when means of transportation and communication were primitive and often non-existent, required the stature of an Amos. Only a prophet could possess the insight to see all the nations standing under the moral judgment of God, who makes no distinction in his ethical demands between the kingdoms of Israel and Judah or between the Hebrew nation and the world community. As we have noted, the prophets taught that the Messianic Age would be worldwide in scope.

Later rabbinic teachers in the *Mishnah* deduce an entire ethical code from the familiar biblical narrative of the creation of Adam. The complete passage in the *Mishnah*, at once naïve and profound, reads as follows:

> Man was created through Adam, a single human being, in order to teach that whoever destroys a single human life is regarded as though he destroyed an entire world,

and he who saves a single human life as though he saved an entire world.

The human race began with a single individual for the sake of peace among all men, so that no man might say, "My ancestor is greater than yours," and to make it impossible for heretics to say, "There are many heavenly Powers."

Moreover, the creation of humanity through one ancestor proclaims the greatness of the Holy One, blessed be He. For man strikes off many coins with a single mold and they are all identical. But the King of Kings, the Holy One, blessed be He, stamps each man in the mold of Adam, and yet no one is identical with his fellow.

Finally, the creation of Adam teaches that each human being is obligated to declare, "For my sake was the world created" [*Mishnah Sanhedrin*, chap. 4].

Thus Judaic ethics finds warrant in the creation of man for the dignity of all human beings, which is the source of their freedom and their right to individuality, and for the equality of all men, which is the foundation of justice, their right to share in the blessings of the world.

From these two principles there derives another significant limitation on national sovereignty as commonly understood—*the absence of the right of any nation to the absolute ownership of the resources of land, sea, or air within its borders.* That a nation is not the master but the steward of its natural wealth is a principle rarely conceded even formally. Yet it is the ethical foundation for all forms of foreign aid and international co-operation. As a rule, these measures are explained in terms of national self-interest, but it is noteworthy that such arguments do not persuade the isolationist and the chauvinist. To be sure, when self-interest is sufficiently enlightened, it becomes a form of altruism, but only because the *ego* has been broadened to include the *alter*. Neither individuals nor nations are islands "entire unto themselves," and they all enjoy the bounty of a world not of their creation. For the more fortunately situated to share their blessings with their less happily situated fellow men is not an act of condescension or even of benevolence. There is a profound truth imbedded in the fact that, in Hebrew, "charity" is expressed by the great term *zedakah*, which simply means "righteousness," the fulfilment of a moral duty, not an expression of sentimentality.

That this approach will be universally accepted and acted upon in the foreseeable future is utopian, but it is in that direction that the ethical education of the world community of nations must proceed.

The interdependence of mankind under the overarching sovereignty of God is therefore the basis for such undertakings as the Marshall Plan, the Point Four Program, and, most recently, the Alliance for Progress. Such activities are therefore not only ethical imperatives of the highest order but basic to a truly practical policy for the United States and other highly developed nations.

International relations are not always concerned with the positive task of establishing avenues of co-operation. At times their goal is more modest but equally important—the avoidance of conflict. Judaic ethics therefore stresses the *importance of negotiation* and the *sanctity of agreements* among nations. The Book of Joshua declares that even though he was tricked into entering upon an agreement with the Gibeonites and so was prevented from conquering them, Joshua adhered scrupulously to the terms of the covenant. Under normal circumstances, when no such deception has taken place, the sanctity of the plighted word is all the greater. The Bible records countless attempts by the Israelites to achieve a peaceful agreement with their neighbors, Edom and Moab. Even in ancient times, when war was regarded as the normal state of international affairs and the scope of the devastation which it could wreak was relatively limited, the Law of Moses ordained that peace must be earnestly sought with any enemy before embarking upon any armed conflict (Deuteronomy 20:10). The great medieval legist and philosopher Maimonides embodied this principle in the section of his law code, *Mishneh Torah*, dealing with "the Law of Kings" (6:4–5).

These considerations have obviously developed infinitely greater urgency in this post-atomic age. The crucial problem confronting international affairs today is the establishment of conditions of peaceful relations with the Communist world, in order to eliminate the peril of atomic warfare. The meaning of nuclear destruction today has been succinctly described, without exaggeration but in awesome and realistic terms, by Harrison Brown and James Real in "Community of Fear." The capacity to wipe out most of the human race and virtually all the painfully achieved products of civilization is omnipresent and real. In spite of all efforts to avert our gaze from facing the issue, the basic question of the age remains: How is this menace to be averted?

A widespread view, which is far more evident in national policy than in theoretical discussion, is that we are helplessly caught in the grip of inevitable circumstances and that therefore the arms race should continue with unabated energy and, if possible, with increased expenditures. The assumption, or, more correctly, the hope, is that if we remain "strong," our foes will be deterred from entering into armed conflict with us. While this viewpoint has been dominant in our government, it is clear that it is ethically untenable. Indeed, the doctrine of men's being caught in a vise from which there is no escape runs counter to the fundamentals of any ethical system. For all ethics rests upon the conviction that man is a free and responsible agent, who is able in significant measure to determine his own destiny.

Moreover, this view of an accelerated arms race as the only course of action open to the free world reflects another ethical drawback—it rests upon the absence of the cardinal

virtue of intelligence. That awesome methods of punishment act as a deterrent to malefactors is a notion exploded
both in the fields of criminology and of history. Capital
punishment has never reduced murder. As for war, when
Alfred Nobel invented dynamite, he confidently proclaimed
that war had now been made so horrible that it was unthink-
able any longer. All that remains of that generous illusion is
the Nobel Peace Prize, which, in certain years, has been left
unawarded. Atomic bombs and missiles serve only to suggest to certain mentalities that "we must do unto the other
fellow as he would do to us, but do it first." Greater than
the danger of calculated war, consciously entered into by
responsible government leaders on either side, is the peril of
an accidental or minor incident which can plunge the world
into war and chaos. That the arms race represents an in-
tolerable drain upon the economic resources of the antagonists, which could well be used for far more constructive
purposes, is an additional consideration of great practical
moment that cannot be ignored.

A more sophisticated defense of the "arms race" is also
proposed in certain quarters. In this version, it is argued that
under certain circumstances, nuclear war, for all its risks and
horrors, is the only ethical course of action open to the
West, since there may be no other way of preserving the
spiritual values of our civilization. We have no alternative
but to echo the words of the biblical Samson in his final
hour, "May my soul perish with the Philistines!" This position may be disputed on practical grounds. Our concern
here is to evaluate it in ethical terms. Basically, we believe
that it makes an error, to which proponents of the ethics of
self-abnegation are particularly liable. It seeks to transfer the
ethical values of individual martyrdom, which ministers to
the advancement of human life, to the condition of the total
group, where mass-murder or mass-suicide would spell not

the enhancement of life but its total dissolution. And it fails to notice the chasm separating the two.

Moreover, from the standpoint of ethics, the advocates of a continuing arms race may be charged with debasing the selflessness of martyrdom through the cardinal sin of pride. For they assume that our way of life is totally good and that of our foes totally evil, so that we are morally justified in holding over the heads of our enemies the threat of their complete destruction. Now one may cherish a passionate loyalty to the democratic way of life because of its achievements in the past and present and its potentialities for the future. And yet one may recognize that those who demand a continuing arms race are guilty of arrogance as well as of moral blindness. For they suffer from a callous indifference to the vast sectors of exploitation, tyranny, disease, ignorance, and insecurity that still plague both the free world and the so-called underdeveloped nations outside the Communist orbit. We need to attain to a much more exalted level of righteousness before we plunge to the depths of unrighteousness that are involved in the total annihilation of our adversaries.

At the other extreme of the spectrum are those who urge unilateral disarmament by the United States even without an agreement with the Soviet Union. Painfully aware of the dangers of the present arms race and conscious of the unspeakable horrors of atomic destruction, many of the advocates of this position would admit that our Russian adversaries might well take advantage of the military superiority that would accrue to them by such a step on our part. Nonetheless, the advocates of unilateral disarmament would insist, such a risk is better than that of total annihilation.

Were the Communist bloc to seize global hegemony without a war, it would mean the physical preservation of the Western world. But the price would be high. It would spell the spiritual asphyxiation of the West, the decay and death of the religious, ethical, and cultural values which Western man has historically regarded as the core of his being. While unilateral disarmament is generally defended on survivalist terms as "practical," it represents an extreme form of the ethics of self-abnegation.

It is true that at times the successful practice of passive resistance in India by Gandhi and his followers is cited to demonstrate the applicability of non-resistance to evil in world affairs. This tactic is a collectivized version of the doctrine that the individual is not to resist evil but is to meet it with good. It is not necessary to point out in detail that there is no analogy between the struggle of India for independence and the present battle for the world, either in the character of the antagonists, in the nature of the struggle, or in the extent of the prize of victory.

It is true that unilateral disarmament would probably safeguard the physical survival of the West, but the ethics of self-fulfilment calls for more—it seeks a policy which is designed to preserve the spiritual values which constitute the personality of Western man. Since intelligence is a cardinal virtue in this system of ethics, it would urge taking a lesser risk than is involved either in the unrestricted arms race on the one hand, or in unilateral disarmament on the other. The only ethical and realistic course is a serious, energetic and unremitting effort by both antagonists to negotiate early mutual disarmament. It is true that negotiations have been carried on over an extended period of time by Soviet and American experts and diplomats. While we feel that the Communists are responsible, the impression is general among nations outside our orbit that we have been dragging our feet and have not recognized the desperate urgency of achieving an agreement. It is to be hoped that energetic steps will be taken to achieve speedy and meaningful disarmament by mutual agreement. There are grounds for believing that the hope is not purely imaginary, even in the face of the continued provocation of Soviet tactics and Communist propaganda that tries one's patience to the breaking point. The flare-up of tempers is infinitely to be preferred to the awesome glare of atomic bombs descending upon cities.

Moreover, these maneuvers, however trying, are themselves part of the strategy of accommodation, by which opposing viewpoints achieve a modus vivendi. In striving for this goal we shall not be yielding simply to expediency. The possibility for success in East-West negotiations still remains, because, however tragically limited in scope our common objectives may be, there still remains a substantial body of ideas, desires, and hopes on which both we and they are in agreement.

There is, first and foremost, the desire by both antagonists to survive and to avoid annihilation or even massive destruction through atomic warfare. If the human race—or any part of it—is wiped out, it is obviously prevented forever from overcoming its shortcomings, correcting its errors, and attaining to a nobler level of being. In the language of religion, death shuts the door on repentance and permanently prevents the return of the sinner to God's ways.

There is also the conviction, held on both sides of the Iron Curtain, that the value of any given society lies in the degree to which the masses of men are freed from the ravages of hunger, disease, and ignorance, though we differ with the Communists fundamentally on the value we set upon liberty and the degree to which we are prepared to surrender some stability for the sake of the free play of men's intelligence and will. We also share with our opponents a concern for the advancement of science, literature, music, and art, though here, too, our stress upon the freedom of the individual allows a far greater measure of experimentation and variety. Be this as it may, there is sufficient ground for common discourse and therefore a measure of hope still exists. It

should be possible to achieve at least an agreement on disarmament and to limit the conflict between East and West
to peaceful competition in the areas of economic and technical aid to underdeveloped areas and in cultural penetration
everywhere in the world.

Some students of foreign affairs have gone further and
spelled out other and more specific bases for possible agreement. Thus, C. L. Sulzberger has proposed three objectives
for a "brush-fire peace" which he feels are attainable (*New
York Times*, Nov. 19, 1960). These are (*a*) reducing tension
on such issues as the non-transference of nuclear arms to
non-atomic states and freedom of outer space; (*b*) agreeing
to a temporary status quo on currently insoluble issues, including reform of the United Nations, until soluble ones are
settled; and (*c*) concentrating on the improvement of the
economy and the educational system of our country and
those of our allies and studying projects to eliminate world
hunger.

Whether we regard these or other objectives as constituting a basis for discussion and ultimate agreement is not as
important as recognizing that such common objectives do
exist and must be found.

Moreover, we shall be able to approach the agonizing and
frustrating task of negotiation with our enemies with more
patience and fewer moralistic pretensions if we endow our
foreign policy with the qualities of honesty and intelligence.
We shall then recognize that we ourselves are far from having fully solved such basic issues as race relations, the proper
distribution of wealth, and the providing of opportunity for
universal education and personal self-fulfilment under our
system of democratic capitalism.

Quite properly, we shall continue to stress the two unique
qualities of democracy fatally lacking in communism: its
inherent capacity for peaceful change and progress and its
creation of the instruments necessary for the free exercise of

the will and intelligence of the people in determining its destiny. But our own unfinished business at home should make it easier for us to meet with our opponents, who are even further from fulfilling their massive goals than are we from ours.

*To keep the avenues of communication and negotiation open among governments is therefore a moral good of the highest order* and the most significant function of the United Nations. Conversely, the refusal to negotiate is the ultimate sin in group relations, not only because it makes impossible the peaceful adjudication of differences and thus increases the incidence of violence and destruction but also because it denies the right of others besides one's self to live.

Judaism is an ancient faith whose classic texts go back many centuries. It therefore cannot be called upon to offer a detailed blueprint for dissipating the countless group tensions confronting our modern age and for reordering the structure of society closer to a pattern of perfection. Ours are not the conditions that prevailed when the Bible and the Talmud were written, nor has the Messianic Age, to which the prophets and the sages looked forward, come to pass. Moreover, those of us who are dedicated to a religious interpretation of life must be constantly aware of the sins of commission and omission which religious men have perpetrated throughout history.

Yet, if it be true that the eternal is always contemporary, there is relevance in the teachings of Jewish tradition for our day. The faith and the insight of the prophets and sages offer for our age the guidance and the courage it desperately needs, in order that the chaos and imminent catastrophe of the present may be overcome and the world order of the future ushered in.

# 13

## NATURAL LAW IN THE MODERN WORLD

Throughout this work, we have sought to explore the resources of the Jewish tradition in the quest for insights and attitudes that can help meet the challenges to world order arising from the boundless variety in human nature. The effort has been made to find within the specific content of Judaism universal norms for dealing with the maze of problems deriving from the religious divergences, the racial differences, the clashing national interests, and the competing social philosophies of the contemporary world.

It is a truism that twentieth-century men have lost a common universe of discourse and no longer share a basic world view. For this very reason, the search has been intensified, in some circles at least, for principles of wide or universal applicability in grappling with the issues of the present and in laying the foundations of the world community of the future. Such a body of doctrine is available in the concept of natural law, which has a long and respectable tradition behind it—one is tempted to say, too long and too respectable for our critical and iconoclastic age.

This new and growing interest in natural law cannot yet be described as a major trend of the age. Yet there is evidence of an increasing concern with this concept, which maintains that there is a basic order of justice discoverable by human reason and conformable to human nature. Moreover, according to the natural law doctrine, this basic order of justice is both the source and sanction of all legitimate legal systems and the standard for appraising and judging the value of all existing positive law.

The eighteenth century, whose classical political documents are the American Declaration of Independence and the French Declaration of the Rights of Man, marked the apogee of the natural law doctrine in a secularized form. In the nineteenth century and the first decades of the twentieth, natural law reached its nadir of decline. In the modern era, it has been generally regarded as a quaint survival of Greco-Roman thought and of medieval scholasticism, and dismissed as totally irrelevant to modern man and his condition. During these last few centuries, the natural law doctrine has remained almost exclusively the province of the Catholic church. This situation seemed entirely appropriate in view of the widely assumed tendency of the church to glorify medievalism in all its forms.

That the sources of natural law were to be sought not only in Hellenistic and Roman thought but also in the Hebraic tradition was all but forgotten even by the advocates of the doctrine. That natural law could help to dissipate the fundamental, ethical, and legal chaos of our age was surely not suspected by its opponents.

But ideas are immortal or, at least, hardy perennials. Bury them deep and they seem decently and permanently interred. But, as time goes on, there are stirrings beneath the sod and the dead doctrine takes on new life—even if in a transfigured form. Circles which have long looked askance at the theory of natural law—philosophers, lawyers, and sociologists—are manifesting a desire to find the viable elements within it. The reasons for this interest at this, the midpoint of the twentieth century, are not far to seek. There is a growing recognition that the moral relativism which has been bolstered by the positivist emphasis in the social sciences in general and by anthropology and sociology in particular is inadequate for the needs of our generation.

Precisely because of the new temper of the age, it is important not to forget the debt we owe to the recent past. "Relativism" fostered some important intellectual and moral virtues of which we are the beneficiaries. It helped create an objectivity in scientific observers and a sympathy for the infinite variety in mores and social structure to be found among men. It fostered a tolerance for systems of society and thought vastly different from our own. It helped to weaken the natural tendency to regard one's own outlook and familar environment as natural and divinely ordained while stigmatizing all other patterns either as senseless aberrations or as sinful violations of the will of God. In creating objectivity, tolerance, and sympathy for the varieties of human experience, relativism made an abidingly valuable contribution, which we may feel impelled to transcend but not to obliterate.

Aside from the natural dialectic of action and reaction which inheres in all branches of human activity and thought, the growing sense of the inadequacy of relativism and positivism stems from the recognition that they offer no firm basis for the preservation of the values of a free society. Robert M. Hutchins highlights the intellectual and moral crisis of the age when he points out that "for any kind of common life or action there must be some consensus."[1] The conception of a consensus associated with the names of Oliver Wendell Holmes and Learned Hand sees it merely as the reflection of the will of the dominant group in society. There are, to be sure, fine distinctions among the formulations of this general position, by Holmes, Hand, and other jurists and lawyers.[2] But the basic position is identical.

[1] Cf. his *Two Faces of Federalism*, p. 14.

[2] For a lucid analysis of these views, see *ibid.*, pp. 17–18.

Here it suffices to note that this view offers no basis for meeting the critical problems of a democratic society today. These include such issues as the nature of sovereignty, the legitimacy of the uses of power, and the limitations to be imposed upon the various competing groups within the nation, as well as the ambivalent threat and promise of technology. Relativism is equally helpless in supplying a rationale for democracy as against its ideological competitors. Whether expressed with greater or lesser sophistication, relativism is ultimately driven to the standpoint of Vyacheslav Molotov, who, when asked about the Stalin-Hitler pact in 1939, answered that "Fascism is a matter of taste."

In a quiet and uneventful age, those whom William James called the "tough-minded" do not feel impelled to reexamine the fundamentals of their world view, and only the "tender-minded" indulge in such philosophic vagaries. But, in an age of mounting crisis, when the foundations of the world are tottering, all men become aware of the necessity for a firm basis by which to decide questions that reach to the very heart of the social order and to the essence of the human situation. If "consensus" represents only the viewpoint of a given segment in society, if its effectiveness derives solely from the power of the group, it has no claim upon men's loyalty once the power of the particular group is spent. Nor can it be defended over any other position, except on the subjective grounds of self-interest or esthetic considerations.

Much more than abstract philosophical interests are involved here. There are radically different consequences that flow from a commitment to natural law on the one hand and to the positivist approach on the other, as Hutchins has clearly shown:

> The jurist committed to natural law reasons back to nature; the jurist committed to any other jurisprudential foundation reasons back, if he reasons at all, to some his-

torical event, like the command of the sovereign, or to some view of social policy, like a feeling that a certain situation or piece of legislation is an affront to "human dignity," a quality that he proclaims, but does not justify.[3]

If a world divided against itself is to survive, it must cease to be divided, or, at least, it must create some common universe of affirmation which all or nearly all men can share. Hence the necessity for some objective standard. Natural law seems to hold out the promise of such an objective standard, whence its growing appeal in our age.

Definitions of natural law are legion, but they are basically not far apart. John Cogley has defined it as "simply the belief that there is a moral order or ethical order which a human being can discover and which he must take account of if he is to attune himself to his necessary ends as a human being."[4] As is frequently the case, the implications of the definition need to be spelled out, because they have often been misstated by its advocates and misunderstood by its adversaries. Basically the postulates of natural law deal with human nature, with law and with reason, and with their interrelationships.

Essentially, natural law declares that only that law is legitimate and has a claim upon men's loyalty which is *in harmony with human nature*. Second, it believes that human nature is *constant* through time, not necessarily unchanging, but with sufficient continuity to make possible generalizations regarding its basic traits, its needs and desires, its limitations and potentialities. Third, it regards human nature as being *universal* in space, modified to be sure by environmental factors but still sufficiently stable to permit a generalized theory. Finally, it regards human nature not as known, but as *knowable* through the canons of scientific investigation and rational thought.

[3] *Ibid.*

[4] In his paper, "Ethics and Natural Law," p. 16.

The caveats we have just noted have unfortunately often been ignored by advocates of natural law, who have treated human nature as *unchangeable, uniform,* and *totally known.* More than a little of the difficulty stems from these distortions. Inherently, however, there is nothing in natural law that negates the exploration of the dimensions of human nature as an ongoing and probably unending enterprise.

Since human nature is constant, universal, and knowable, law represents the effort by society to safeguard the requirements and proper needs of its members through the theory and practice of justice and not merely by the establishment of a structure of legal procedures. Legality is not distinct from justice, but neither is it identical with it. It bifurcates into legal procedure and equity. Ideally viewed, the law begins in the effort to codify the dictates of justice.

For several reasons, the legal system never becomes coterminous with justice. First, the law develops a life of its own and elaborates a complex of procedures which ultimately become codified in the statute books. By that time, however, society has often moved on to new insights or it has been modified by new conditions requiring new and often radical applications of the time-honored principles. Hence a cultural lag between positive law and the new frontiers of justice is an all but universal feature of every social system.

Second, justice is not identical with law, because justice includes aspects of human relationships that are beyond the power of the law to govern—what the Talmud calls "matters handed over to the heart." The law makes it punishable to injure one's fellow; justice requires that we help him. Beating one's father is a legal crime enforceable with sanctions; no system of law can compel a man to love or reverence his parents. There thus emerges the paradox that law, which arises in order to make justice operative in society, falls perpetually behind it. In a rational and just society, the goal will always be to close the gap and bring legal practice as close to equity as possible. Believing in the existence and knowability of human nature and in the reality and rationality of justice, natural law regards a theory of justice as the necessary foundation for any legal system worthy of the name.

Finally, natural law believes in man's reason as an ever present instrument for evaluating both human nature and the law and for evaluating the law by the touchstone of the legitimate needs and aspirations of human nature.

These three elements—human nature, justice, and reason—are all that are required by the doctrine of natural law. One may hazard the guess that, had natural lawyers restricted themselves to these three elements, the doctrine would not have aroused the widespread suspicion with which it is viewed in many quarters. Historically, however, many advocates of the doctrine have gone further and insisted that natural law is rooted in the universe and therefore is divinely ordained. Moreover, the practitioners of natural law have frequently—one is tempted to say, generally—utilized the doctrine to justify contingent judgments and historically conditioned prejudices on specific issues by giving them an aura of the "eternal, rational and God-given," in Brand Blanshard's phrase.

It is no service to the cause to underestimate the substantial roadblocks in the way of a rehabilitation of natural law or to minimize their validity. The fundamental dilemma felt by many who stand outside the dominant tradition of natural law but are sympathetic to its value has been succinctly expressed by Hutchins in his observation that natural law appears to be "a body of doctrine that is either so vague as to be useless or so biased as to be menacing."

Brand Blanshard[5] has spelled out the two unhappy alternatives that confront modern advocates of natural law: "The natural law which we are to take as our guide remains

5 *New York Times Book Review*, Feb. 12, 1961.

deplorably misty. If natural law is to be usable, we must be able to tell what is natural." He then adds two more objections, "The advocates of natural law fix some absolute rules which often turn out to be incredible." He quotes John Henry Newman as saying that it would be better for millions of men to die in extreme agony than for a single man to commit the slightest venial sin. He also cites George P. Grant as maintaining that it would be wrong to convict an innocent man even if it were the price of averting a world war. Third, Blanshard argues, "It is not true that if we abandon the Law of Nature as our test, we have nothing left to fall back upon. We can still fall back on the majority view of modern moralists, namely that we should so act as to produce the greatest good."

This last argument is by no means difficult to meet. Blanshard proposes that instead of natural law as the norm we use the standard of "producing the greatest good," yet he fails to recognize that the next question, "What is the greatest good for men?" catapults us at once into a discussion of human nature—its needs, its fears, and its hopes. In a word, natural law has been driven out of the door only to enter by the window.

Far weightier is his second objection, repeated by virtually all critics of natural law—the argument from the history of the doctrine. It is undeniable that the theory of natural law has been subjected to not a few misinterpretations, unwarranted conclusions, and downright errors, both intellectual and moral, and the end is not yet in sight. The history of a doctrine, including the uses to which it has been put, is not necessarily the determining factor as to its inherent validity—that is indeed one of our basic theses. But neither can its *curriculum vitae* be ignored, if only because a knowledge of its history can help alert us to congenital weaknesses to which the concept is exposed.

The instances cited by Blanshard do not exhaust the bill

of particulars. Thus it has been noted[6]—and with substantial justice—that in natural law

> those aspects that can be linked to the given physical nature of man are made to predominate over those aspects that arise from the possibilities of developing human culture. . . . The natural law emphasis would appear to incline toward an undue bias toward the former—toward static and fixed guide lines rooted primarily in elemental facts. Thus, it would appear to have an undue conservative bias.

Specifically, it has been asked, "Has the natural law tradition helped in emancipating woman?" It is doubtful whether the record of history would bear out the contrary view that "It is easy to show that natural law can be and *often has been in fact* an instrument of social reform." The most that can be said for the history of natural law in modern times is that it has at times provided a rationale for some social reforms that were initiated and fought for under other auspices, by men and movements far removed from its presuppositions.

The conservative bias of natural law that has been so widely noted does *not* derive from a misinterpretation of the facts. Moreover, it is too common a phenomenon to be merely accidental. Rarely are the advocates or practitioners of natural law to be found on the frontiers of ethical thought. Historically, natural law has been far more in evidence as a limiting and restraining factor in human activity than as a liberating principle making for growth and development. As Dr. Hutchins has noted, natural lawyers have been more active in defining "a just war" than in furthering disarmament or a new conception of sovereignty. The conservative bias in natural law, which is undeniable, is the consequence of its tendency to see human nature as essentially given rather than growing, as fixed rather than flexible.

[6] By William Lee Miller, "Comments on Natural Law," prepared for the Center for the Study of Democratic Institutions, from which the quotations in this paragraph are drawn.

It is, however, not enough to make this observation, whether neutrally or critically. There are two interrelated questions that should be asked: First, what accounts for the generally conservative approach adopted by natural lawyers? Second, is this standpoint inherent in the doctrine of natural law itself?

I would suggest that the reason natural law has tended to be "static" in its application lies in its cultural origins, in the two periods in which it arose and in which it reached its highest development. As we shall note below, the roots of natural law are not to be sought only in Greco-Roman culture. The Hebraic component, as embodied in the Old Testament, the apocrypha, the New Testament, and rabbinic literature, is of comparable antiquity and, as seventeenth- and eighteenth-century scholars knew, it possesses substantial significance. The fact is, however, that the dynamism of the Judeo-Christian world view, the sense of history moving toward a great consummation, was not present in Greek and Roman thought, which saw life as unchanging and human history as going through repetitious cycles. And it was classical civilization that fathered natural law.

The Middle Ages, in which natural law reached its apogee, were also marked by a static conception of life. To be sure, the Jewish and Christian religions looked forward to a divine intervention in human affairs but only at "the end of days," which was taken to mean "beyond history." On the other hand, in this temporal world, here and now, medieval thought had no conception of change and growth. The feudal system, with its permanent stratification of classes, gave expression to this static view in the social and political order.

Natural law necessarily took on the coloration of these two periods, which saw its gestation and its maturity. From these eras it derived its bias in favor of the static, the unchanging, the immovable. The august authority of Aquinas

virtually made *epigoni* of all his successors. The later practitioners of natural law did little more than elaborate on the
work of their predecessors. The spirit remained largely the
same.

The modern world, however, is marked by its dynamism
and by its perpetual flux. Growth and change are not merely realities of life today—they always were—but are consciously recognized and even welcomed. Moreover, the
vastly enlarged horizons of understanding opened up to
modern man by the physical and life sciences make it possible to do far more justice to the nature of man and of his
environment than was possible in the past.

A cynical observer might therefore argue that natural law
needs only to be saved from its friends in order to convert
its enemies! A fairer and more sympathetic view would be
that natural lawyers today need to remember that the doctrine in its classic form had its birth and maturation in static
cultures. From them it absorbed this characteristic, for
which it had an innate predisposition, because of its emphasis upon the permanent elements of human nature. Today
we can undoubtedly find valuable material for a viable conception of natural law in the tradition of the past, but we
must go beyond it in its static conception of human nature.

If natural law is to be a vital resource in the modern age
and not merely vestigial remains from medieval times, it
will need a generous infusion of the modern consciousness
of development. On every issue before it, natural law theory
must be aware of the dialectic of continuity and change
which constitute the phenomenon of growth.

And on the negative side, natural law theory will need to
reckon with the deep propensity in the human soul to self-
seeking and self-deception, to which our age has become
painfully sensitive. It cannot ignore the insights of traditional religion regarding the innate weakness of man, whether
expressed in the Christian doctrine of "original sin" or in the

Jewish concept of the two *yetzers*, "the evil impulse" and "the good impulse." Nor can natural law overlook the universal phenomenon of "rationalization," the seemingly boundless capacity of men to disguise their instinctual drives and submerged desires and to project them in rational and moral terms. What modern psychiatry has amply documented was intuitively felt by the prophet: "The heart is deceitful above all, and desperately sick; who can know it?" (Jeremiah 17:9).

These insights will necessarily complicate the task of delineating the attributes of human nature which is basic to the natural law enterprise. But they do not negate the conception of human nature as constant, universal, and knowable. Nor do they refute the conviction that human reason remains the only available standard for creating and evaluating the norm of justice as the foundation of law.

The essential difficulty with the concept of natural law lies in a misunderstanding of its basic affirmation. This error has given rise to questionable interpretations or doubtful applications of principles that are in themselves sound. Thus, it is an axiom of natural law that the proper norms of social conduct and legal injunction are derived from "nature." The full meaning of this affirmation becomes clear, however, only if we understand what it negates. Without denying the affinities of man for other living creatures or his relationship to the universe as a whole—quite the contrary—it is *human* nature, not animal or physical nature, which is the proper norm for natural law.

It therefore follows that the investigation of human nature cannot be limited to those physical aspects which man has in common with the lower animals. Unlike them, man is a sociobiological being. Hence, such manifestations of human nature as friendship, love, reason, and culture are not artificial grafts upon human nature but are inherent elements in it, no less than the instinct for self-preservation or the sexual drive which he shares with other animals. There are, undoubtedly, great difficulties involved in the objective description and analysis of these specifically human traits, particularly since they are not susceptible to quantitative techniques. But these problems of the investigator do not invalidate either the reality of these attributes or their "natural" character. The "morally relevant nature of man" cannot be delineated unless we reckon with the entire complex of human nature. Within its dimensions we must include its physical, intellectual, aesthetic, and spiritual aspects, without which human nature is not human.

When all these factors are taken into account, an advocate of natural law may come to conclusions radically different from some that are being maintained and defended today on the ground that they and they alone represent the application of natural law to contemporary questions.

Perhaps one striking example will help make the point clear. We are frequently told that birth control is a violation of natural law and that therefore the prohibition is binding upon all men, whatever their religious views. Brand Blanshard makes this contention basic to his criticisms, as already cited above: "If natural law is to be usable, we must be able to tell what is natural. Is birth control natural as a step to race improvement, or unnatural as an interference with physiological process?" But Blanshard's alternatives disappear when we equate the "natural," not with the biological, but with the human. For man, at least, and perhaps in rudimentary form for some animals, procreation does not exhaust the meaning of the intersexual relationship. Invariably, the physical aspects of sex seek a larger framework in the primary commitment of personal love and in the permanent setting of family life. This is particularly true in the case of man, where the birth of a child marks the beginning of a long period of dependency in which he requires the care of his parents and the protection of society. It is noteworthy that in the Bible the creation of Eve is explained on the ground of her capacity to fulfil Adam's need for human companionship, "It is not good for man to dwell alone" (Genesis 2:18), long before her function as the child-bearing sex is envisaged (3:16).

The profound biblical metaphor which declares that man is created in the image of God has been variously interpreted through the ages as equivalent to man's immortal soul, the gift of reason, or his dominion over the lower orders of creation. Implicit in all these views of the metaphor is man's possessing *in parvo* the basic attribute of God, his creativity. Aside from some rudimentary or instinctual forms of this quality to be found in the lower animals, it is man alone who has the capacity to be master of his world and not simply its creature, being able to mold his environment and modify his instinctual drives. When the specifically human aspects of the sexual relationship are given due weight, one may well conclude that natural law is not being violated and on the contrary is being obeyed when there are genuine physical, psychological, economic, or social grounds for limiting the number of children in a family.

If impediments such as these to the doctrine of natural law are removed, one may reasonably hope that many who now stand outside the tradition may find their place within it.

Unfortunately, however, I suspect that many of the new recruits that may have been inveigled into joining the ranks of the proponents of natural law may be driven away by another consideration. The opponents of natural law are right in suspecting that lurking in its shadow are some metaphysical and theological presuppositions. Because of the disrepute into which theological affirmations have fallen, many of the latter-day advocates of natural law seek to deny or sever what now appears as a marriage of inconvenience and of non-necessity. Thus, speaking as a religious believer, John Cogley maintains that "the natural law doctrine found in Aristotle, Cicero, and *Antigone* is much older than Catholicism and I believe would have developed from its dim beginnings in antiquity even if the Catholic Church had never existed." He is undoubtedly correct in his view that natural law is not linked to any specific theology. But, if the assumptions underlying the natural law and the implications flowing from it are analyzed, it would appear that some conclusions regarding the purpose of life and the nature of the universe do emerge.

From the secular standpoint of a social scientist, Philip Selznick[7] has argued for a modern conception of natural law, emphasizing two basic postulates. For him, as for the present writer, natural law must rest upon the basis of rigorous scientific inquiry which is the only firm foundation of our knowledge of human nature. Second, it must possess a demanding character upon the conscience and the actions of men. Then, in order to free natural law from any "entangling alliance" with metaphysics or theology, Selznick maintains that "it is not necessary for natural law supporters to prove that man has any inherent duties, including the duty to live at all, or to choose the good and avoid evil. It is the system that has the commitment."

I do not believe this position can stand up under analysis. It must be obvious that "the system" has no meaning or existence apart from its establishment and maintenance by human beings. Moreover, Selznick himself concedes, "If there is to be a legal order it must serve the proper ends of man." But the proper ends of man require an analysis of the nature of man and evaluational judgments are therefore inescapable. Finally, unless we accept as basic the duty to live and to choose the good and avoid evil, there is no virtue in any system of law that claims, however imperfectly, to embody the principle of justice. If we adopt the rule of power as the

---

[7] In his paper, "Sociology and Natural Law," scheduled to appear in the *Natural Law Forum.*

normative principles of society or make the denial of the life-impulse basic, a radically different legal structure neces-sarily emerges, as under naziism.

Selznick has made too far-reaching a concession to the positivist proclivity for identifying the quest for truth ex-clusively with sociometric techniques. Thus he declares, "It is enough to study any normative system always from the standpoint of the normative system itself." Now, if his words are taken at face value, he has surrendered what is perhaps the principal value inherent in the doctrine of nat-ural law, its utility as a standard of moral judgment and rational discrimination. If his contention is right, the systems of communism, fascism, naziism, and democracy are all of equal validity, since each may be studied from the stand-point of the normative system itself. The canons of justice and reason would shed no light on the crucial question as to which system deserves the loyalty of modern man.

Selznick may be correct in insisting that, strictly speaking, the doctrine of natural law requires no metaphysical foun-dations, merely the full and unbiased observation of human nature. But, as he himself recognizes, facts cannot be insu-lated from values. Human nature exhibits the qualities of friendship, love, co-operation, the appreciation of beauty, the hunger for righteousness. But it also reveals aggressive-ness, greed, lust, irrationality. Which constellation of attri-butes is to be regarded as the norm of human nature and which as aberrations or perversions of the essential nature of man? Which traits, accordingly, can be made the basis of natural law? The answer cannot come from a mythically "objective" scientific investigator whom only the naïve imagine to exist. On the contrary, a scientist approaches the phenomena he seeks to understand with a theory, a view-point, a prejudice, if you will, previously arrived at. A true scientist differs from his counterfeit in his willingness to modify or discard his hypothesis on the basis of the evidence, but he begins with a hypothesis before surveying the evidence.

But even if we grant the possibility of an "unbiased" observation of human nature to serve as the basis for a scientific sociology, such objectivity could suffice only for science, but not for the scientist. A scientist is not merely a scientist, but a human being, and a natural lawyer is more than a lawyer. The refusal to explore philosophical implications here, as in any other positivist approach, is possible only by an arbitrary decision to avoid asking ultimate questions and stopping the inquiry midway in its path. The contention of positivism that questions that are not experimentally verifiable or subject to sociometric treatment are meaningless is a purely wilful and gratuitous assumption. A question is not meaningless merely because we have no answer or cannot all agree on one.

Moreover, even from the standpoint of the scientific method itself, it is unnecessary—and impossible—to exclude value judgments from the arcanum of the scientific enterprise. It is a truism even in the natural sciences that the scientific observer is himself part of the material being observed. Finally, the processes of selecting the data to be studied and of establishing a hierarchy of values among them constitute prior conditions for any meaningful investigation.

When we speak of love and friendship as illustrating "the primary relation," we are giving to these relationships more than a numerical designation. We are suggesting that the deep and extensive communication and mutual commitment to be found in love and friendship represent in some sense a higher relationship than the "constrained and guarded arm's-length contact of individuals which exists among neighbors or in business or in the economic realm."

One of Selznick's most significant ideas is his recognition of the existence of "latent values in the world of fact" which endow physical relationships like parenthood and sexuality with their specifically human character. But we cannot stop with merely noting the quality of "invaluation" which exists in human nature, this capacity to endow with supraphysical values the physical attributes with which man enters the world. Its presence tells us something not only about human nature but also about the world of which man is a part, unless we are prepared to interpose an impenetrable wall between man and the lower rungs of the evolutionary ladder, an approach contradicted by the findings of the sciences of chemistry, biology, and psychology at every turn.

We may, of course, insist that there is no "proof" of any direction or meaning in the history of the earth which is marked by the emergence and evolution of life. But the evidence is abundant that as we ascend the evolutionary ladder from the ameba to man, we encounter an ever greater complexity of physical structure, a corresponding growth in the specialization of function among the various organs, together with an increased degree of efficiency, and an ever more developed nervous system with a heightened degree of consciousness, which reaches the maximum of self-awareness in man. Nor is this all. This self-awareness in man is more than a consciousness of self; it expresses itself in the love of beauty, in moral aspiration, and in the capacity to reason.

These attributes of man's nature reveal something about the universe, just as an apple discloses the nature of the tree upon which it has ripened, and it itself in turn was present in the seed from which the tree grew. In a sense not intended by Anaxagoras, it is true that man creates God in his own image or, more accurately, that man's nature bears witness to his Creator's image, in which he was fashioned. While, therefore, the natural lawyer *qua lawyer* may properly set limits in his activity and refrain from asking ultimate questions, his human concerns will lead him to recognize that his growing understanding of human nature sheds light upon the nature of all life and of the universe which is its home.

For reasons of temperament or economy of effort, we

may decide to place a perfectly proper yet arbitrary restriction upon our rational faculty—"thus far shalt thou go and no further." But if we impose no limits to the scope of our thinking, we shall find that espousing the natural law doctrine means exploring its implications for the nature of the universe and thus moving inescapably toward a religious world view.

Moreover, in treating reason and justice rather than irrationality, greed, and cruelty as the basic traits of human nature, we are, quite legitimately, bringing value judgments to bear upon the observable phenomena of human behavior. These value judgments, whether we are aware of the fact or not, have their source in a world view fashioned by a theistic metaphysics.

This theoretic conclusion is buttressed by a consideration of the Hebraic sources of natural law, which have been largely lost sight of during the last few centuries. To be sure, history cannot replace the canons of logic in demonstrating the truth or falsity of a proposition. It can, however, alert us to relationships which might otherwise be overlooked. Though not always fully appreciated, the ethics of the Western world is rooted in two traditions, one, the Greco-Roman, the other, the Judeo-Christian. Largely under the impact of the academic approach, the sources of natural law are generally traced to the Greeks, while the Hebraic component tends to be ignored or minimized.

The Hebraic sources of natural law are all explicit in linking the ethical imperatives they set forth to belief in a Supreme Being. Basic to the biblical world view is the conviction of the unity of God, so that the natural order and the moral order represent two facets of the same divine nature.

The pathos of the patriarch Job in the Bible lies in the fact that he challenges the justice of God in whom he has

believed because he has been victimized by the God of
power, but he refuses to accept a dichotomy between them.
Job's reconciliation with God is effected by the God-
speeches, the import of which has been generally misunderstood, because, in accordance with a characteristic feature
of Semitic poetry, the theme is not explicitly set forth but
is suggested and left to be inferred by the reader. Through
the vivid and joyous description of the glories of the universe, the analogy is borne in upon Job that just as there are
order and harmony in the natural world, so there must be
order and meaning in the moral sphere. Man cannot fully
fathom the meaning of the natural order, yet he is aware of
its beauty and harmony. Similarly, though he cannot expect
fully to comprehend the moral order, he can believe that
there are rationality and justice within it. For the author of
Job, God is one and indivisible, governing both nature and
human life. If there is pattern anywhere in the universe,
there must be pattern everywhere. As nature is instinct with
morality, so the moral order is rooted in the natural world.

This conception is tersely phrased by the psalmist:
"Truth springs forth from the earth." Such classic statements of biblical ethics as the Decalogue (Exodus, chap. 20;
Deuteronomy, chap. 5) or the Holiness Code in Leviticus
(chap. 19) are, or may be viewed as, unsophisticated adum-
brations of natural law. Both these formulations offer no
detailed theological doctrine and are largely devoted to
spelling out ethical injunctions. But both codes are rooted
in faith in the one living God and in the prohibition of
paganism. Moreover, both specifically motivate obedience
to the law in terms of loyalty to the divine Lawgiver: "I am
the Lord," a formula repeated again and again (Exodus
20:2, 5; Leviticus 19:2, 3, 4, 10, 12, 14, 16, 18, and *passim*).

Less familiar is the great Confession of Innocence spoken
by the patriarch Job (Job, chap. 31) in which he sets forth
the code of conduct by which he has lived. It is noteworthy

that of the fourteen elements in his code of practice virtually all are ethical, with a single but significant exception—his lifelong avoidance of paganism through the worship of heavenly bodies.

As we have noted above, in another connection, an explicit doctrine of natural law is first set forth in the Book of Jubilees, which was written before the beginning of the Christian era. In it Noah is described as enjoining upon all his descendants a system of "ordinances and commandments" (Jubilees 7:22). In the Talmud, the Seven Laws of the Sons of Noah are set forth as universally binding. They forbid, as we have seen, idolatry, murder, sexual immorality, theft, blasphemy, and cruelty to animals, and enjoin the establishment of law and order (B. *Sanhedrin 56a–60a; Tosephta Abodah Zarah* 8:4–8).

The New Testament, as we have observed, seems to refer to the Noachide Laws in one passage (Acts 15:20, 29). In another, Paul explicitly refers to the doctrine of natural law as the endowment of all men in his statement:

> For when the Gentiles, which have not the law, do by nature the things contained in the law, these, having not the law, are a law unto themselves; which show the work of the law written in their hearts, their conscience also bearing witness, and their thoughts the meanwhile accusing, or else excusing one another [Romans 2:14-15].

The rabbinic doctrine of the Noachide Laws makes ethical conduct rather than creedal adherence obligatory upon all men. It is therefore a code of law rather than a system of belief which it enjoins. Yet though there is little theological content in the Noachide Laws, they are by no means lacking in a metaphysical foundation. They do include the prohibition of idolatry and of blasphemy and therefore rest upon the recognition of a divine creator and governor of the world.

Among medieval thinkers, this doctrine of the Noachide

Laws merged imperceptibly with that of natural law in the Middle Ages, as in the work of Bahya ibn Paqudah, the most popular Jewish moral philosopher of the Middle Ages (eleventh century, Spain). Before him, the tenth-century philosopher Saadia, influenced by the concept of natural religion (*fitra*) maintained by the Arab Kalam philosophers, virtually identified the truths of divine revelation with those achievable by human reason. Leo Strauss has shown that Judah Halevi equates the law of reason which underlies all codes with the law of nature. On the Christian side, John Selden, whose work *De Jure Naturali et Gentium Juxta Disciplinam Ebraeorum* (1665) identified the Noachide Laws with natural law, represented the effort of the natural-law school in the period of the Enlightenment to establish points of contact with the biblical tradition. With the growth of secularism in the last few centuries, however, the Greco-Roman source of natural law has continued to be cited, while the Judeo-Christian element has tended to be relegated to theologians.

It may be merely a historical accident that a nexus existed between belief in a divine source of justice and reason on the one hand and loyalty to a law of justice and reason on the other. And it may be argued that now the link can be dispensed with. I do not think so. But, at the very least, the centuries-long tradition linking religion and natural law should lead to re-examination of the notion that a commitment to natural law does not involve any conception of man's place, his duties, and his purposes in the cosmos.

Some reasons have already been suggested for the conviction that there is more than a purely adventitious link between natural law and religious commitment. In brief, they inhere in the recognition of an organic relationship between man's endowment and the nature of the lower animals on the one hand and between him and the universe of which he is a product on the other.

If this metaphysical basis for man's existence and nature is granted, a firm basis emerges for some fundamental legal and ethical conclusions. Some of these implications have long been part of the tradition of the West. Others are still in the emergent stage but give every sign of becoming integral to the outlook of the free world.

All of these doctrines have two features in common. The first is that only a natural law which is rooted in a religious world view is capable of supplying a valid theoretic foundation for them. It is no accident that the American Declaration of Independence, which appeals to "the laws of nature and nature's God," affirms the existence of "self-evident truths" and "unalienable rights" with which men "have been endowed by their Creator."

The second aspect of all these ethico-legal issues is that they transcend the positivist concept of ethics as "governing the relation of man and his fellows." The ethical consciousness is given an enormously broader scope by being set within a cosmic framework that encompasses the non-human elements of nature, the lower animals, and the physical resources of the plant and mineral kingdoms. The recognition has been growing that man has duties to his "little brothers," the animals, and even to his more distant cousins, the trees and the flowers, as well as to the mineral resources and the earth itself, which is his mother. But the conservation of natural resources is more than good husbandry or, to use the term in its etymological sense, good economics. That a profound ethical imperative, irrespective of any individual or group advantage or disadvantage, is involved here —that conviction can flow only out of an acceptance of natural law rooted in a perception of a cosmos in which man is not the sole or supreme arbiter of his destiny and that of his fellow creatures.

Some of these moral imperatives have the demanding power of law or are on the road to developing this quality. They can be indicated here only briefly.

The prohibition of cruelty to animals, which is one of the Noachide Laws, is a principle written large in biblical thought. Such laws as those forbidding plowing with a mixed team of an ox and a donkey (Deuteronomy 20:10) or muzzling an animal during the threshing season (25:4) or taking a mother bird and her young from the nest at the same time (22:6 f.) or slaughtering a cow and her calf on the same day (Leviticus 22:28) reflect a deep feeling of pity for the lower creatures. The Hebrew dietary laws represent a complex of sources, practices, and values which have as yet been incompletely explored. Nonetheless, the humanitarian motive is unmistakable among them, as in the insistence upon the speedy and accurate slaughtering of animals for food to minimize the pain.

The love of hunting is amply attested for the ancient world both in oriental and Greco-Roman literature, as well as for the modern age. This popular sport has developed an elaborate ethic and etiquette in Western society. It is generally overlooked that this universal practice is quite at variance with the biblical outlook, which relegates hunting to Nimrod and Esau but regards it as unworthy of an Israelite to take the life of animals for sport.

The compassion for the lower orders of creation reaches its climax in the last two words of the Book of Jonah. The prophet, indignant that his prophecy of doom for the hated Ninevites has been set aside by their genuine repentance, is admonished by God in words marked by supreme irony and compassion:

> And the Lord said, Thou wouldst have spared the gourd, for which thou hadst not labored, neither hadst thou made it grow; which came up in one night, and perished in one night;

> And shall I not spare Nineveh, that great city, wherein
> are more than twelve times ten thousand persons who
> know not how to discern between their right hand and
> their left hand, and also much cattle? [Book of Jonah,
> 4:11–12].

It is true that in Genesis 1:28 man is given "dominion"
over all living things:

> And God blessed them, and God said unto them, Be
> fruitful, and multiply, and replenish the earth, and subdue
> it: and have dominion over the fish of the sea, and over
> the fowl of the air, and over every living thing that
> moveth upon the earth [Genesis 1:28].

But, in biblical thought, a monarch's rule was never absolute. The kingship in ancient Israel was a limited monarchy
with the sovereign subject to countless checks upon the
exercise of arbitrary power, including the all-important
right of dissent utilized by the prophets. Always inherent in
the status of the ruler was the obligation to those ruled, a
sense of responsibility for the welfare of those whose destiny was in his hands.

The right of the lower creatures to life is innate and inalienable, with the single exception of the use of certain
types of animal flesh for food. Yet even here "the reverence
for life" must be given tangible expression, hence the biblical prohibition of the eating of the blood of animals, because "the blood is the life" of the creature (Deuteronomy
12:23).

Characteristically, the ethical attitude toward animals expressed in the Bible became a legal norm enforcible by
sanctions in the Talmud, under the rubric of "the pain of
living creatures" (*tza'ar ba'alei hayyim*). Man's obligation
not to inflict cruelty and unnecessary pain upon animals,
as a principle of natural law, is rooted in the recognition that
no less than man they represent the handiwork of the Crea-

tor. Hence, the prohibition is included in the Noachide Laws.

Cruelty to animals is generally accepted as evil. Much slower has been the recognition of the duty that man owes to the natural world, to the rivers and forests, to the mountains and valleys that are man's hearth and home. This innate reverence for the handiwork of God is entirely distinct from a concern for personal property. Its legal source in biblical thought is to be found, paradoxically enough, in the laws regulating warfare (Deuteronomy 20:19 f.). The Law of Moses forbids the Israelites, when laying siege to a city, to cut down the fruit trees surrounding the town. Nor did it matter whether the wood was needed for military purposes or the act was part of a campaign of *Schrecklichkeit* designed to bring the enemy to submission. The reason assigned for the interdiction is deeply moving: "For is the tree a human being that it can seek refuge from before thee during the siege?"[8]

The biblical phrase used in the passage, "Thou shalt not destroy" (*bal tashhet*), later becomes the basis in rabbinic law of a far-reaching doctrine, the prohibition of destroying any object, be it natural or man-made. The principle includes, but goes far beyond, the abhorrence of vandalism. It applies to one's own possessions as well as to *res nullius* (ownerless property). The prohibition inheres in the reverence due to the creative element, the energy and ability, however humble, that enters into every existent thing. The wanton destruction of natural resources is therefore forbidden, even if the so-called owners are themselves the willing agents of the process.

Another ethico-legal principle with which a positivist law encounters difficulty is the prohibition of suicide. The

[8] This is my version of the Hebrew text, far more defensible on linguistic and exegetical grounds than the renderings in the standard translations. The substance of the argument is, however, unaffected by these variant views.

Judeo-Christian tradition has always regarded suicide as a cardinal sin, wherein it differed sharply with the Greco-Roman outlook. That man has no right to commit suicide is a doctrine which can be validated in reason only by the conviction that life, even one's own life, is not man's own possession but a trust from a power beyond himself.

It has been maintained in many quarters that a new conception of property is needed for the free world, in order to do justice to the realities of our present economic order, which is a far cry from that of early individualistic capitalism on the one hand and from communism on the other. What we call private property today, in an era of government regulation, corporate management, the diffusion of ownership through stocks and bonds, the existence of a recognized and powerful labor movement, and a vast network of international economic machinery, is far removed from the concept of the private property of individuals as most of the proponents and opponents of "the free enterprise system" commonly understand it. A new and more adequate conception of property needs to be worked out. Such a theory can conceivably find a basis in the biblical doctrine of all wealth as the property of God, with man as its temporary trustee.

This is explicitly affirmed as the guiding principle underlying the law of the Jubilee, according to which all land that had been sold by its original owner reverted to him or his descendants at the fiftieth year (Leviticus 25:8–24; esp. 23). The same doctrine of God being the only true owner of wealth is implicit in the biblical ordinances of the sabbatical year. Every seventh year all debts were canceled (Deuteronomy 15:1 ff.), and all land was left fallow, with its produce to be the property of the poor, who were free to glean it at will (Exodus 23:10 f.; Leviticus 25:1–7). The sabbatical year, like other aspects of the social legislation of the Bible (Leviticus 19:9–10), was designed to prevent the undue concentration of wealth in the hands of the few and the impoverishment and eventual enslavement of the many. But its rationale was religious—the seventh year was "a Sabbath unto the Lord" (Leviticus 25:4) when he reasserted his ownership of the land.

No such simple procedures will avail to solve the complex economic issues confronting the few islands of an affluent society in a world-wide sea of penury. But the principle that neither men nor nations possess absolute ownership of the wealth of the world may well serve as the basis for creating the just social order which is yet to be born.

Finally, the doctrine which is perhaps the basic article of faith of the free world, the concept of the inalienable dignity—not merely the equality but the dignity—of every human being, likewise finds its clearest basis in the recognition of each man as a child of God, fashioned in the Divine image (Genesis 1:27; 5:1; Psalm 8:5–9).

An event of recent history, the Eichmann case, may serve to highlight the role of natural law in the modern world. Because of the sensationalism, the complexities and the charged emotions of the Eichmann trial, it is difficult to comment on it dispassionately. It is, however, noteworthy that the defense opened with four principal contentions. Eichmann's attorney argued that his client had been illegally abducted from Argentina. He challenged the jurisdiction of the Israeli court in connection with crimes allegedly committed outside its borders. Dr. Servatius then denied the validity of the Israeli statute involved since it was adopted in 1950, after the date of the alleged offenses. Finally, he contended that Eichmann was merely executing the orders of his superiors in accordance with his duty.

From the standpoint of positive law, these contentions have a substantial degree of force and the prosecution went to great lengths to refute them. With regard to the first two arguments, the attorney general of Israel cited American legal decisions, in which the U.S. Supreme Court upheld the right to try prisoners without regard to the means by which they were apprehended. As for the right of jurisdiction, the analogy of international piracy was invoked, whereby a pirate could be tried by any of the countries whose nationals he had victimized.

The last two arguments were not as easily disposed of. That the Israeli statute under which Eichmann was being tried was adopted after the crimes had been committed was undeniable, and the principle forbidding retroactive punishment is deeply imbedded in the jurisprudence of the free world. The attorney general's staff sought to meet the technical objections by pointing out that there was no other court either in The Hague, in West Germany, or elsewhere competent or willing to try Eichmann. But this was manifestly insufficient to counter the moral principle inherent in the prohibition of ex post facto legislation or punishment. Ultimately, the prosecution found itself compelled to rest its case upon a law forbidding murder that antedates the Israeli statute of 1950 by nearly thirty-four centuries, the command, "Thou shalt not kill" in the Decalogue. It insisted that the mass extermination of human beings is a crime even if the Genocide Convention before the U.N. is never placed on the statute books of the nations.

In sum, the moral responsibility of a mass-murderer and consequently his conviction are possible only from the standpoint of natural law and not from the positivist conception of law as the articulated will of the sovereign. It is this recognition of a fundamental theory of justice as basic to law that makes it possible to hold a William Wirt responsible for the atrocities suffered by federal prisoners at the Andersonville, Georgia, Confederate prison during the Civil War or to charge an Eichmann with the murder of millions of human beings during the Nazi era. The doctrine of natural law insists upon the existence of a moral order that takes precedence over the accepted formula of "following orders." It is the imperatives of the natural law that undergird the provisions of positive law when they are just and override them when they are not.

The nub of the Eichmann case lay precisely here—the defendant contending that he was merely obeying orders and thus acting legally and was not properly subject to punishment, the prosecution insisting that antecedent to all other regulations stood a higher law which should command obedience and which Eichmann had violated. It was upon this doctrine and not upon the Israeli statute of 1950 making genocide a crime that the prosecution built its case. Thus, natural law, though not mentioned by name in the proceedings, constituted the gravamen of the Eichmann trial.

Nor was it being invoked in the State of Israel for the first time and merely in order to serve as a weapon against the Nazi offender. In his summation the prosecutor, Gideon Hausner, recalled the painful and tragic incident which occurred in the Arab village Kfar Kassem in 1956. During the Arab-Israeli hostilities, a curfew on the Israeli-Jordanian frontier had been imposed. The Arab villagers had returned to their homes unaware of the curfew and forty-three were massacred by an Israeli border patrol.

Several officers and men of the Israeli border police were tried for murder. They pleaded that the orders to shoot curfew breakers had come from higher echelons and that they had not acted according to their personal wishes. However, Judge Binyamin Halevi, who was to be one of the judges of the Eichmann trial, convicted the Israeli military on the ground that the orders they had received were "manifestly unlawful." He observed that the unlawfulness of the orders "strikes any eye and makes the heart resentful, provided that the eye is not closed to see and the heart is not closed or vicious." Justice Moshe Landau, later to serve as the presiding judge of the Eichmann tribunal, presided over the Kfar Kassem appeal. He upheld the conviction, declaring, "A soldier, too, must have a conscience."[9] Here again, the doctrine of natural law, studiously avoided in contemporary jurisprudence, persisted in making its appearance, albeit incognito!

We may now summarize the conclusions and imperatives that emerge from our discussion of the role of natural law in the past and its potential value in the present:

1. The doctrine of natural law is profoundly needed today to supply a standard of guidance and criticism for dealing with the tensions of power and the conflict in authority among individuals and groups within a free society and for evaluating the respective claims to men's loyalty by competing ideologies.

2. Natural law is not so vague as to be valueless with regard to any specific situation, nor does it offer a detailed blueprint for dealing with each problem. Its role is to provide a concept of human nature and justice to serve as the rationale for the legal and social system of society. From it, individuals and groups may, at times quite legitimately, draw varying and even contradictory conclusions. This is precisely what happens under any constitution or enabling document, be it a principle like "due process" derived from the American Constitution or the concept of "the dignity of man" emanating from the Judeo-Christian tradition.

3. If natural law is to prove fruitful, and not stultifying, it is important to recognize the human component of human nature, which, though linked to animal nature and physical nature, nevertheless is different from both. Human nature is dynamic and rich in potentialities which must be reckoned with in any viable theory of natural law.

4. Natural law must be concerned with the ends of human life as well as with the means men employ to achieve

[9] Quotations from Homer Bigart in the *New York Times*, August 10, 1961, p. 4.

their ends. It is not objectivity but self-deception for the scientific student of human nature or of society to proclaim his abstention from any personal commitment. On the contrary, he will attain to a greater measure of truth if his commitment, which is always present implicitly if not explicitly, is brought to the surface and is constantly present before his consciousness. When he is aware of the bias to which he is prone, he is more likely to be on guard against being misled in his conclusions.

5. The natural lawyer may, for reasons of economy of effort, limit his field of concern to the study of human nature and human institutions in action and decline to ask any "non-operational" questions. But the basic human propensity for asking ultimate questions, at least by the "tender-minded," cannot be denied. Granted the existence of rationality and creativity within man, far-reaching consequences do emerge with regard to the nature of the universe of which man is the offspring. The nature of man *in esse* sheds light upon the character of the universe *in posse*, which, therefore, emerges as rationally created, dynamic, and possessing within itself the seeds out of which have developed the specific human traits in human nature. These are pre-eminently the attributes of rationality, moral aspiration, and creativity.

Those who find themselves unable or unwilling to accept any religious or metaphysical basis for natural law need go no further than they wish. They should recognize, however, that beyond their stopping-point, the road goes on. For many men, if not for all, it leads inevitably back to the starting-point of the biblical world view: "In the beginning God!"

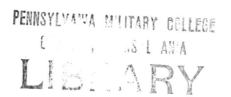

# GENERAL INDEX

Aaron, 122–23
Aaronides, 29
Abraham (patriarch), 7, 23, 57, 135, 187
Abraham ben David of Posquières, 36
Abyssinia, 134, 191
Adam, 9, 194, 217
Adams, John, 81
Aeschylus, 27
Africa, Africans, 86, 116–17, 135, 176, 183
Age of Reason, 15, 139
Agricultural Society of South Carolina, 157
Akiba, 123, 157–58, 160, 163–64
*Alenu* (prayer), 24–25
Alexandrian post-biblical Judaism, 7
Aliens, 123, 160, 163; Jews as, 35
Alliance for Progress, 196
America, Americans, 7, 12–13, 16, 42, 47, 54–55, 61, 66–67, 79, 82, 85–87, 89–96, 100, 102–9, 113–17, 119, 125, 129, 133, 136, 154, 170, 172–73, 205, 226, 231, 234; *see also* United States
American Council on Education, 109
American Indians, 133
American Jews, 108–9
American Revolution; *see* Revolutionary War
American Union; *see* Union, the American
Ammonites, 23

Amos, 2, 23–24, 58, 74, 123, 163, 178, 188
Amsterdam, 38
Anastasius I, 70
Anaxagoras, 221
Ancient world, 53, 160
Andersonville, Ga., 232
Angels, 29
Anglo-Saxons, 84, 103, 127
Animals, 46, 99, 215–17, 224–29, 234
Anthropology, 206
Anticlericalism, 84, 89
Anti-Negro prejudice, 126
Antinomianism, 8, 148
Antirationalism, 27
Antireligionism, antireligionists, 84, 86, 114
Anti-Semitism, 13, 15, 63, 126, 150
Apocrypha, apocryphal literature, 7, 46, 62, 169, 213
Apologetic literature, apologetics, 45, 155
Apostles, 5
Aquinas, Thomas, 35, 213–14
Arab States, Arabs, 43, 173–74, 176, 233
Arabia, 134
Arabian Desert, 43
Arabic Kalam philosophers, 225
Aram, 188
Architecture, 184
Argentina, 231
Aristobulus, 45
Aristotelianism, 36
Aristotle, 27, 118–19, 218
Army, 40, 92

237

Heathenism, heathens; *see* Paganism, pagans
"Hebraic-Christian heritage"; *see* Judeo-Christian tradition
Hebraic spirit, Hebraism, 11–12, 72, 81
Hebraic tradition; *see* Tradition, Jewish
Hebrew Bible, Hebrew Scriptures, 7, 25–26, 33, 57, 74, 82–83, 142, 148, 166, 168, 174, 177; *see also* Bible; Scripture; Torah
Hebrew language, 3–5, 28
Hebrew prophets; *see* Prophets
Hebrew religion; *see* Judaism
Hebrews, Hebrew nation, 27, 43, 73, 121, 123, 163, 179, 185–86, 194, 222
Hegel, Georg Wilhelm Friedrich, 139, 177
Hellenistic Judaism; *see* Judaism, Hellenistic
Hellenists, Hellenizers, Hellenism, 5, 20, 27, 73, 205
*Herem*, 37, 39; *see also* Ban; Excommunication
Heretics, heresy, 32, 35–36, 38, 62, 64, 77
*Hesed*, 59
Hesiod, 74
Hess, Moses, 14
Hierocracy, 73
High schools, 110, 112
Hillel, School of; Hillelites, 34–35
Hindus, Hinduism, 86, 155
History, 7, 27–28, 52–53, 71, 73, 78, 107, 110, 123, 139, 154, 177–79, 181, 198, 213, 222
Hitler, Adolf, 63, 85, 140, 207
Hogben, Lawrence, 128
*Hokmah*, 167
Holiness Code, 160–61, 223
Holland, 13, 31, 38, 97, 105; *see also* Netherlands, the
Holmes, Oliver Wendell, 206
Home, the, 103–4, 113
Hosea, 57, 74, 84, 177–78, 188
Hospitals, 93
Humanism, 72, 80, 109, 139
Humanitarianism, 84, 227
Humanity, human nature, human

race, 11, 14, 20, 30, 72, 137–45, 170, 185, 204–5, 208–12, 214–16, 218–22, 234–35; *see also* Man, mankind
Hume, David, 84
Hunting, 227
Hutchins, Robert M., 206–8, 210, 212
Hyatt, J. Philip, 56

Idolatry, 44, 46, 49, 51, 157, 224
Idumeans, 45
Immigration, 103
Immorality, 157, 178–79, 224
Immortality, 217
Impulses, good and evil; see *Yetzer hara; Yetzer hatobh;* Yetzers
Incarnation (in Christianity), 10, 64
Independence, Declaration of; *see* Declaration of Independence
Independence, political, 3
India, 176, 192, 200
Indifference, religious; *see* Religious indifference
Individual, the; individualism, 11, 15–18, 26, 53, 77–78, 84, 150–51, 156, 165, 171–73, 187, 195, 201
Indonesia, 176
Industrial Revolution, 12, 16, 84
Industry, 13
Inheritance, 40
Injustice, 169
Inquisition, 38
Integration, 95, 129, 131
Interfaith relations, 17, 54–55
Intergroup relations, 17
Intermarriage, 131–33, 135
International Court of Justice, 191
International law; *see* Law, international
International relations, internationalism, 17, 137–38, 170, 173, 183–85, 188, 190–203
Intolerance, religious; *see* Religious intolerance
Iraq, 134
Irish, 103
Iron Curtain, 192, 201
Isaac (patriarch), 187
Isaac the Tosafist, 49
Isaiah, 44, 74, 178–79, 182, 186, 188–89

INDEX



139, 164, 166–69, 172, 177–81, 185–90, 194, 203, 215, 228
Proselytes, proselytization, 23–24, 45, 123, 135
Protestant Reformation; see Reformation
Protestantism, Protestants, 29, 31–32, 51, 66, 68, 77, 89, 93–94, 103, 105, 109, 111–12, 142
Proverbs, Book of, 168–69
Psalmist, 33, 193, 223
Psalms, 27, 168
Pseudepigrapha, 62
Pseudo-Darwinism, 144
Pseudo-Marxism, 144
Psychiatry, 215
Psychology, 145, 221
Public schools; see Schools
Public schools, religion in the, 66, 94–114
Puritans, 31, 81
Put, 121

Qumran Scrolls, 6
Qumran sectarians, 34

Rab (talmudist), 24
Rabbinic Judaism; see Judaism, rabbinic
Rabbinic law; see Law, rabbinic
Rabbinic literature, 7, 124, 213
Rabbis, rabbinate, 8, 29, 39, 75–76, 111, 118, 144; see also Chief rabbi; Sages
Race, racialism, 21, 30, 86, 95, 115–36
Raphall, Morris J., 118
Rashi, 51
Rationalism, rationalists, 16, 26, 28, 33, 36, 53, 81, 84, 141, 145, 168, 205, 208, 210, 215, 219, 221–23, 225, 235
Rationalization, 215
Reaction, 15
Real, James, 197
Realism, 172
*Realpolitik,* 166
Reason; see Rationalism
Reason, Age of; see Age of Reason
Reconstructionist movement, 39
Red Sea, 82

Redeemer, redemption, 5
Reform Judaism; see Judaism, Reform
Reformation, 1, 12
Relativism, 206–7
Religion, 14, 25, 38, 40, 42, 48, 55, 66–67, 70–71, 74, 79–136, 145, 149, 156, 162, 172, 181, 188, 190–203, 214, 222, 225, 235
Religion, disestablishment of, 42
Religion, natural, 225
Religion in the public schools; see Public schools, religion in the
Religions, oriental; see Oriental religions
Religious authority; see Authority, religious
Religious belief; see Belief, religious
Religious conformity, 39
Religious disputations; see Disputations, religious
Religious education, 40, 90, 101, 108, 111–14; see also Education
Religious Education Association, 109
Religious indifference, 48, 113
Religious intolerance, 38, 42–43, 53, 78
Religious liberty, 31–54, 69, 95, 114
Religious life, 110
Religious observance; see Observance, religious
Religious schools, 92, 97, 109, 112–13, 127, 135
"Religious test," 111
Religious tolerance, 42, 44–45, 47–48
Religious tradition, 115–36
Renaissance, 12
Renan, Ernest, 7, 43
Renunciation, 155
*Republic* (of Plato), 27, 118
*Responsa,* 11, 62
Resurrection, 5, 34, 64
Revelation, 7, 34, 48, 166, 225
Revolutionary War, 81–82, 84–85
Richards, J. M., 184–85
Righteousness, 20, 34, 180, 188, 196, 219
Rights of man, 84
Rites; see Ritual

# INDEX OF
# BIBLICAL PASSAGES

254 THE ROOT AND THE BRANCH